Getting the Runaround

Getting the Runaround

FORMERLY INCARCERATED MEN AND
THE BUREAUCRATIC BARRIERS TO REENTRY

John M. Halushka

UNIVERSITY OF CALIFORNIA PRESS

University of California Press
Oakland, California

Library of Congress Cataloging-in-Publication Data

Names: Halushka, John M., 1985– author.
Title: Getting the runaround : formerly incarcerated men and the
    bureaucratic barriers to reentry / John M. Halushka.
Description: Oakland, California: University of California Press, [2023] |
    Includes bibliographical references and index.
Identifiers: LCCN 2023005941 (print) | LCCN 2023005942 (ebook) |
    ISBN 9780520388680 (cloth) | ISBN 9780520388697 (paperback) |
    ISBN 9780520388703 (ebook)
Subjects: LCSH: Prisoners—Deinstitutionalization—New York (State)—
    New York. | Ex-convicts—New York (State)—New York—Social
    conditions. | Ex-convicts—Effect of imprisonment on—New York
    (State)—New York. | Civil service—New York (State)—New York.
Classification: LCC HV9306.N6 H35 2023 (print) | LCC HV9306.N6 (ebook) |
    DDC 364.809747—dc23/eng/20230524
LC record available at https://lccn.loc.gov/2023005941
LC ebook record available at https://lccn.loc.gov/2023005942

Manufactured in the United States of America

32 31 30 29 28 27 26 25 24 23
10 9 8 7 6 5 4 3 2 1

For Michelle, Lily, and Sienna

CONTENTS

...

PREFACE

This book was written at a time of growing bipartisan support for scaling back the excesses of mass incarceration. There is widespread cultural and political consensus that people convicted of nonviolent drug offenses do not deserve prison time. They should receive treatment and support rather than being locked in cages.

Many of the men featured in the book fit the profile of the "deserving" nonviolent offender: men with long histories of trauma, addiction, and chronic health conditions. Rather than receiving the treatment and support they needed, they cycled through the carceral system for a series of nonviolent offenses. As these men struggle to recover from histories of trauma and addiction, they live in the shadow of their criminal records and continue to struggle at the margins of mainstream social and economic life. Many criminal justice reforms are aimed at this population of returning citizens. These men represent a vulnerable population who have slipped through our frayed social safety net and become caught in the gears of the carceral state. Most of the harm they have caused has been to themselves. Locking them up is a burden to taxpayers that does little to address their underlying addiction issues. In short, these men are deserving of sympathy and mercy.

But many other men featured in this book are not so sympathetic. This book tells the stories of men who were convicted of serious violent felonies: armed robbery, domestic violence, sexual assault, attempted murder, manslaughter, and murder. These men have caused physical and psychological harm to others. They have violated the social contract in its most fundamental sense. And for that we have decided that these men are not deserving of our sympathy. They deserve long prison sentences in harsh conditions. Even after they serve their sentences, they should be permanently excluded from mainstream social life in the name of public safety and justice for victims.

In telling the stories of these unsympathetic men, this book asks us to consider extending sympathy and mercy to them. It argues that if we are to truly confront the problem of mass incarceration, we cannot just focus on those we deem deserving; we must confront the difficult question of how we treat people who have harmed others after they are released from prison. Does it make us safer to cast them out as permanent social and economic outsiders? Does perpetually punishing these men deliver justice—in the form of healing and accountability—to survivors of violence? What does it cost our society, not just fiscally, but also socially and morally, to cast these men out? What would it mean to create a system of prison reentry that is truly inclusive, that reintegrates not only vulnerable and sympathetic people convicted of nonviolent offenses but *all* those released from our nation's swelling prisons, including people who have committed violent acts?

In asking these questions, we are forced to confront a more fundamental question about public safety and security. What does public safety truly mean? Does it mean the coercive powers of police, courts, and prisons to exert state violence on those who violate the law? Is defining public safety in this narrow sense worth the vast human toll of locking up large swaths of our nation's population, most of whom are poor people of color? Or can we define public safety and security differently? Can public safety come to mean protecting our most vulnerable citizens from the social, economic, and political forces that produce poverty, violence, and human suffering in the first place? Can it mean investing in public infrastructure to support healthy communities rather than relying solely on our most coercive forms of state social control to create security? In the pages that follow, this book challenges us to reckon with these questions and to imagine a different future.

ACKNOWLEDGMENTS

This book is the product of over a decade of work, and it would not have been possible without the support and inspiration of a community of mentors, colleagues, and family members.

First and foremost, I extend my deepest gratitude to the research participants who made this book possible. The people I met at Second Chances and Uplift changed my life. I am forever grateful for the opportunity you gave me to document your struggles.

This book began as a humble class project in Lynne Haney's ethnography seminar at NYU. Lynne showed me that it was possible to make bold claims with ethnography. Her theoretical insights, methodological rigor, and clear writing style inspired me to embrace ethnography at a time when I wasn't sure where my academic career was headed. She took my ideas seriously and gave me the confidence to dive headfirst into fieldwork. And she always pushed me to make my work more theoretically sophisticated and empirically grounded. Thank you, Lynne, for continuing to inspire me.

I owe a great deal of thanks to Colin Jerolmack. Whenever I needed advice during grad school, Colin's door was always open with a hot cup of espresso in hand. Colin recognized the potential of my work early on and helped me to find confidence in my voice. Thank you, Colin, for always having your door open and for always pushing me to be the best ethnographer I could be.

David Garland has been an intellectual inspiration since my days as an undergraduate student. When I was working on my senior thesis, I stumbled across a copy of *The Culture of Control* in the library. The book blew my mind, and it was a major inspiration for me to pursue graduate education. At NYU, David always pushed me to do my best work. Whenever my writing was vague, or I tried to cover up a bad argument with a rhetorical flourish, David always called me out. Thank you, David, for always pushing me to think and write with precision.

Many others helped me to develop this project during graduate school, including Dee Royster, Jo Dixon, David Greenberg, Ruth Horowitz, and Iddo Tavory. The Ethnography Workshop, the Crime, Law, and Deviance Workshop, and various informal writing groups provided much needed community. My colleagues Jon Gordon, Matt Canfield, Alexis Pang, Michael Gould-Wartofsky, Robert Riggs, Max Besbris, Jacob Faber, Peter Rich, Francisco Vieyra, Stacy Torres, Amaka Okechukwu, Issa Kohler-Haussman, and Chris Seeds all provided advice and support along the way. Tim Leffel's friendship sustained me during the many trials of graduate school.

My colleagues in the Department of Justice Studies at SJSU have provided a welcoming intellectual home. Thank you especially to Alessandro De Giorgi for providing comments on multiple drafts of my book proposal and several chapters of the book.

Since graduate school, several colleagues have continued to support this project. Jon Gordon has generously provided feedback on my writing. I am grateful for his friendship and generosity. This book would not have been possible without Reuben Miller. Reuben's work has been a constant source of inspiration, and our conversations over the years have helped shaped many of the ideas in this book. I am also grateful to Reuben for going out of his way to put me in contact with Maura Roessner at University of California Press. Max Besbris, Spencer Headworth, and Allison McKim generously shared their book proposals with me and helped me to write a successful one of my own. Tim Black also generously read the proposal and provided insightful feedback. Frank Prior read parts of the manuscript and provided helpful comments. Kimberly Spencer Suarez helped me to develop the article upon which this book is based. A few years ago at a conference, Forrest Stuart asked me, "So when's your book coming out?" At the time I didn't think I was capable of writing a book, but Forrest's encouragement planted the seed of confidence that I needed to get this project started.

Thank you to the amazing staff at University of California Press for making this book possible. Special thanks to Maura Roessner for being a dogged advocate for this project from the start and for giving me the chance to share my research with the widest possible audience. Thank you to Sam Warren and Madison Wetzell for their editorial assistance, and to Jon Dertien and

Sharon Langworthy for their assistance with copyediting. And thank you to the two anonymous peer reviewers for the thorough and thoughtful comments.

The research for the book was supported by the Henry MacCracken Fellowship for Graduate Studies and the Dean's Diversity Fellowship at NYU, the National Science Foundation and National Institute of Justice (grant no. SES-1424309), and the Research, Scholarship and Creative Activity Reassigned Time Grant at SJSU.

Thank you to the Darnall Family: Bill and Patty; Stephanie, Andrew, Charley, Noa, and Izzy; and Billy and Ariel. You welcomed me with open arms and treated me as family since day one. This work would not be possible without your support.

Thank you to the Halushka family. To my Mom and Dad, thank you for making the sacrifices that made my education possible. To my Dad, thank you for teaching me the Jesuit principle of *age quod agis*. In my Latin classes I learned that it literally translates as "Do what you are doing," or focus on the task at hand. But growing up, you always told me it meant, "If you're gonna do something, do it right!" I like your translation better. This book is a testament to doing things the right way.

To my Mom, thank you for giving me the tools to discover faith and social justice in my own way. Although there were many things I resisted about Catholic education, it is also where I learned the moral imperative to stand up for "the least among us," especially prisoners and outcasts; that no one is beyond forgiveness; and that we all deserve God's love. The countless hours we spent reading the newspaper together at the kitchen table were instrumental in shaping my sociological imagination and honing the principles of social justice that guide my work.

To my siblings, Steve, Mark, Natalie, and Dave, thank you for always watching out for me. Thank you to my nieces and nephews, Kiani, Jack, Luke, Leila, Alex, Adam, Kellan, and Griffin, for the joy you bring to our lives. Special thanks to my brother Dave, who gave me my first Bad Religion cassette and my first sociology textbook. I wouldn't be here without those.

Finally, I'd like to thank my wife, Michelle, and our two daughters, Lily and Sienna. Michelle, you have been a constant source of love and support in my life. We met when I was just starting graduate school, and you have stood by my side through all the struggles of my academic career. Every time this book took me away from our family, you picked up the slack and supported me in countless ways. This book would not have been possible without you. Your unconditional love and boundless belief in me are the greatest gifts in my life. Thank you.

Lily and Sienna, you are two perfect miracles of the universe. Thank you for helping me become a father. This book took shape in the first years of your life. Learning to become your father played an important role in shaping how I wrote this book. It helped me to understand the struggles that formerly incarcerated fathers endure, and it gave me a deeper understanding of the devastating toll mass incarceration takes on families throughout our country. I hope that in some small way this book will help make the world you inherit a more just and equitable place.

Introduction

EVERY YEAR MORE THAN 640,000 PEOPLE are released from state and federal prisons in the United States. One of them is Andre.[1] When I interviewed him in 2014, Andre had been home for about 6 months, having served a 20-month sentence in New York state prison for real estate fraud.[2] At the time he was 43 years old, unemployed, estranged from his family, and living in a sober-living facility in the Bronx. I was interviewing Andre for a study about how men of color with criminal records manage the dual stigmas of race and criminality on the labor market. But when I asked Andre what he thought was his main barrier to employment, he didn't mention his status as a Black man with a criminal record. "The first barrier that I faced was time management," he told me. "Because when you first come home, it's like, a bunch of different agency appointments that they have you maintain. And then the process of maintaining that, you can't really do anything else."

Andre began discussing the sheer amount of time he had to spend to access public assistance. His only source of income at the time was food stamps and general assistance. He also received a monthly rental allowance check and Medicaid coverage, which paid for his rent and treatment sessions at the sober house. But maintaining access to these benefits was a constant struggle. Andre said his welfare application was denied "two or three times" because letters for follow-up appointments kept getting lost in the mail, necessitating a months-long process of phone calls and office visits before Andre could access his benefits. In the age of workfare Andre was required to sign a personal responsibility contract, meet regularly with his case manager, and participate in mandated work assignments or job training programs as conditions of receiving aid. Maintaining his housing posed its own set of challenges. As structured living environments, sober-living facilities require residents to follow a set of house rules or face eviction. Most significant were the mandatory treatment sessions Andre had to attend, which included up to four group meetings and one individual counseling session per week. Other conditions included a nightly curfew, random drug tests, household chores, and regular visits from his parole officer (PO).

Andre felt that the process of maintaining access to public assistance and transitional housing required so much time and effort that he had little time left to pursue employment or housing independence. "It's debilitating," Andre told me. He wondered how he could ever find a job if he had to constantly leave work to attend treatment sessions at the sober house. "And from here, unless I do something else, it can only get worse." Andre claimed that he never really had a substance abuse issue to begin with; instead, he said, he was living in the sober house as a low-cost housing solution. But his time living there is temporary, and he'll eventually have to figure out another place to stay to avoid living on the streets or in a homeless shelter. "So, what the hell do I do?" Andre asked rhetorically. "I find myself another situation. I tell another program, that, you know, I have a substance abuse issue, and I go there. Because, obviously, I know this system now. But now you've made me professionally poor. This is what I do for a living. And there's nothing else I can do, because you haven't given me the time to go and find a job or the work experience."

As Andre's case illustrates, people returning home from incarceration cycle through an "institutional circuit" of parole, transitional housing facilities, public assistance programs, and community-based service providers as they struggle with conditions of severe deprivation.[3] Yet most research on reentry has overlooked how formerly incarcerated men navigate this patchwork of bureaucracies.[4] Based on three years of ethnographic fieldwork and 45 in-depth interviews with formerly incarcerated men returning to New York City, *Getting the Runaround* takes readers into the bureaucratic spaces of reentry, revealing how the mundane rules and practices of parole offices, welfare programs, and transitional housing facilities function as bureaucratic barriers that contribute to the ongoing marginalization and social control of formerly incarcerated people.[5]

This book makes three distinct contributions. First, it draws attention to the bureaucratic barriers to reentry: the collection of impersonal bureaucratic practices that obstruct returning citizens from basic elements of social inclusion. Much of the literature on the barriers to reentry conceptualizes them as a combination of formal laws, discriminatory practices, and demographic risk factors that obstruct returning citizens from accessing employment, housing, education, public assistance, and voting. But Andre's experience reveals how returning citizens are not only excluded through legal disqualification, outright discrimination, or social vulnerability, but also through the litany of bureaucratic hassles, degradations, and costs that they experience in their efforts to comply with parole mandates and to access public aid—an experience I call "getting the runaround."

The concept of the runaround expands our understanding of the barriers to reentry by shifting our focus to the *institutional mechanisms* that undermine reintegration. By placing returning citizens' interactions with the institutional circuit at the center of the analysis, the book is among the first to draw attention to the hidden ways in which mundane bureaucratic practices amplify inequality and contribute to the social exclusion of returning citizens.[6] I argue that "the runaround" exacerbates material poverty, reinforces distrust of state authorities, and ultimately undermines successful reintegration. Men experiencing the runaround find themselves on a relentless treadmill of appointments, programs, and curfews. It requires so much time, energy, and financial resources to keep up with this grind that they are left without the resources necessary to pull themselves onto the road toward employment and economic independence.

The runaround teaches men to expect arbitrary and abusive treatment from institutional gatekeepers, reinforcing an already distrustful relationship with the state. Some men respond to this sense of disempowerment through noncompliance and system avoidance, which results in losing access to material resources and, in some cases, arrest and reincarceration. By repeatedly diminishing returning citizens' rights and communicating symbolic stigma, the institutional circuit pushes men to be the kinds of subjects the system is designed to govern: defiant and disengaged men in need of discipline and punishment.[7]

However, not everyone who experiences the runaround responds with resistance and noncompliance. The book shows how formerly incarcerated men develop creative ways to cope with the stress of the runaround and adapt to the demands of bureaucratic processing. The book's second major contention is that formerly incarcerated men express reformed masculine identities through their ability to cope with the runaround. On average, the

TABLE I. Interview Sample Demographics,
45 Formerly Incarcerated Men

Sample Characteristics	Number (N = 45)	Percent
Age (years)		
23–30	7	15
30–39	13	29
40–49	16	36
50–65	9	20
Race and ethnicity		
Black	28	62
Latino	14	31
White	3	7
Fatherhood		
Yes	43	96
No	2	4
Child support order		
Owed to state	13	29
Owed to mother	4	9
Owed to both	1	2
None	27	60
Time in prison (most recent)		
Less than 1 year	15	33
2–5 years	16	36
5–10 years	6	13
More than 10 years	8	18
Incarcerated more than once		
Yes	25	56
No	20	44
Time since release		
Less than 1 year	18	40
2–5 years	15	33
5–10 years	7	16
More than 10 years	5	11
Parole supervision (ever as adult)		
Yes	37	82
No	8	18
Parole supervision (current)		
Yes	19	42
No	26	58
Public assistance (ever as adult)		
Yes	39	87
No	6	13

Sample Characteristics	Number (N = 45)	Percent
Public assistance (current)		
Yes	33	73
No	12	27
Housing (current)		
Federal halfway house	3	7
Homeless shelter	10	22
Treatment facility	13	29
Family/partner	16	35
Independent	3	7

SOURCE: Halushka (2020)

men I interviewed were in their forties, and almost all of them were fathers (see table 1). The men narrated how growing older gave them a new perspective on life and pushed them to atone for their failures as fathers. In their efforts to remain out of prison and "be there" for their kids, they adopted a law-abiding lifestyle marked by a transition away from a hostile relationship with the state to a more cooperative one.

Much of the literature on the relationship between marginalized men and the state focuses on antagonistic relationships between men of color and the criminal legal system.[8] This research has documented how marginalized men experience patterns of abuse and harassment at the hands of criminal legal actors, especially the police, leading to a deep mistrust of state authority that often results in noncompliance with the criminal legal system.[9] However, much of this literature focuses on the experiences of young men in their teens and young adulthood and focuses almost exclusively on their relationship to criminal legal institutions.[10] As a result, we know little about how men experience state power over the life course and how their interpretations of state power are shaped by interactions with state institutions beyond the criminal legal system.

By contrast, *Getting the Runaround* focuses on the experiences of formerly incarcerated men at middle age and explores their relationships with a spectrum of state bureaucracies. The book traces the life histories of men of the "mass imprisonment generation," showing how they transitioned from a hypermasculine street lifestyle characterized by active avoidance and defiance of state authorities to a more mature and domesticated sense of manhood rooted in work, fatherhood, and compliance with state authorities. These shifts in gender identity reflect not only life course transitions but also the productive powers of the state to shape and mold subjectivities. Through repeated cycles of incarceration and reentry, the men learned to discipline their behavior to conform to the rules and rhythms of the institutional circuit. Drawing on institutional narratives of individualism and personal responsibility, they learned to reinterpret the runaround as a short-term inconvenience that can be overcome through tenacity and a positive attitude. They also learned to orient themselves to treat system navigation as a full-time job, what Andre called being "professionally poor." They developed skills and sensibilities to navigate complex bureaucratic systems and learned to leverage their reformed identities to negotiate interactions with institutional gatekeepers. In the course of learning how to manage the stress of the runaround, they molded themselves into kinds of masculine citizens the state seeks to produce: men who are sober, docile, and willing to take any available work.

And yet despite complying with state authorities, avoiding reincarceration, and internalizing the state's messages of personal responsibility, most study participants continued to struggle with persistent unemployment and housing insecurity for years after release. The book's third major contribution is to document the lives of returning citizens who have avoided criminal legal contact for several years yet continue to struggle at the margins of mainstream social life. Most scholarship on reentry focuses on the period immediately following release.[11] By contrast, *Getting the Runaround* tells the stories of formerly incarcerated men beyond the initial shock of reentry. Almost half of the men interviewed for the study had avoided reincarceration for at least three years. Despite their nominal reentry "success," they did not experience full social and economic reintegration. Their goals of wage work, fatherhood, and political participation were often stymied by insurmountable disadvantages born of their race, class, and criminal records. They experienced repeated bouts of unemployment and housing instability and cycled repeatedly through low-wage jobs, public assistance programs, and transitional housing facilities. The systems designed to facilitate their reintegration continually failed to extend their life chances beyond basic survival and low-wage work, all while diminishing their basic civil rights through ongoing surveillance, behavioral mandates, fees, and sanctions. Ultimately, *Getting the Runaround* reveals the deep limitations of current reentry policy, demonstrating the urgent need to reconceptualize how we measure reentry "success" and shift conversations around reentry beyond the narrow goals of public safety and austerity to encompass a broader vision of social justice and inclusion.

It has been five decades since the United States began the unprecedented policy experiment of mass incarceration. Today, the United States boasts the world's highest per capita incarceration rate, locking up people at a scale unseen in our nation's history and with few international comparisons.[12] Because almost all incarcerated people will eventually be released, mass incarceration has produced a corollary phenomenon: mass prisoner reentry. Every year more than 640,000 people are released from state and federal prisons in the United States, a fourfold increase since 1975.[13] Researchers estimate that by 2010 there were 4.9 million formerly incarcerated people living in the United States, accounting for 2 percent of the adult population.[14] Communities of color disproportionately bear the costs of mass incarceration. Nearly 40 percent of people with prison records are African American men. One in ten African American men is formerly incarcerated, a rate five times the general population.[15]

While reentry marks the transition from incarceration to community life, returning citizens typically experience it as a transition into poverty.[16] Returning citizens disproportionately return home to the same impoverished and racially segregated urban neighborhoods where they grew up, places where employment is scarce, family budgets are strained, and mechanisms of informal social control are weak.[17] The stigma of their criminal records, coupled with human capital deficits and histories of trauma, substance misuse, and mental illness, makes finding employment difficult.[18] People who have been to prison on average earn lower wages, experience longer bouts of unemployment, and are more likely to work in the secondary labor market than individuals without prison records.[19] In the Boston Reentry Study, a longitudinal study of 122 formerly incarcerated men and women returning to the Boston area, half were unemployed after a year, and a quarter never found work at all. The median annual income was just $6,500, about half the federal poverty line for a single adult.[20]

Given these levels of deep poverty, the vast majority of returning citizens experience hunger. One survey found that 91 percent of returning citizens experienced food insecurity in the year after release, and over a third had not eaten for an entire day in the past month.[21] Researchers estimate that returning citizens are twice as likely to experience food insecurity in a given year as people without incarceration histories.[22] Returning citizens also face significant barriers to establishing stable housing. Rising housing costs, discrimination by private landlords, and restrictions on applying for public housing make it difficult for returning citizens to establish stable living situations.[23]

These persistent hardships draw returning citizens into the orbit of various social safety-net bureaucracies. As we saw in Andre's case, returning citizens stitched together a patchwork of safety-net support after release, relying on public assistance programs, transitional housing facilities, and community-based service providers to meet their basic material needs. Prerelease programs, parole referrals, and mandatory parole conditions also channel returning citizens into safety-net programs, rehabilitation facilities, and shelters.

Formerly incarcerated men also become entangled with family welfare bureaucracies, particularly the child support system. There are 1.1 million parents of minor children serving time in state and federal prisons in the United States, over a third of whom have open child support cases.[24] Incarcerated fathers accrue significant child support debt while they are incarcerated. Indeed, "close to 40% of child support debt is owed by men with no reported income, in part because of imprisonment."[25] With typical support orders ranging $225–300 per month, fathers commonly enter prison with $10,000 in child support debt and leave with $20,000 or more due to the accrual of interest and fees.[26] In her study of 145 formerly incarcerated fathers, sociologist Lynne Haney found that men owed an average of $36,500 in child support debt, three times the amount owed by low-income fathers without incarceration histories.[27] The accumulation of child support debt during incarceration, as well as disputes over child custody, draw formerly incarcerated men into contact with the Office of Child Support Enforcement and the family court, both of which can mandate men to participate in job training programs and various therapeutic programs such as drug treatment, responsible fatherhood programs, and anger management classes. Child support authorities can also sanction men for nonpayment, including suspending drivers' licenses and imposing jail sentences.

I conceptualize this loosely integrated network of criminal legal and social welfare bureaucracies as the "institutional circuit" of prisoner reentry.[28] This network of agencies, programs, and facilities acts as a gatekeeper that governs access to public aid and community freedom. The concept of the institutional circuit draws our attention to the ways in which the state governs prisoner reentry as a hybrid project of poverty governance that straddles state systems of punishment and welfare.[29] The term "poverty governance" refers to the ongoing activities of governments to manage "the needs and disorders" of marginalized populations and to transform them "into cooperative subjects of the market and polity."[30] Scholars of poverty governance argue that the purpose of social welfare policy is not so much to eradicate poverty as to contain and manage the problems and populations associated with it.[31]

Conceptualizing reentry as a site of poverty governance allows us to see how the state governs the lives of criminalized men across a range of institutions, not just the criminal legal system. While parole supervision loomed large in the daily lives of study participants, their interactions with the state were not confined to the criminal legal system. However, we know little about how formerly incarcerated men navigate the intersection of punishment and welfare in their daily lives. Much of the literature on reentry has focused on men's entanglements with criminal legal institutions, with little attention paid to their experiences navigating social welfare bureaucracies.

Literature on the "punitive turn" suggests that rehabilitation and social welfare interventions have evaporated from the lives of criminalized men in an era of carceral expansion and welfare state retrenchment. According to sociologist Loïc Wacquant's influential account of "neoliberal penality," the state governs social marginality through a gendered regime of social control. A masculine "right hand" regulates poor men through a coercive carceral apparatus designed to incapacitate the surplus population of low-skill men of color left behind by deindustrialization. At the same time, a feminine "left hand" regulates poor women of color through a disciplinary workfare regime designed to push single mothers off public assistance and into low-wage jobs. Taken together, "the rollback of welfare state protections for the most downtrodden" and "the rollout of a vastly enlarged police and penal state" have created the conditions that all but ensure formerly incarcerated men remain trapped in cycles of incarceration and recidivism.[32] Lacking access to rehabilitation and social welfare programs, they are left to fend for themselves in impoverished urban neighborhoods awash with criminal opportunities and saturated with police and parole surveillance.

However, recent scholarship has complicated this account, showing how release from prison functions as a pathway that connects marginalized men to the welfare state. Prerelease programming and POs act as intermediaries connecting formerly incarcerated men to public assistance programs, transitional housing facilities, and community-based service providers.[33]

Sociologists Reuben Miller and Forrest Stuart argue that despite being excluded from a variety of aspects of conventional citizenship, formerly incarcerated men are also *included* in alternate systems of governance that are unavailable to conventional citizens, such as access to "prisoner reentry programs and prisoner-specific social service agencies, healthcare and housing services administered through public and private organizations, counseling provided by state and non-governmental agencies, and services through probation, parole, and alternative court systems."[34] The ability of formerly incarcerated men to access these services belies the notion that rehabilitation and social welfare have disappeared from the lives of formerly incarcerated men in the era of "neoliberal penality." Far from being a gendered division of control, the left and right hands of the state converge in the daily lives of formerly incarcerated men in the form of the institutional circuit of reentry.

Although returning citizens are able to access public goods and services through the institutional circuit, accessing these forms of aid exposes them to a continuum of social control that cuts across multiple state systems of punishment and welfare.[35] Navigating the institutional circuit requires men to submit to ongoing surveillance, acquiesce in behavior modification programs, pay fees for supervision and services, and live under the constant threat of sanctions for noncompliance. These forms of social control multiply as men accumulate entanglements across the institutional circuit.

At the same time, these forms of social control are spread out across a decentralized and underfunded bureaucratic infrastructure. Each bureaucracy on the circuit had its own unique rules, procedures, and paperwork requirements. Men often had to supply the same information and documentation over and over again to access services. Agency offices were often located on opposite ends of the city, sometimes requiring men to travel dozens of blocks or to multiple boroughs to attend appointments. What's more, these agencies routinely failed to communicate or coordinate supervision, leading to complex entanglements that made it difficult for study participants to keep track of their intersecting obligations and comply with state authorities.

The combination of disciplinary social control and bureaucratic fragmentation that characterizes the institutional circuit of reentry is a reflection of broader trends in US political development that political scientists Joe Soss, Richard Fording, and Sanford Schram call "neoliberal paternalism." This policy regime is characterized by a "mode of poverty governance . . . [that] is, at once, more muscular in its normative enforcement and more dispersed and diverse in its organization."[36]

Contemporary poverty governance is "neoliberal" in the sense that responsibility for managing poverty has become increasingly devolved, privatized, and organized around market logic. Policymakers have transferred authority for social policy administration from federal agencies to state and local lawmakers, who in turn have outsourced responsibility for service delivery to private actors. Market-based performance accountability systems monitor service delivery and award public funds to organizations that meet output quotas. As a result, poverty governance is increasingly decentralized and fragmented, with responsibility for managing the poor dispersed across a range of public and private actors. In the context of prisoner reentry, the state subcontracts almost all reentry-related services to private nonprofits, including substance abuse treatment, workforce development training, transitional housing, and mental health services, among many others.

Poverty governance is "paternalistic" in the sense that the overarching ideological project of contemporary poverty governance is aimed at transforming the poor into disciplined market actors. Neoliberal paternalism begins from the assumption that the poor cannot act in their own self-interest. They lead disordered lives that keep them trapped in cycles of generational poverty. The role of the state is to act as a strict parent who instills order and discipline by restricting welfare benefits, enforcing work mandates, and meting out harsh punishments for those who cause disorder. This paternalistic approach to poverty governance valorizes ideals of citizenship traditionally associated with masculinity, particularly labor market participation and economic independence.[37] This masculine conception of citizenship devalues domestic care work and instead prioritizes paid employment as the most essential duty of citizenship, for both men and women.[38]

We can see this valorization of paid work and family breadwinning throughout the institutional circuit of prisoner reentry. The state enforces work obligations at virtually every juncture of the institutional circuit through parole conditions, workfare mandates, transitional housing requirements, and child support orders. If men fail to find work or pay child support, they are threatened with a cascade of sanctions, ranging from loss of public benefits and driving privileges to return to prison. Through these intersecting forms of social control, the state seeks to transform formerly incarcerated into idealized masculine citizens: men who engage in paid labor and fulfill their roles as family breadwinners.

Thus, the institutional circuit of prisoner reentry is simultaneously highly disciplinary and grossly fragmented. Formerly incarcerated men experience intersecting forms of social control spread out across a decentralized bureaucratic network. This contradictory mixture of disciplinary social control and bureaucratic fragmentation creates the structural conditions for formerly incarcerated men to experience the runaround.

GETTING THE RUNAROUND

Formerly incarcerated men experience a series of interlinking hassles, costs, and degradation as they flow through the institutional circuit of reentry, an experience I term "the runaround." Simply avoiding reincarceration and maintaining access to public aid drains men's time and resources. The effort it takes just to manage the competing demands of parole, public assistance, and transitional housing saps their energy, drains financial resources, and leaves little time left over to reforge family relationships or pursue economic independence.

The concept of the runaround draws together insights from research on "administrative burden" and "procedural punishment" to shed light on the ways in which mundane, and often hidden, bureaucratic processes undermine reintegration. By documenting these "bureaucratic barriers" to reentry, the runaround helps to "render invisible punishments visible" and to uncover the hidden forms of bureaucratic labor that returning citizens must endure to avoid reincarceration.[39]

The runaround draws inspiration from Pamela Herd and Donald P. Moynihan's concept of "administrative burden."[40] Herd and Moynihan identify a variety of material and psychological costs that citizens incur when they attempt to access basic rights and services, including public assistance, abortion, voting, health insurance, and Social Security. These burdens are not distributed equally. The poorest and most vulnerable citizens disproportionately bear the costs of administrative burdens. What's more, administrative burdens are the result of deliberate policy choices to limit access to rights and benefits, particularly for stigmatized groups. For example, contemporary public assistance programs are intentionally designed to deter the poor from seeking aid. By creating complicated application procedures, imposing work requirements, and subjecting aid recipients to stigmatizing surveillance tactics, policymakers argue that administrative burdens are helping the poor by incentivizing paid work and preventing welfare dependency.[41]

While Herd and Moynihan largely focus on the administrative burdens associated with various social policy programs, sociologists of punishment have focused on the administrative burdens associated with the criminal legal system. In particular, research on criminal courts has shown how mundane court procedures—such as the ordeal of arrest and pretrial detention, the stress and frequency of multiple court appearances, long waits in security lines and courtroom waiting areas, lack of information about the court's processes, and racist and degrading treatment from court officials—function as "procedural punishments" that stigmatize criminal defendants and deprive them of civil rights above and beyond formal criminal sanctions.[42]

The concept of the runaround extends these insights to the case of prisoner reentry. Much of the literature on the barriers to reentry focuses on the "collateral consequences" of criminal convictions, foregrounding the "over 48,000 laws, regulations, and administrative penalties" that block people with criminal records from accessing employment, housing, education, public assistance, voting, and a host of other facets of social inclusion.[43] Other researchers draw attention to the structural disadvantages that block formerly incarcerated people from achieving reentry success. These studies focus on the ways in which histories of poverty, trauma, and discrimination create conditions of "human frailty" that lead to ongoing social exclusion.[44]

However, a full accounting of the barriers to reentry must extend beyond formal laws and individual life histories to also include the diffuse set of bureaucratic practices that functions to destabilize and discourage reintegration. By focusing on these *bureaucratic barriers* to reentry, this book draws attention to the institutional mechanisms that undermine reintegration, showing the ways in which mundane bureaucratic processes function to restrict returning citizens from accessing basic elements of social inclusion.

The runaround also draws our attention to the relational dynamics of reentry, highlighting how social exclusion unfolds in the context of ongoing interactions and relationships *between* returning citizens and state actors.[45] This relational approach foregrounds how the runaround is the outcome of "extreme asymmetries in power" between returning citizens and institutional gatekeepers.[46] Institutional gatekeepers wield power over returning citizens' ability to access material resources and maintain community freedom. As a result, men on the institutional circuit become "vulnerable to the decisions of others."[47] Parole officers, welfare caseworkers, and transitional housing staff can decide whether a person has access to food or shelter; they can invade a person's privacy and dictate where they go and how they spend their time; and they can cut a person off from services or send them back to prison for violating rules. What's more, returning citizens often feel unable to hold institutional gatekeepers accountable. The complexity and opacity of the institutional circuit makes it difficult for returning citizens to understand the rules and procedures that govern their lives. This lack of transparency undermines their ability to locate the source of their frustrations and seek redress from institutional gatekeepers.

Returning citizens experience these profound power asymmetries as an extension of the state's power to punish.[48] Although they are no longer incarcerated, returning citizens continue to lack control over their daily lives. They experience an ongoing diminishment of their civil and social rights, and they are routinely silenced, degraded, and stigmatized by state actors.[49] However, punishment is not only repressive and exclusionary; it also has productive effects. Punishment "molds, trains, builds up, and creates subjects."[50] It elicits emotional responses, conditions interpretive frameworks, trains habits and routines, and shapes practices of identity work. We can see the productive effects of punishment through the ways in which men respond to the runaround.

The runaround provokes a variety of negative emotional responses. When institutional gatekeepers impose long waits, deny access to services, and silence their complaints, men become frustrated and angry, especially when they are already burdened by the stress of poverty and social exclusion. Under these conditions, they become vulnerable to interpreting unintentional errors or the routine application of rules as forms of personal disrespect. They may even come to believe that institutional gatekeepers are intentionally conspiring to set them up for failure. Men respond to these frustrations through resistance. They engage in verbal confrontations with institutional gatekeepers, disobey institutional rules, or engage in systems avoidance. Although these "compensatory manhood acts" allow men to reassert a sense of control over their lives, they confirm cultural expectations that criminalized men are aggressive, lazy, and oppositional to authority.[51] When men resist, they become the kinds of defiant and disengaged men the system is designed to govern.[52]

Men routinely narrated having this kind of oppositional relationship to the state during their youth. However, as men grew older and embraced identities as fathers, they transitioned from an antagonistic relationship with the state to a more cooperative one. Seeking to atone for their past mistakes as fathers, men embraced roles as caretakers and moral guides for their children and grandchildren. They yearned to "be there" for their kids, spending time with them to make up for everything they had lost to incarceration, violence, and substance misuse. But in order to "be there" for their kids, men had to remain out of prison. This meant adopting identities as law-abiding citizens and complying with the mandates of the institutional circuit. In response, men learned to reinterpret the runaround as a short-term inconvenience that can be overcome through hard work and a positive attitude. Through repeated experiences of incarceration and reentry, they internalized the state's messages of individualism and personal responsibility, and they developed a set of skills and sensibilities to more easily navigate the institutional circuit. The routine hassles and indignities of the runaround trained men to conform to dominant cultural expectations of deservingness. In order to access public aid and avoid reincarceration, formerly incarcerated men learned how to demonstrate their ability to follow rules, control their emotions, remain sober, and accept the most immediate and available work. Through these experiences, men transformed themselves into the idealized worker-citizens the state seeks to produce.

In these ways, the runaround produces exactly the kinds of subjects the state seeks to govern: on the one hand, unruly and defiant men who break rules and violate laws—and are thus in need of control and incapacitation—and on the other hand, heroically tenacious men who possess the discipline and personal responsibility to become autonomous worker-citizens—and are thus deserving of social inclusion.[53] However, this promise of social inclusion was often an empty one. Even when men embraced ideologies of personal responsibility and complied with state authorities, they experienced persistent material hardship for years after attaining nominal reentry "success." They continued to live on the edge of poverty, just a job loss or an eviction away from severe hardship.

RESEARCH METHODS

Setting

The book is primarily based on ethnographic fieldwork conducted at Second Chances and Uplift, two community-based nonprofits in New York City. Second Chances is a community-based prisoner reentry agency. Established in the late 1960s, today it serves more than 4,000 clients annually and operates two residential housing facilities and a "one-stop" service center, where I conducted fieldwork. In addition to service provision, it also engages in advocacy campaigns to promote progressive criminal legal reforms. Uplift is a community-based workforce development program. Formed in the early 1980s, today it serves more than 1,000 clients annually in its New York City office and administers a network of community-based affiliates in over 20 cities nationwide. While Second Chances exclusively serves justice-involved people, Uplift serves a more diverse population of "difficult-to-employ" individuals, including returning citizens, but also individuals with histories of substance misuse, homelessness, and welfare receipt. Both programs have long track records of success, boasting multimillion-dollar budgets that include government contracts and partnerships with private charitable foundations.[54]

Between 2011 and 2014 I spent 17 months conducting fieldwork. My research focused on the employment- and family-based services at each organization. At Second Chances I conducted fieldwork in two programs: The Workforce Development Workshop (September 2011–December 2011; September 2012–May 2013) and the Parents in Transition Program (April 2014–September 2014). The Workforce Development Workshop is a 10-day, 80-hour "job readiness" course that teaches returning citizens basic job search skills, such as filling out job applications, creating résumés, behaving during a job interview, networking, dealing with conflicts at work, and addressing their conviction when interacting with employers. After completing the workshop, clients are matched up with an employment specialist, who provides job interview referrals to clients based on their skill set. Once a client is placed in a job, Second Chances continues to provide various retention services and incentives to ensure clients remain employed for their first year. Clients also have the option to participate in vocational training programs in "green" construction and culinary arts. During my fieldwork, the workshop annually enrolled between 300 and 500 clients, and each workshop usually consisted of 20–40 clients.

The Parents in Transition Program was another option for people who completed the workshop. The program was designed to increase formerly incarcerated parents' emotional and financial contributions to their children. The program provided formerly incarcerated parents with a part-time, paid internship for three months. The internships paid $8 per hour for 21 hours per week. Program participants also received an unlimited subway pass, called a MetroCard, every week to allow them to travel to their internship sites and search for work during their off time. As a condition of participating in the program, participants were required to attend weekly Responsible Fatherhood classes, where they learned about their financial and emotional responsibilities toward their children, as well as to participate in a "Work Circle," where participants would discuss their internships and strategies for landing permanent employment.

At Uplift, I conducted fieldwork in its Responsible Fatherhood Program (April 2014–December 2014). The program was also designed to promote the financial and emotional contributions of noncustodial fathers to their children. Clients at Uplift were required to attend parenting and healthy relationship classes for four days a week for two weeks. Clients could either attend in the daytime from 9:00 a.m. to 2:00 p.m. or in the evening from 3:00 p.m. to 8:00 p.m. Clients were provided with a free MetroCard to commute to and from the facility as well as a free meal for attending. Once they completed the parenting and relationships curriculum, clients were required to attend a four-day Job Readiness workshop in the third week, which taught clients basic job search skills, such as preparing for job interviews and crafting a résumé. Upon completion of this workshop, clients were set up with an employment specialist, who worked with clients to place them in a job that suited their skill set. Clients were also eligible to participate in a free Occupational Safety and Health Administration (OSHA) 10 hour training session.

Second Chances and Uplift provided windows into the institutional circuit of reentry. Prisoner reentry programs represent junctions where various tributaries of the institutional circuit converge. Both programs relied on parole, public assistance agencies, child support authorities, and transitional housing facilities for client referrals, and returning citizens utilized the services at Second Chances and Uplift to fulfill various work-related obligations mandated by these bureaucracies. The book builds out from observations at Second Chances and Uplift to chart the wider network of criminal legal and social welfare bureaucracies that govern study participants' daily lives.

The study's setting in New York City may raise questions about whether the findings presented here are generalizable to other cities. While New York City may not be a "typical" or "representative" city to study reentry, it is precisely the city's unique features that make it a powerful case study.[55] The city's deep socioeconomic inequalities and its complex social service infrastructure allow us to observe the bureaucratic barriers to reentry in stark relief.[56] While the exact empirical conditions may be different in other cities, the findings of this book reveal generalizable social processes about how criminal legal and social welfare bureaucracies shape reentry processes.[57]

New York is also a powerful case study because it represents a receptive reentry context in which we might not expect returning citizens to experience significant barriers to reentry. The state offers a relatively generous safety net to returning citizens. It was among the first states to opt out of federal mandates banning people convicted of drug offenses from receiving food stamps. It is also one of only a handful of states that offers cash assistance to single adults without children, many of whom are formerly incarcerated men. New York policymakers have adopted an "evidence-based" approach to prisoner reentry that focuses on providing a variety of prerelease services and reentry programs to facilitate the transition from incarceration to community. New York City has a high density of community-based service providers, and it has a relatively accessible public transit system compared to other cities. And yet even in this receptive context, I find that returning citizens persistently encounter bureaucratic obstacles that undermine economic independence and diminish their civil rights.

Fieldwork at Second Chances and Uplift

When I began graduate school in 2009, a burgeoning body of scholarship had emerged documenting the profoundly negative impact mass incarceration was having on American society.[58] These studies were among the first to empirically document the myriad barriers formerly incarcerated people faced to achieve reintegration. Yet none of these studies had provided a ground-level account of how returning citizens navigated these barriers in their daily lives. How do people released from prison make sense of the immense challenges they face? What strategies do they develop to navigate the obstacles to reintegration? What happens to returning citizens who avoid reincarceration? What do their lives look like?

I set out to find a field site where I could observe people navigating the barriers to reentry firsthand. In September 2011 I saw an announcement for an event called "Dismantling Mass Incarceration" through the NYU Sociology Department listserv. The event was a national symposium of prison reform advocates held in New York City. It was at this event that I first learned about Second Chances after picking up one of its brochures. I contacted the volunteer coordinator the following week and began volunteering soon afterward. By chance, I was asked to assist with the program's Workforce Development

Workshop. Because of my placement in the workshop, I became interested in how returning citizens negotiate the barriers to employment.

After volunteering for a semester and writing a paper about my experiences for a class project, I decided to expand the project and gain formal approval from New York University's institutional review board (IRB). With the organization's permission and IRB approval, I began conducting formal ethnographic fieldwork between September 2012 and May 2013 in the Workforce Development Workshop. During this period, I was fully integrated as a volunteer staff member, spending two to three days per week at the facility for four to eight hours per day. I performed a variety of tasks. I designed and taught a curriculum on résumé writing, conducted mock job interviews, edited internal documents, and made outreach phone calls. I also worked one on one with 63 clients to help them craft résumés. These informal "résumé interviews" not only allowed me to document program participants' work and incarceration histories but also provided some of my first insights into clients' entanglements with parole and safety-net bureaucracies outside of Second Chances. I also conducted several informal focus groups. These class discussions would often unfold when I would introduce myself to the class at the start of every workshop. At other times workshop facilitators would leave me in charge of the class, and I would use the opportunity to lead a class discussion. These focus groups had a loose and informal structure and covered a range of topics, including the barriers to reentry, racism, the war on drugs, parole, the prison-industrial complex, addiction, and personal responsibility, among other topics. I made audio recordings of three of these focus groups.

As busy as this may sound, I was able to spend a considerable portion of my days simply observing what went on at the facility and interacting with clients and staff members over lunch and during breaks. I carried around a notepad and took handwritten field notes throughout the day. Since I was in an office setting, this did not draw very much attention. I would transcribe my field notes on a computer after returning home each day. I also had a desk and a computer at Second Chances, which I would use to write up field notes during breaks.

My class and race background initially made me an outsider at Second Chances. I grew up in Manhattan Beach, California, a wealthy, White suburb of Los Angeles. This was worlds away from the disadvantaged New York City neighborhoods where most Black and Latinx clients and frontline staff members had grown up.[59] For most program participants, their highest level of education was a GED. By contrast, I had recently graduated from UC Berkeley and was working toward my PhD at New York University. I come from a mixed ethnic background. My mother grew up in a Mexican American household in East Los Angeles. My father was born in Hawaii to a Japanese American mother and a Polish American father. Throughout my life, I have primarily identified as Mexican and Japanese American. At Second Chances, however, most people perceived me as White. My relatively light skin tone; Polish last name; educational background; and upper middle-class, southern California style of self-presentation set me apart from clients and frontline staff members, who were predominantly formerly incarcerated people of color. Instead, these attributes aligned me more closely with the managerial staff at Second Chances, who were predominantly White and college educated.[60] My age also set me apart. When I began fieldwork, I had just turned 26, making me about a decade younger than most clients, who were in their late thirties, forties, and fifties. Finally, I have never had contact with the criminal legal system in my life. Although I have family members who have struggled with addiction and have had scrapes with the law, they have largely been able to avoid serious prison time. Instead, they were able to achieve sobriety through family support, insurance-funded rehabilitation programs, and ongoing participation in Alcoholics Anonymous. Thus, at the outset of my fieldwork my understanding of incarceration and reentry was based entirely on academic literature and pop culture, not lived experience.

Despite my outsider status with clients and frontline staff members, I was able to develop working relationships with research participants by being willing to help out in any way I could. I gained notoriety early on by becoming the local "résumé expert." One of the main goals of the Workforce Development Workshop was for program participants to graduate with a high-quality résumé. Since most staff members were too busy to spend the time working one on one with clients to craft résumés, I was put in charge of this task.[61] I would sit with program participants for 30–45 minutes at a computer, documenting their employment histories and asking questions to draw out qualities that made them unique employees. In the course of a few months, I developed a reputation as the resident "résumé expert." Program participants would seek me out for help, and staff members relied on me to produce high-quality résumés.

I also developed rapport by positioning myself as an ally who could give voice to the formerly incarcerated community. Eric, one of the workshop facilitators, played a crucial role in vouching for me as an ally. Eric was a

Latino man in his forties with a long history of addiction and incarceration. Eric was passionate about helping people overcome the barriers to reentry and had a keen interest in criminal legal reform movements. He was well read on the subject and participated in various public speaking events advocating for reform. Eric and I had regular conversations about the injustices of mass incarceration and the politics of criminal justice reform. Eric seemed to appreciate my academic perspective and would pick my brain about the academic literature on mass incarceration. Likewise, I valued Eric's perspective as someone with firsthand knowledge of the hardships of reentry, and I relied on him as a key informant throughout my fieldwork.

Every two weeks, Second Chances would welcome a new cohort of workshop participants. On the first day of class I would introduce myself and discuss my research project. These presentations were often quite awkward. The audience was either indifferent to my study or actively skeptical of my motivations for wanting to pry into their lives. However, as I developed rapport with Eric, he would help warm up the crowd for me. Before my presentation, he would often introduce me as his "partner" and an "advocate who does very important work." He would tell the class that participating in my research project was a way for them to "get your voices heard." I would often play off this framing, explaining to clients that the goal of my research was to learn about the reentry process from their point of view. My hope was that in doing so, we could one day change the "hearts and minds" of policymakers so that they will design criminal justice policies that are more closely aligned with the lived realities of returning citizens. I was also transparent about the fact that I came from a privileged background and did not know the first thing about what it was like to grow up in a disadvantaged neighborhood or experience incarceration. I was there to listen and learn from them, and hopefully to use my privilege to amplify their voices to a wider audience. Although some people were still skeptical of my presence, Eric's endorsement helped to normalize my outsider status in the space.

In addition to my work within the workshop, I also assisted staff at Second Chances with recruitment efforts at a local parole office from March 2013 to May 2013. We would arrive at the parole office when it opened at 8:00 a.m. and stay for two to four hours before returning to Second Chances. Every hour we made an announcement in the waiting area about Second Chances's employment program and attempted to enroll participants. These outings allowed me to observe the general workings of a parole office and helped to contextualize returning citizens' descriptions of parole.

My initial round of fieldwork at Second Chances ended May 2013, but I returned to Second Chances for follow-up fieldwork between March 2014 and September 2014. In contrast to my initial round of fieldwork, which was focused primarily on how returning citizens navigate the barriers to employment, my next round of fieldwork focused specifically on how men navigate issues related to fatherhood and child support. As a result, my fieldwork shifted from the Workforce Development Workshop to the Parents in Transition Program.

During this time, I was concurrently conducting fieldwork at Uplift's Responsible Fatherhood Program, which began April 2014 and concluded in December 2014. I found Uplift's program through an internet search. I emailed the program coordinator about conducting research. He invited me for an interview and shortly afterward granted me formal permission to conduct research at the facility. Since I was splitting time between two organizations, I took on a less active role than I had in my initial round of data collection. I visited each facility once or twice a week and spent two to four hours at each facility observing classes and interacting with clients and staff. Since I spent significantly more time collecting data at Second Chances, the majority of data presented in the book is derived from my fieldwork there.

Interviews

The fieldwork was supplemented by 45 audio-recorded, in-depth interviews with formerly incarcerated men whom I recruited from classes at Second Chances and Uplift. I chose to focus my sample on men not only because they represent over 90 percent of released inmates in New York state, but also because we know little about men's experiences navigating social welfare bureaucracies. In-depth interviews were conducted in private offices at Second Chances and Uplift, and these ran between one and two hours. The average age of interviewees was 41, and most were either Black or Latino men, except for three who were White. While all the men I interviewed were unemployed and embroiled in various institutional entanglements, they varied in terms of age, incarceration history, and time since release, which allowed for comparisons across age cohorts and reentry experiences.

The book largely focuses on the experiences of men of the "mass imprisonment generation" as they grow into middle age and embrace identities as fathers. However, the book also explores the experiences of men in their midtwenties who are still struggling to construct reformed identities and leave behind criminal lifestyles. By comparing the experiences of men from different age cohorts, we are able to explore variations in how men experience the runaround and form relationships with the state at different stages of the life course.

The sample also draws comparisons between men at different stages of the reentry process. Like previous reentry ethnographies, the book explores the experiences of men during the initial period after release.[62] However, the book also draws on interviews with men who have avoided criminal legal contact for at least three years. While we know that men experience significant "stress and hardship" during the initial transition from prison to community life, we know significantly less about the long-term socioeconomic outlook of returning citizens.[63] By focusing on the experiences of men who have avoided reincarceration for over three years, the book illustrates how men experience material hardship not only during the initial shock of reentry, but also for years after attaining nominal reentry "success."

Since returning citizens are a difficult-to-reach population, I took every opportunity to conduct interviews with willing participants as long as they were men and had been incarcerated at some point in their lives.[64] Interviews occurred in two rounds. The first round occurred between September 2012 and November 2014. During this time I conducted 15 interviews with formerly incarcerated men I had met in classes at Second Chances and Uplift. These men agreed to participate in interviews on a completely voluntary basis and were not paid.

These interviews broadly focused on men's life course narratives before and after incarceration, but they evolved over the course of my fieldwork. I was initially interested in how men navigate the labor market after prison, particularly men's employment histories and how they strategize about managing stigma during interactions with employers. However, early in the course of my fieldwork I began to notice how men's entanglements with parole, public assistance programs, and transitional housing facilities created their own set of obstacles. Some men even downplayed the significance of their criminal records in holding them back from employment. Instead, they cited what I began to call the "runaround" of parole, public assistance, and transitional housing appointments as being the most significant barriers to employment. They felt they could land a job, despite their criminal records, if only they had enough time to conduct a job search instead of running around the city to attend various appointments. As I heard this narrative more and more,

I began to reorient data collection to focus on how these entanglements with the institutional circuit shaped reentry processes.[65]

The second round occurred between July 2015 and July 2016. These interviews were part of a larger study on the effects of incarceration and child support debt on men's reintegration, cofunded by the National Science Foundation and the National Institute of Justice.[66] During this time I conducted 30 interviews with formerly incarcerated men recruited from classes at Second Chances and Uplift. Men were paid $25 in cash for their participation. These interviews also focused on men's life histories and entanglements with the institutional circuit. However, these interviews probed deeper into men's experiences of fatherhood and their entanglements with the child support system.

I exercised caution when interpreting interview data. In some cases, I was able to corroborate statements made during interviews with ethnographic observations at Second Chances, Uplift, and the parole office.[67] However, since I was unable to directly observe men's interactions across the institutional circuit or follow them over their life courses, I was unable to corroborate statements regarding these topics. Instead, I relied on study participants' retrospective accounts. I did not treat these narratives as objective accounts of what had happened in the past. Instead, I treated them as men's partial, subjective interpretations of what they *thought* had happened in the past.[68] These subjective narratives were analytically useful because they provide insights into how formerly incarcerated men interpret their interactions with institutional gatekeepers, how they anticipate future experiences with the institutional circuit, and how they think about their young adulthood in relation to the present.[69]

I center the voices of study participants throughout the book. Words enclosed in double quotation marks or set off as block quotes represent direct quotations from audio transcripts of interviews and focus groups, as well as transcripts of handwritten field notes. When quoting from field notes, I follow ethnographic convention to only quote words that I wrote down in my field notes in real time.[70] As noted earlier, my handwritten field notes were transcribed on a computer immediately after leaving the field every day. In many cases I was able to transcribe field notes at my desk at Second Chances within minutes of writing down dialogue. Although audio recordings offer a higher degree of fidelity, I am reasonably confident that these handwritten quotations are faithful representations of the dialogue that unfolded in situ because of the immediacy with which I transcribed my field notes every day.

PLAN OF THE BOOK

Chapter 1 maps the institutional circuit of prisoner reentry in New York City. The chapter traces returning citizens' journeys across a series of institutional domains, documenting the flow of bodies, money, and social control across the various tributaries of the institutional circuit. The chapter reveals how formerly incarcerated men experience the institutional circuit as a contradictory combination of disciplinary social control and bureaucratic fragmentation, which creates the structural conditions for formerly incarcerated men to experience the runaround.

Chapters 2 and 3 unpack the experience of "getting the runaround." Chapter 2 focuses on the material costs of the runaround. The runaround exacts a series of financial and opportunity costs on returning citizens, which act as bureaucratic barriers to reentry. Returning citizens must keep up with these "compliance costs" to avoid reincarceration and maintain access to public aid, but doing so undermines their ability to attain economic independence and rebuild family relationships.[71] Chapter 3 focuses on the subjective effects of the runaround. The repeated hassles of the runaround leave men feeling confused, frustrated, and disempowered. These negative experiences exacerbate the physical and emotional strains of reentry and reinforce men's distrust of state authorities. Men attempt to reassert their sense of masculine autonomy and express hostility toward the state through noncompliance and system avoidance, but these acts of resistance push them further to the margins of mainstream social life. By repeatedly subjecting men to "procedural injustice," the institutional circuit produces exactly the kinds of defiant and disengaged men it is designed to govern.[72]

Chapters 4 and 5 explore how formerly incarcerated men learn how to cope with the strains of the runaround. Chapter 4 explores how men developed a set of interpretive frames to view the runaround as a short-term inconvenience that can be overcome through tenacity and a positive attitude. The chapter traces the life histories of middle-aged men of the "mass imprisonment generation" and explores how they express reformed masculinity through a cooperative relationship with the state. These reformed masculine identities were rooted in cultural narratives of individualism and personal responsibility, which aligned with men's biographies as entrepreneurial "hustlers" and were reinforced by the curriculum of rehabilitation programs throughout the institutional circuit of reentry. Men drew on these narratives to construct symbolic boundaries between themselves and "undeserving" others.

Chapter 5 explores the hidden forms of bureaucratic labor formerly incarcerated men undertake to comply with the mandates of the institutional circuit, what Andre called being "professionally poor."[73] Men had to constantly labor to make themselves "institutionally legible."[74] That is, they had to translate their complex experiences of reentry into coherent bureaucratic narratives that resonated with dominant institutional understandings of rehabilitation. By making themselves institutionally legible, formerly incarcerated men are able to avoid reincarceration and access material resources. But in doing so, they reinforce symbolic boundaries between the deserving and undeserving poor and reify the state's categories of deservingness.

Chapter 6 explores the experiences of formerly incarcerated men who continue to struggle with economic insecurity, despite internalizing cultural narratives of individualism and learning the skills to be professionally poor. Almost half the men I interviewed had avoided reincarceration for at least three years but continued to find themselves in dire economic straits. Even though they had attained nominal reentry "success," these men constantly lived their lives on a razor's edge of poverty. In many cases, a job loss, a relapse, or an eviction had derailed relative economic stability and pushed them back into poverty. Even formerly incarcerated staff members at Second Chances and Uplift lived at the precipice of poverty. The chapter illustrates how dominant metrics of reentry "success" miss the ongoing material struggles returning citizens face long after they leave behind criminal careers. And it shows how the institutional circuit functions to keep returning citizens trapped in cycles of poverty and bureaucratic processing rather than serving as a conduit for social inclusion.

The conclusion provides an overview of the major themes of the book and offers suggestions to chart a new path forward for reentry. By closely examining how formerly incarcerated men navigate the institutional circuit of reentry, we gain deeper insights into the bureaucratic mechanisms that undermine reintegration and diminish the citizenship rights of formerly incarcerated people.[75] The book concludes by outlining an agenda for creating a social justice approach to reentry policy.

ONE

The Institutional Circuit
of Prisoner Reentry

VICTOR WAS RELEASED from prison just over two months ago. A Latino man in his fifties, he had served 30 years in state prison for what he claimed was a "justified homicide." As we ride the subway together downtown, Victor tells me that his main hobbies are reading books and writing postcards to his friends who are still incarcerated. But since his release, he hasn't had the time to read a single book, and he's barely written to any of his friends upstate. Instead, he's spent the last two months running around the city to attend appointments.

In a given week, Victor travels an institutional circuit that takes him across New York City. Parole conditions mandate that Victor reside in a homeless shelter located in East New York, Brooklyn. He was originally paroled to a shelter in the Bronx near his mother's apartment, but he was transferred to the shelter in Brooklyn for his safety after a resident on his floor was killed in a stabbing. His PO also requires him to attend anger management classes and receive substance abuse treatment at an outpatient facility located in the Lower East Side of Manhattan, which is over an hour away from his shelter by subway.

As a condition of living in the homeless shelter, Victor is required to enroll in public assistance and comply with all requirements to maintain eligibility.[1] In addition to regular appointments with his case manager, he is also required to participate in a back-to-work (BTW) program. At the BTW program, Victor is required to participate in job readiness classes and engage in independent job search activities. He must produce two business cards per day to prove that he is actively searching for work. Victor is also required to participate in an offsite work experience program (WEP). The WEP requires welfare recipients to participate in "structured work assignments in

City agencies or non-profit organizations . . . to 'work off their benefits.'"[2] WEP assignments usually involve performing menial tasks, such as picking up garbage; raking leaves; or polishing surfaces in city parks, subway platforms, or city offices.

When I met Victor, he was fed up with his BTW program and WEP assignments. He was trying to enroll in the Workforce Development Workshop at Second Chances to fulfill his welfare requirements instead. He hoped Second Chances would be more responsive to his needs as a person with an incarceration history. But he worried that if Second Chances did not process his paperwork correctly and coordinate with his welfare case manager, he could receive a failure to comply (FTC) sanction from welfare. This would not only cut him off from his welfare benefits but also jeopardize his housing and even his freedom. The shelter requires Victor to comply with all welfare requirements. Failing to do so could lead to being evicted from the shelter, which could cascade into a parole violation if he did not report a change in his housing promptly.

Frustrated, Victor tells me that his experience coming home so far can be summed up by two things: waiting and paperwork. He vents to me in an exacerbated staccato, "Wait, wait, wait; paperwork, paperwork, paperwork." Victor opens his backpack, revealing a cluttered mess of documents he's accumulated from his various bureaucratic entanglements: a jumble of informational handouts, flyers, and worksheets from various rehabilitation programs along with what look to be hundreds of pages of official records from prison, parole, public assistance, and the shelter system. "I already did a bunch of programs in prison," he tells me. "Now I have to do more programs, except the infrastructure is all jumbled."

Victor feels that in addition to being geographically fragmented, the various programs and agencies that govern his life are more exploitative than supportive. He tells me, "Everyone is making money off of me." He notes that his substance abuse treatment program is paid for through his Medicaid benefits, and he thinks that Second Chances profits off his participation in the Workforce Development Workshop. "I know it's a 501(c)(3) [nonprofit], but if I wasn't here, no one would be getting paid." He continues, "I mean good for you, you get a salary, but you wouldn't be getting paid if I weren't around. . . . It's nothing personal, I'm not personally mad at anyone. . . . It's the way the system is set up."

Victor returns to his frustration about having to run around the city to attend programs. "Who's paying for me to get around to all these appointments?" he asks rhetorically. Victor receives a paltry $45 per month in cash assistance, which he is supposed to use to cover personal expenses like subway passes. I commiserate with Victor, "It's like they design it to make it harder on you." He replies, "Oh they set you up to fail. They want you to fail."

. . .

As Victor's case illustrates, returning citizens find themselves enmeshed in an "institutional circuit" upon release: a loop of agencies, facilities, and programs that supervise and provide services to the formerly incarcerated.[3] Victor feels that the institutional circuit of reentry has set him up to fail. To comply with parole conditions and access public aid, he must circum-navigate the city every week, spending most of his time and meager income riding the subway, waiting at offices, and filling out paperwork. Rather than addressing his underlying needs, he thinks that rehabilitative programs view him solely as an avenue for extracting public funds and generating grant dollars. And he feels constantly at risk of losing access to public aid or returning to prison, with a simple paperwork error potentially triggering a cascade of sanctions. Victor's experience suggests that rather than facilitating reintegration, the institutional circuit of reentry perversely undermines it.

This chapter examines the structural conditions that underpin Victor's experiences. It maps the network of criminal legal and social welfare bureaucracies that constitute the institutional circuit of prisoner reentry in New York City. Building out from interviews and ethnographic observations, it traces formerly incarcerated men's experiences navigating various bureaucratic systems across the city. The chapter is framed around the metaphor of "circulation" to describe how the institutional circuit manages the problems associated with reentry by continually circulating and displacing returning citizens across a series of institutional domains. As physical bodies move through the institutional circuit, public funds and grant dollars attached to their caseloads follow them. Forms of social control accumulate in the daily lives of returning citizens as they move from one institution to the next.

The chapter homes in on two significant nodes of institutional overlap: community-based reentry programs and transitional housing facilities. Both sites represent junctions where various tributaries of the institutional circuit converge, allowing us to follow the flow of bodies, money, and social control across various institutional domains. The chapter traces how transformations in penal and social policy in the last decades of the twentieth century—particularly the "punitive turn" in community corrections and the implementation of neoliberal "welfare reform"—have created a symbiotic division of labor between community-based reentry programs; transitional housing facilities; and various state agencies, including parole, public assistance programs, and child support authorities.

By tracing the flow of bodies, money, and social control across the institutional circuit of reentry, this chapter reveals the structural underpinnings of the runaround. Formerly incarcerated men experience the institutional circuit as a contradictory combination of disciplinary social control and bureaucratic fragmentation. On the one hand, the various agencies that make up the institutional circuit of reentry are engaged in a shared neoliberal project to discipline the behavior of criminalized men and transform them into productive market actors. On the other hand, these disciplinary efforts are spread out across a fragmented network of public and private bureaucracies. I argue that this context of disciplinary social control and bureaucratic fragmentation creates the structural conditions for formerly incarcerated men to experience the runaround.

POVERTY GOVERNANCE AND THE INSTITUTIONAL CIRCUIT

Anthropologist Kim Hopper and his colleagues coined the term "institutional circuit" to describe the cycles of institutionalization homeless adults experience as they circulate between hospitals, shelters, treatment facilities, and jails.[4] Through "largely haphazard and uncoordinated transfers across institutional domains" homeless populations are constantly displaced and their underlying needs are not met as they are shuffled between institutional spaces.[5] Hopper and his colleagues argue that rather than facilitating long-term housing placements, homeless service systems perversely perpetuate homelessness by constantly recirculating marginalized populations through the institutional circuit.

This circular logic of poverty management plays out in institutional spaces beyond homeless services. Ethnographers studying the day-to-day work of poverty governance illustrate how frontline actors, such as ambulance crews, jail intake staff, and hospital triage nurses, are constantly circulating the physical bodies of marginalized populations across institutional domains.[6]

Sociologist Armando Lara-Millán argues that this work of "redistributing the poor" allows frontline actors to displace responsibility for managing burdensome caseloads onto other institutional actors. This allows underfunded state bureaucracies to resolve budget crises, all while appearing to comply with legal mandates to provide minimal care. By moving bodies and money across institutional domains, frontline actors are able to create the "illusion of policy success."[7]

Research on the daily lives of marginalized populations has documented how this constant circulation leads to ever-increasing forms of social control. As marginalized people flow through institutional circuits, they experience "multidirectional" bureaucratic entanglements.[8] Their displacement from one institution to the next results in a cascade of social control, with each new institutional entanglement triggering new forms of surveillance and discipline.[9] These forms of social control begin to "link, loop, and overlap across state terrains," working "in circular ways to form feedback loops of disadvantage."[10] Marginalized people become trapped in unending cycles of institutionalization, an experience sociologists Susan Starr Sered and Maureen Norton-Hawk call "institutional captivity."[11]

In the context of reentry, returning citizens navigate a loop of agencies, facilities, and programs following release. This institutional circuit includes community corrections agencies such as parole, probation, and "problem-solving" courts; public assistance agencies and community-based workforce development programs; transitional housing facilities, such as halfway houses, residential treatment facilities, "three-quarter" sober houses, and homeless shelters; outpatient therapeutic programs related to substance abuse, anger management, and "responsible fatherhood"; and family welfare agencies such as the office of child support enforcement, family court, and child protective services. This network of agencies, programs, and facilities acts as a gatekeeper that governs access to public aid and community freedom. While jails and prisons were certainly stops on the institutional circuit for study participants, I have bracketed correctional facilities from this discussion to highlight the fact that formerly incarcerated men circulate through a variety of institutional settings while living in the community and to show that formerly incarcerated men navigate a web of social control even in the absence of reincarceration.

We can see the circular logic of poverty governance play out on the institutional circuit of reentry. For example, to keep up with overlapping appointments and obligations, formerly incarcerated men circulate between various offices and facilities throughout the city. For men like Victor, this means circumnavigating the city every week to keep up with mandated appointments. Over months and years, formerly incarcerated men churn through programs and facilities multiple times, as they are forced to repeat classes, resubmit applications, and return to housing facilities following sanctions, job losses, relapses, and evictions. As their bodies flow across these institutional spaces, funds attached to their caseloads follow them. These funds are often extracted from returning citizens' welfare benefits in the form of Medicaid reimbursements, as Victor observed, and, as we will see later, in the form of rental allowance checks and food stamps.

The more returning citizens become enmeshed in the institutional circuit, the more they experience techniques of social control in circular ways. As returning citizens accumulate institutional entanglements, forms of surveillance, behavioral mandates, and sanctions form "feedback loops" across institutional spaces, with entanglements with one institution triggering oversight from other institutions.[12] For example, parole conditions required Victor to participate in anger management and substance abuse treatment and to take up residence in a homeless shelter. Living in the shelter triggered entanglements with public assistance programs, which in turn triggered entanglements with a BTW program. Victor is now caught up in a loop of social control as he juggles parole appointments, treatment sessions, and public assistance requirements. Failing to successfully manage any one of these obligations can trigger a cascade of sanctions: a missed welfare appointment can lead to lost benefits, which can trigger an eviction from housing and potentially a parole violation.

The institutional circuit of prisoner reentry is composed of over a dozen public and private agencies. However, there are "watersheds" within this network of bureaucracies "into which other streams on the institutional circuit flow in and out."[13] The next sections focus on two of those watersheds: community-based prisoner reentry programs and transitional housing facilities.

MAPPING THE INSTITUTIONAL CIRCUIT OF REENTRY

It's orientation day at Second Chances. Every two weeks a new cohort of formerly incarcerated jobseekers begins the Workforce Development Program.

The program begins with an orientation session, in which participants learn about the rules of the program and fill out the required paperwork to become officially enrolled. A group of about 30 formerly incarcerated jobseekers, mostly Black and Latino men in their thirties and forties, are packed into a small, windowless classroom for today's orientation. The men wait impatiently for the orientation to start: fidgeting with phones and newspapers, bouncing their legs, and sighing as they wait for the facilitator to begin. Their impatience reflects their desperation to find a job. Struggling with acute poverty and under pressure from parole, transitional housing facilities, public assistance programs, child support authorities, and family members to find on-the-books employment, the men are here today with the hope that the Workforce Development Workshop will change their luck.

The orientation gets underway. Casey, a Black formerly incarcerated career counselor, explains how the program works. It begins with a mandatory 10-day, 80-hour "job readiness" workshop, which starts the following Monday at 9:00 a.m. If clients complete the workshop, they move on to job placement and retention services, with the option of enrolling in additional vocational skills training. Many in the room take issue with the program's steep time commitment, citing various obligations that conflict with the workshop. They begin bombarding Casey with questions: "I have a drug treatment appointment every Monday. Will I be able to leave early for that?" "I have court on Monday. Can I be excused that day?" "I have to be back at the halfway house by 3:30. Can I get a note?" "I have a parole appointment next week. Can you call my PO?" Casey deflects most of these questions, assuring them that the program will provide letters of participation to excuse them from other obligations.

These orientation sessions at Second Chances provide a window into the institutional circuit of prisoner reentry. They reveal how community-based service providers function as hubs where state systems of punishment and welfare converge. Programs like Second Chances rely on parole, public assistance agencies, and transitional housing facilities for client referrals, and their budgets reflect a patchwork of funding contracts from criminal legal and welfare agencies at various levels of government. At the same time, returning citizens utilize the services at Second Chances and Uplift to fulfill their obligations to parole, public assistance programs, child support agencies, and transitional housing facilities, all of which require returning citizens to engage in work-related activities as a condition of maintaining freedom or receiving aid. Community-based service providers are also important sources of other therapeutic programs mandated by the state, including substance abuse treatment, anger management classes, and "responsible fatherhood" programs. To understand why community-based service providers play such a prominent role in the reentry field, we first need to unpack broader transformations in penal and social policy over the last several decades that have led to the privatization of rehabilitation.

Community-Based Reentry Programs, Parole, and the Privatization of Rehabilitation

The ascendance of community-based service providers as the primary purveyors of rehabilitation reflects deeper shifts in the institution of parole that occurred as a result of the "punitive turn" in the corrections field.[14] For most of the twentieth century, the work of POs straddled the boundary between social work and law enforcement. Parole officers supported the rehabilitative needs of former prisoners through direct services, such as counseling, housing assistance, and job placement, while also enforcing sanctions to protect public safety.[15] However, since the 1970s the professional balance of parole has shifted heavily toward law enforcement. Sociolegal scholar Jonathan Simon documents how during this period experts declared that "nothing works" to rehabilitate offenders, undermining parole's institutional identity as a social work profession.[16] At the same time, the collapse of the industrial labor market and the hardening of urban poverty removed many of the informal mechanisms of social control that POs had relied upon to monitor people under parole supervision. With people under parole supervision now unmoored from the routines of work, family, and community, POs had to turn to new technologies of surveillance, such as actuarial risk predictions, offender databases, and drug testing, to monitor people under parole supervision and craft a coherent institutional narrative.[17]

By the 1990s this law enforcement approach to parole had become firmly institutionalized, with the "old penology" of social work and rehabilitation replaced by a "new penology" focused on surveillance, risk management, and systems efficiency.[18] Today, this law enforcement approach is exemplified by the fact that POs in many jurisdictions carry firearms and handcuffs, and their daily work focuses almost exclusively on surveillance activities, such as monitoring compliance with conditions, drug testing, collecting fees, and arresting violators.[19] To the extent that POs continue to engage in rehabilitative activities, it is largely in the form of resource referrals to third-party service providers. Indeed, a division of labor has emerged in the community corrections field, with parole handling the surveillance and law enforcement aspects of community supervision and community-based non-profits handling the provision of rehabilitation services.[20]

The ability of parole to rely on community-based nonprofits to deliver rehabilitative services also reflects broader transformations in the delivery of social services in the age of neoliberalism. Since the 1970s, "neoliberal re-forms have strengthened the state's capacities to serve markets, restructured its operations around market principles, and extended its reach through collaborations with civil society organizations."[21] Thus, at the same time that parole was becoming more punitive, the social service infrastructure in the US welfare state was becoming increasingly privatized. Throughout this period, policymakers devolved responsibility for social service administration from federal authorities to state and local governments. State and local governments, in turn, outsourced responsibility for service provision to private charities, community groups, and nonprofit organizations.[22] Between 1973 and 1995 federal funds flowing to nonprofits increased by 400 percent, from $23 billion to $175 billion.[23] Today, local nonprofits are the "linch-pins of the contemporary safety net."[24] In major cities across the country, community-based organizations represent the majority of social service providers responsible for "job training, adult education, child care, temporary emergency food or cash assistance, and substance abuse or mental health treatment."[25]

Although the criminal legal system has always relied on the help of churches and private charities to manage the needs of returning prisoners to some degree, the scale on which contemporary "community-based" nonprofits receive state funding to deliver rehabilitative services is unprecedented.[26] Policies such as the Second Chance Act of 2007 and the White House Office of Faith-Based and Neighborhood Partnerships have dramatically expanded federal funding for community-based prisoner reentry programs. The number of community-based prisoner reentry programs more than tripled between 1996 and 2007, from fewer than 400 in 1996 to more than 1,300 in 2007.[27]

The privatization of rehabilitation has also accelerated in recent years due to the growing legitimacy of the "smart-on-crime" movement. Since the onset of the Great Recession in 2008, state governments throughout the country have struggled to reduce public spending in the face of shrinking revenue and growing budget deficits.[28] Rather than continuing costly and inefficient "tough-on-crime" policies of the past, lawmakers today are seeking to get "smart-on-crime" by reorienting criminal justice policy making around the principles of technical expertise and empirical evaluation.[29] Their goal is to find cheaper and more efficient ways of achieving public safety than simply warehousing offenders in costly, overcrowded prisons. With more inmates released from federal and state prisons every year than ever before, the issue of prisoner reentry has emerged as a centerpiece of this reform movement. Reformers hope that by expanding access to community-based rehabilitation programs, they can prevent cycles of recidivism that contribute to prison overcrowding and drain correctional resources.[30] For their part, community-based reentry programs promote themselves as being small-scale, local initiatives that are more flexible and cost-effective than large-scale government bureaucracies and thus better suited to developing and implementing state-of-the-art "evidence-based" practices proven to reduce recidivism. Moreover, by being embedded in the fabric of local communities, these programs promote themselves as being more "culturally competent" and responsive to the needs of the populations they serve.[31]

Although smart-on-crime reformers have revitalized faith in the rehabilitative ideal after decades of tough-on-crime hegemony, it is important to emphasize that smart-on-crime reformers in New York and elsewhere justify rehabilitation primarily in terms of risk management and cost savings.[32] The ultimate aim of these interventions is to lower recidivism rates, reduce prison overcrowding, and maximize public safety returns on corrections spending.[33] In this context "rehabilitation is viewed as a means of managing risk, not a welfarist end in itself."[34] Thus, smart-on-crime lawmakers are only concerned with addressing returning citizens' rehabilitative needs insofar as "these needs correlate with recidivism."[35]

Three of the most prominent needs deemed worthy of intervention are violent behavior, drug addiction, and unemployment. A network of community-based service providers has emerged in recent years to address these rehabilitative needs through anger management classes, substance abuse treatment programs, and workforce development training. Parole officers utilize these community-based programs not only to address the rehabilitative needs of people under their supervision but also as risk management tools to monitor the whereabouts of people under supervision and test their capacity for rule compliance.[36]

Indeed, participating in substance abuse treatment and anger management was a mandatory parole condition for many study participants, regardless of whether men felt they actually needed these interventions. When Kenneth, a 33-year-old Black man, was released from prison in 2012, he was mandated to attend outpatient substance abuse treatment and anger management classes. Kenneth felt that the only reason he was mandated to drug treatment was because of his conviction for selling drugs, not because he was actually in need of treatment. Kenneth said he was a recreational marijuana user but didn't have any addiction issue. To him substance abuse treatment is "for a person that really has a drug problem. . . . That's like for [a] crackhead, [a] dope [fiend]. . . . Not a person that just smokes weed. It's just not for that." A person's self-reported history of drug use can also be grounds for mandatory treatment. For example, Peter, a 34-year-old Black man, said that when he was paroled in 2010, one of his parole conditions was to participate in a mandatory outpatient drug treatment because he had reported a history of marijuana use. He tells me, "I've never been arrested for any drug related charges whatsoever. I've never been arrested under the influence of any drugs. But because I've used marijuana, they made me take the program."

Men like Kenneth and Peter often questioned the therapeutic value of these programs and complained about the hassles they created in their daily lives. Because rehabilitation programs are dispersed across a fragmented network of service providers throughout the city, returning citizens must spend their limited time and resources to attend appointments. As we saw in Victor's case, this could mean circumnavigating the city to attend mandated rehabilitation programs.

In addition to violence and drug abuse, unemployment is another prominent target of rehabilitative intervention. A guiding assumption of smart-on-crime policy is that developing the human capital of former prisoners will keep them sober, employed, and out of prison.[37] Indeed, employment had been a centerpiece of New York governor Andrew Cuomo's smart-on-crime platform.[38] In 2012 he launched Work for Success, a jobs initiative designed to reduce high rates of unemployment among formerly incarcerated New Yorkers by expanding access to job readiness training. The initiative was led by a coalition of policymakers, government agencies, and community-based service providers. In line with smart-on-crime tenets, the Work for Success initiative involved evaluating existing employment programs, utilizing "evidence-based, action-oriented research to identify which strategies work best."[39] The initiative was also designed to bolster partnerships between government agencies and community-based organizations. Indeed, the executive committee was composed of over a dozen community-based service providers, who worked with the governor's office to expand access to evidence-based job readiness training programs. In addition to expanding access to job readiness training, New York has also been at the forefront of removing legal barriers to employment. In recent years, lawmakers have removed barriers to licensure for a variety of professions, implemented ban the box legislation, and created laws to limit access to criminal records.[40]

Parole plays a central role in implementing this "work first" approach to reentry. Indeed, POs play a prominent role in impelling employment among returning citizens.[41] For example, study participants reported that finding employment or participating in job training was a common parole condition, and that parole supervision intensified during periods of unemployment. They experienced longer waits at parole offices and more frequent parole appointments when they weren't working. Because they were unemployed and had nowhere to be, they surmised that POs would use long waits and frequent appointments as a way to monitor their behavior and keep them out of trouble. Conversely, when study participants found employment, they reported that parole supervision became less intense and their relationship with their PO improved. For example, Walter, one of the formerly incarcerated workshop facilitators at Second Chances, told the class, "I think parole was easy for me because [of] the fact that I came home and two [weeks] out of being out, I started working. So, by me having a job, all this time, my PO never messed with me."

Parole also facilitates employment through service referrals to community-based workforce development programs. As the Work for Success initiative illustrates, partnerships between government agencies and community-based service providers are central to New York's smart-on-crime approach. I observed how this system of service referrals worked while conducting outreach work at a local parole office for Second Chances. As a volunteer intern, my job was to shadow Selena, a Latina woman in her early twenties fresh out of college, who was in charge of recruitment efforts for the workforce development program at Second Chances. During my time working alongside Selena, I observed a symbiotic relationship between POs and nonprofit outreach workers. Parole officers relied on community-based organizations for service referrals to meet the rehabilitative needs of people on their caseloads. The office employed a dedicated reentry program coordinator, who maintained a kiosk of information pamphlets for reentry programs and worked with community-based organizations to schedule recruitment activities. On my first outing to a parole office with Selena, we were welcomed by the bureau chief, who told us, "The building is yours." We were allowed to occupy an empty cubicle in the office and were free to make announcements in the waiting area to enroll potential clients as often as we wanted. We would make our rounds through the office, introducing our program to POs, who would escort interested jobseekers after their appointments were over.

At the same time, community-based service providers, like Second Chances, rely on parole offices for client referrals. Second Chances was under constant pressure to keep up with contractually mandated performance metrics.[42] The program risked losing funding if it could not enroll enough program participants, and parole offices provided fertile grounds for recruiting potential clients. However, despite the abundance of potential recruits, Selena and I faced stiff competition. Two other community-based employment programs were also recruiting clients at the parole office. Although we maintained collegial relationships with the other outreach workers, we were nonetheless competing for a limited number of client referrals.

One of the main challenges Selena and I faced was that many of the people we were trying to recruit had already cycled through in our competitors' workforce development programs. They had completed job readiness training and been placed in jobs but were unemployed a few months later. People in this situation were seeking a job referral from Second Chances, not another mandatory job readiness class. For example, one potential recruit explained to me that he had already been through our competitor's workforce development program: "Like I said, I already did [a job readiness program.] . . . I'm job ready. . . . I have a résumé and all that." Another potential recruit was uninterested in going through the routine of another job readiness class: "You wear the suit; you take notes on what to say and what not to say. . . . Yeah I did all of that in the drug treatment program."

The relationship between parole and community-based service providers illustrates how bodies, money, and social control flow across the institutional circuit. Formerly incarcerated men circulate through outpatient substance abuse treatment programs, anger management classes, and workforce development programs to comply with parole conditions, often churning through multiple programs. Community-based nonprofits rely on client referrals from parole to meet mandated performance metrics and maintain the flow of grant funding. If formerly incarcerated men do not fully comply with the rules and requirements of these programs, they face potential parole sanctions.

Community-Based Reentry Programs
and Neoliberal Welfare Reform

Parole is not the only state agency that relies on community-based non-profits to deliver employment services. New York City's Human Resource Administration (HRA), the agency responsible for administering public assistance programs, relies heavily on a network of private service providers, including Second Chances and Uplift, to provide employment services to welfare recipients. Although single mothers are the population most commonly associated with public assistance, formerly incarcerated men also rely heavily on these programs to meet their basic needs.[43]

New York is among 11 states that offer cash assistance to single adults, through a state-funded program called Safety-Net Assistance.[44] The program is designed for adults who fall outside the eligibility requirements for Temporary Assistance for Needy Families (TANF), the country's largest cash entitlement program for households with dependent children. New York also allows individuals convicted of drug-related felonies to receive Supplemental Nutrition Assistance Program (SNAP) benefits, also known as "food stamps." Although the 1996 "welfare reform" law banned people convicted of drug-related felonies from receiving federally funded public assistance for life, almost all states, including New York, have modified or opted out of this ban in recent years.[45]

A typical benefits package for a single adult in New York City includes a monthly cash allowance between $45 and $400, monthly SNAP benefits between $160 and $400, a monthly shelter allowance voucher of $215, and Medicaid coverage.[46] But in the age of workfare, receiving public assistance comes with strings attached. Since the passage of the Personal Responsibility and Work Opportunity Reconciliation Act (PRWORA) of 1996, also known as so-called welfare reform, public assistance in America has shifted from a focus on income maintenance to work activation.[47] The primary goal of contemporary public assistance is rapid job placement, "regardless of the wage, the relevancy of the job to a person's career interest or experience, or the barriers facing the individual."[48] Policymakers aim to reduce welfare caseloads by discouraging people from seeking aid altogether through complex application procedures and punitive noncompliance policies. Indeed, public assistance agencies have increasingly "criminalized poverty" by utilizing the tools and rhetoric of the criminal justice system to root out fraud and punish rule breakers with criminal sanctions.[49] For those who navigate these bureaucratic obstacles, the goal is to move aid recipients off welfare rolls and into employment as quickly as possible by setting strict time limits on aid receipt and imposing work-related behavioral requirements.

Like public agencies across the country, New York City's HRA has adopted this "work first" approach to public assistance. HRA offices, renamed "job centers," process public assistance applications and determine eligibility for benefits. Like parole, HRA outsources responsibility for delivering job training and job placement services to the private sector. HRA contracts with a network of for-profit and nonprofit vendors to administer BTW Programs, which provide job readiness and job placement services to welfare recipients.

During these initial screenings, caseworkers assess whether an applicant faces any significant barriers to employment. If the applicant is found to be "employable," they are referred directly to a BTW program while they wait for the approval of their application.[50] It takes approximately 45 days for a public assistance application to be approved, during which time the applicant is required to report to their assigned BTW program from 9:00 a.m. to 5:00 p.m., five days per week and participate in job readiness classes and job search activities. Once the recipients' application is approved, they are required to report to their BTW program two days per week, while the other three days they are required to report to an offsite WEP. WEP requires welfare recipients to participate in "structured work assignments in City agencies or non-profit organizations . . . to 'work off their benefits,'" usually by performing janitorial work like picking up garbage or polishing surfaces.[51] Failing to meet these requirements results in an FTC sanction, which leads to benefits being temporarily reduced or denied altogether. Reasons for receiving an FTC include missed appointments, unexcused absences, inappropriate behavior, or not accepting a job offer.[52]

Many of the men I met at Second Chances and Uplift had cycled through BTW programs with little success. They had heard through word of mouth that they could fulfill their BTW requirements at Second Chances and Uplift, programs that catered specifically to the needs of people with criminal records. Indeed, both organizations employed a "culturally competent" staff of formerly incarcerated individuals who could provide support and mentorship to program participants. Their job readiness curriculum was tailored specifically to the needs of people with criminal records, and both worked with a network of employers willing to hire people with criminal records. Second Chances also provided a menu of wraparound services, including mental health and substance abuse counseling, family services, housing, and food support.

Although both programs had ties to parole and HRA, coordinating with these systems was difficult. For example, Second Chances received funding from HRA to provide free subway passes, called MetroCards, to program participants to attend training. In order to be eligible for a MetroCard, program participants needed to produce an official HRA budget letter showing they were receiving SNAP benefits. But many program participants did not have immediate access to their budget letters or had lost them in the deluge of paperwork they had accumulated through various bureaucratic entanglements. In order to access their budget letters, they would have to visit an HRA office in person. However, for some men the extra $4.50 for roundtrip subway fare was simply not in their budget. This put men in a difficult bind.

For example, during a break at Second Chances, Jerome, a Black man in his thirties or forties, approaches me to ask for help with getting a MetroCard. He explains to me that he spent the last of his subway fare getting to class today, and he needs a new MetroCard to get home today. "Did you turn in your budget letter today?" I ask him. Jerome tells me that he wasn't able to obtain a budget letter because he didn't have enough money for subway fare to get to the HRA office last week. He explains to me the irony of the situation: he needs a MetroCard to get home today. In order to get a MetroCard, he needs to produce his budget letter from HRA, but in order to get to an HRA office to obtain a copy of his budget letter, he needs a MetroCard to get there first.

In some cases, staff at Second Chances would authorize MetroCards for men in Jerome's situation or provide access to MetroCards through other funding streams. But Jerome's case is illustrative of the flow of bodies, money, and social control that circulates through the institutional circuit of reentry. Formerly incarcerated men must shuffle back and forth between offices to obtain official paperwork. This paperwork opens a flow of funding that allows them to access a MetroCard to participate in job readiness training. A cascade of sanctions hangs over their heads if they fail to complete the program, with an FTC sanction from HRA potentially triggering sanctions across the institutional circuit.

Other prominent state agencies that partner with community-based nonprofits are the Office of Child Support Enforcement and the New York City Family Court Division. Second Chances and Uplift both administered Responsible Fatherhood programs. Funded through various government grants, Responsible Fatherhood programs provide parenting classes and job training to noncustodial fathers, many of whom are formerly incarcerated, with the ultimate goal of fostering financial stability and compliance with child support orders. Indeed, one of the central goals of so-called welfare reform was to reduce welfare dependency by impelling noncustodial fathers to pay child support through aggressive enforcement measures.[53] In Responsible Fatherhood classes, formerly incarcerated fathers are taught that it is their moral obligation to take financial and emotional responsibility for their children. They also learn about the rules and procedures of the child support and family court systems as well as lessons about cultivating healthy relationship dynamics with their children and co-parenting partners.

While a handful of men attend these programs because they genuinely want help in improving their parenting and relationship skills, most have ulterior motives for participating. Most commonly, formerly incarcerated men participate in Responsible Fatherhood programs to gain access to job training programs and job placement services. At Second Chances, participating in the Responsible Fatherhood program allowed program participants to access a paid internship program, while at Uplift, program participants were able to access a vocational skills training class. For those receiving public assistance, participating in these job training programs allowed them to fulfill work-related mandates required to maintain program eligibility. For men facing domestic violence charges or contempt of court charges for nonpayment of child support, participation in these classes was mandated by court orders and backed up by criminal sanctions. Still for others, participating in Responsible Fatherhood classes was a way for them to get help modifying child support orders or addressing outstanding arrears that they had accumulated while incarcerated. Others were embroiled in court battles over child custody or child support payments. Participating in these programs would help them officially document their efforts to improve their parenting skills and employment prospects. Men hoped that documenting these efforts would lead to positive court outcomes.

Responsible Fatherhood programs provide yet another example of how formerly incarcerated men are shuffled through various agency offices, in this case family courts, child support offices, and community-based service providers. Their participation in Responsible Fatherhood programs opens a flow of grant dollars for community-based service providers, and a potential cascade of sanctions looms over the heads of program participants if they fail to successfully complete the program.

Transitional housing facilities, such as halfway houses, homeless shelters, residential treatment programs, and "three-quarter" sober houses, were another significant site where state systems of punishment and welfare converged. Parole requirements funneled returning citizens into transitional housing facilities, and these facilities covered operating costs by extracting fees from residents through their public assistance benefits.

Among the men interviewed for this book, nearly three-quarters were receiving public assistance and almost 60 percent lived in a halfway house, homeless shelter, or residential treatment facility. A number of pathways lead formerly incarcerated men into transitional housing facilities. For example, certain parole conditions may prevent parolees from living with family members. When I interviewed Curtis, a 27-year-old Black man, in 2016 he was living in a homeless shelter despite the fact that his family owned a brownstone home in Brooklyn where he had grown up. Curtis had been convicted of forgery. He had used his family's home address to receive forged checks and credit cards through the mail. Because his home address was tied to his conviction, parole considered it a "high risk area" and prevented him from residing there. In other cases, parole conditions require returning citizens to be released directly into a transitional housing facility. Ricardo, a 45-year-old Puerto Rican man, served eight years in federal prison for conspiracy to distribute crack cocaine. As a condition of his federal probation, Ricardo is required to live in a halfway house until he completes the remaining eight months of his prison sentence.

For others, residence in a transitional housing facility was the result of parole or probation sanctions.[54] When I interviewed him in 2016, Dwight had been living in a residential treatment program for three months. Before that, he was living with his brother-in-law, a convenient arrangement that allowed him to see his two kids often. Dwight is a recovering heroin user and relapsed three months ago. After testing positive for heroin at a parole appointment, his PO gave him two options: either go back to prison or complete a one-year residential treatment program. Dwight chose the program and hopes to get his life back on track.

While parole conditions played an important role in funneling formerly incarcerated men into transitional housing facilities, many study participants turned to these facilities voluntarily. When I interviewed Cedric in 2015, he was 48 years old. He had spent most of his adult life using drugs and cycling in and out of prison. "I fight my demons every day," he told me. He voluntarily enrolled in a residential treatment program hoping to "get some structure" in his life and to repair the damage he had done to his family through decades of addiction and incarceration.

Still others turn to transitional housing facilities out of acute need. Felipe, a 36-year-old returning citizen, turned to the shelter system after experiencing years of housing instability. When I interviewed him in 2016, Felipe had been cycling in and out of prison and jail since 2007, mostly for parole violations and minor crimes. For most of this time Felipe had been living with his parents and bouncing around to various family members' homes. Felipe grew tired of couch surfing and wanted an apartment of his own so he could visit with his kids more often. A year prior to our interview he had decided to enter the shelter system, hoping that it would lead to a permanent housing placement. Over the last year Felipe has cycled through six different shelters, never spending more than 90 days at any one site. These frequent "administrative transfers" are common experiences for shelter residents. Administrators must constantly circulate bodies throughout shelter facilities to manage bed space across the system.[55] Felipe has tolerated these frequent transfers because he does not want to be evicted from his bed and lose his place in line for supportive housing.

Residential treatment facilities and three-quarter houses also served as housing resources for men facing street homelessness. Four interviewees reported long-term sobriety but had taken up residence in treatment facilities as short-term housing solutions. Roland is a Black man in his late fifties. When I interviewed him in 2015, he had been home for about six months, having served a 30-year prison sentence for aggravated murder.[56] Roland was initially paroled to his daughter's apartment but moved out after a month because he didn't want to be a burden on her family of four. He was referred to a treatment facility through a friend who works for a social service agency, who promised the program would help him find permanent housing. Although Roland was a heavy cocaine and heroin user for most of his adult life, he says he has been sober for 15 years, which he attributes to his strong Christian faith. He resents having to participate in addiction treatment to access housing. The facility's strict rules and lack of privacy remind him of prison, and he feels that the staff are incompetent. "They ain't got nothing to offer me, man," he tells me.

Jesse was charged with armed robbery 16 years before I interviewed him in 2014, an accusation he vehemently denies. To avoid a lengthy prison sentence, he pleaded guilty to theft, but his criminal record has haunted him ever since. Over the years he has struggled to maintain steady employment and housing, working a series of temporary jobs and bouncing around to several family members' homes. After he had worn out his welcome with a cousin, Jesse's formerly incarcerated brother suggested he move into a treatment facility where he could get help with employment and housing.

"He was telling me, you know, you can come here to this program. They help you get with the housing; you can start working, you know, there's programs that can help you with . . . your felony, this and that. And come to find out none of that's true." He continues, "The things that I'm doing while being in this program, I can do them without having to be there. Without having to pay them a client fee. Without having to deal with HRA paying them, and they, you know, giving me flack about them not being paid from HRA. You know, I wouldn't have to go through all that, these things I can do myself. So, I said, if I was able, if I was working, I wouldn't be there. I would've left yesterday." He continues, "Next month would be 14 years clean from drugs. But I'm in a drug program because I was on the verge of becoming homeless because I'm not able to work. You know, so it's like a trickle-down effect. You know, and it's one of the most humiliating things for me, to be in a drug facility when I'm not using any drugs, you know?"

Residing in a residential treatment program or homeless shelter connects former prisoners to other organs of the welfare state. Facility rules typically require residents to enroll in public assistance programs. Residents of the city's homeless shelters must enroll in public assistance as part of an independent living plan (ILP).[57] Men living in inpatient treatment programs and "three-quarter" houses are required to enroll in public assistance programs to cover the costs of rent and treatment.[58] As Jesse mentioned, state and federal public assistance programs play a significant role in subsidizing the costs of residential treatment programs in New York City. Treatment facilities cover operating costs by pooling residents' public assistance benefits and receiving Medicaid reimbursements for providing substance abuse treatment.

For example, Dwight explained that his shelter allowance and SNAP benefits are paid directly to the residential treatment facility where he lives to cover the costs of rent and food, while his Medicaid coverage pays for the costs of his substance abuse treatment sessions. The facility is holding his cash benefits in a savings account. Some respondents reported that facilities extracted a $30–50 client fee from these benefits, although Dwight did not report this. The facility gives Dwight a $30 allowance out of his cash benefits every other week to purchase personal items. Once he advances in the program, he will be given $30 every week, and then $60 every week. Once he graduates, he will be given the balance of his savings account, which he estimates to be roughly $500.

These facilities provided crucial resources for formerly incarcerated men seeking shelter and treatment with meager public assistance benefits. Indeed, the shelter allowance of $215 has remained constant since 1988, while housing costs in the city have skyrocketed. At the time of the study, the median rent in the city was $1,200.[59] Although homeless shelters were an option for men in these situations, many study participants viewed shelters as stigmatized and dangerous places to avoid at all costs. Jesse had spent one night in a homeless shelter a few years earlier. All of his possessions were stolen, and he refused to ever return to one. Recall that Victor reported a man was killed in a stabbing during his first night at his shelter. Thus, residential programs were lifelines for destitute formerly incarcerated men with few other options.

However, the men's desperation meant that they were vulnerable to being exploited by predatory program operators. This was especially the case for men who took up residence in three-quarter houses. Three-quarter houses are private, for-profit residences (usually two- to three-family homes) that house and provide treatment services to up to 100 single adults, mostly men returning home from incarceration. Their name denotes their liminal status between a regulated halfway house and a private home.[60] Unlike regulated halfway houses and residential treatment programs, however, three-quarter houses are largely unregulated and operate with little oversight, despite the fact that they are almost entirely subsidized by public funds.

Andre, a 43-year-old Black former prisoner, had firsthand knowledge of the unscrupulous practices that occur at three-quarter houses. Andre not only currently lived in a three-quarter house; he also used to be a three-quarter house operator. His conviction for real estate fraud stemmed from a scheme he had developed to fraudulently acquire foreclosed properties and turn them into three-quarter houses.[61] Andre explained how three-quarter house operators can turn large profits from shelter allowances and Medicaid reimbursements:

ANDRE: So, a whole three-quarter housing structure, the way that it works is basically, get a bunch of guys who don't have any place to live. And usually they're coming home from jail. And you get $215 a month for each one of those individuals, from Public Assistance [shelter allowance]. So, if you happen to have a space that can hold upwards to 50 or 100 guys, and you can work the numbers right insofar as, you know, electric, um, water, gas, so on and so forth. You can see significant numbers. You can see upwards of $5,000 to $10,000 a month in profit from a situation like that.

Indeed, three-quarter house operators "work the numbers right" by leaving buildings in disrepair and spending minimal amounts on basic utilities.[62] However, Andre explained that the most profitable aspects of three-quarter houses are Medicaid reimbursements:

ANDRE: So, whether you have a [substance abuse] issue or not, you're gonna go to their [treatment] program. They get $56 a swipe from Medicaid, every time you go to their program. So that's their money. You've gotta do three groups a week, and you've gotta do one individual a week. If you miss them, trust me you'll know about it because they will kick people out at 03:00 in the morning. That's their bread and butter. The $215 a month that they get from you [in shelter allowance], is pretty much [the] operational budget for that particular house. So, you got 100 guys, and you know, the running of the house, the leasing, or the mortgage on that particular property, the paying the salary of the house managers, that's what those checks cover. After that, just [to] see their actual profit, even though they're a nonprofit, they have to get $56 a visit from you. That's the business, that's how it works.

In 2015, a year after I interviewed Andre, a *New York Times* investigation uncovered the "housing netherworld" of three-quarter houses.[63] The investigation corroborated much of what Andre had told me: a system of decrepit and overcrowded homes run by unscrupulous businessmen interested in fleecing the government. The investigation revealed that in order to avoid eviction, sober residents were forced to relapse so that they could remain enrolled in lucrative treatment programs, effectively "doom[ing] tenants to a perpetual cycle of treatment and relapse, of shuttling between programs and three-quarter houses."[64] Indeed, Andre told me that once he finished his 18-month program at his current three-quarter house, he would have to "tell another program that . . . I have a substance abuse issue and go there" in order to avoid living in a shelter. Shortly following the *Times* investigation, the city launched a task force to investigate three-quarter houses. In 2017 the city council passed a series of laws to protect tenants' rights and provide greater oversight over three-quarter houses.[65]

Although the city has taken steps to regulate three-quarter houses and prosecute the most abusive and exploitative building operators, the city nonetheless still relies on these facilities to house populations vulnerable to street homelessness. Indeed, these findings reveal a symbiotic relationship between the state and private treatment providers: inpatient treatment programs and three-quarter houses rely on public assistance programs to subsidize their operating costs, while government agencies utilize three-quarter houses and treatment facilities to reduce shelter rolls and house formerly incarcerated people excluded from private housing markets.

Indeed, transitional housing facilities provide windows into the flow of bodies, money, and social control across the institutional circuit. For example, formerly incarcerated men are routinely circulated across the shelter system to open bed space or to protect residents' safety, as Felipe and Victor experienced. Parole and probation conditions funnel men into homeless shelters or halfway houses, as Curtis and Ricardo experienced, and sanctions can trigger forced moves into residential treatment facilities, as Dwight experienced.[66] Significant housing barriers lead formerly incarcerated men to circulate repeatedly between family members' homes and various transitional housing facilities.

The flow of public money into transitional housing facilities occurs through the routine extraction of fees from residents' public assistance benefits. Indeed, state and federal public assistance programs play a significant role in subsidizing residential treatment programs and three-quarter houses. In many cases this has led to predatory and exploitative relationships between building operators and residents, as Andre explained in the context of three-quarter houses.

Finally, transitional housing facilities illustrate how returning citizens experience a cascade of social control as they flow through the institutional circuit. While these facilities are crucial resources for men with few housing options, they also extend practices of confinement and control.[67] Indeed, men often described living in transitional housing facilities as akin to being incarcerated. Andre described his three-quarter house as "a prison without bars." Curtis said of his shelter, "It feels like you're back in jail, you know what I'm saying? It's like you just leave from jail to go to another jail."

As they had in prisons and jails, the men experienced crowded and filthy living conditions where drug use and violence were pervasive. Within housing facilities, they were under constant surveillance and their personal liberties were significantly curtailed. They had to abide by curfews, submit to drug tests, and participate in mandatory programs. In residential treatment programs, men were restricted from leaving the facility, controlling their finances, using cell phones, or receiving visitors until certain treatment milestones were reached. These forms of social control are linked across the institutional circuit. Parole officers constantly surveilled housing facilities and monitored residents' compliance with housing rules, threatening parole revocations for men who broke rules. Men's residence in facilities was contingent on abiding by HRA mandates. An FTC sanction could trigger not only a loss of benefits, but also a loss of housing.

CONCLUSION

By tracing men's entanglements with the criminal legal and social welfare bureaucracies across New York City, this chapter reveals how the state manages the problems associated with reentry through a logic of "circulation." We see how the physical bodies of returning citizens circulate through offices, facilities, and programs throughout the city as men struggle to keep up with mandatory appointments and rehabilitation programs. Public funds and grant dollars flow between agencies as caseloads move throughout the institutional circuit. Practices of surveillance and control extend deeper into the lives of returning citizens as they bounce from one institution to the next. In the end, the state is able to contain the problems associated with reentry by continually redistributing and displacing returning citizens across the institutional circuit without addressing the deeper institutional failures and structural inequalities that undermine reintegration in the first place.[68]

This chapter also reveals how formerly incarcerated men experienced the institutional circuit as a contradictory combination of disciplinary social control and bureaucratic fragmentation. Rather than conceptualizing the institutional circuit as being *either* a tightly coordinated regime of social control *or* a dysfunctional hodgepodge of bureaucratic systems, this chapter demonstrates how both tendencies coexisted to varying degrees at different junctures of the circuit. On the one hand, a common paternalistic ideology pervaded the institutional circuit, with each agency organized around a common goal to discipline and reform the behavior of formerly incarcerated men. Community-based reentry programs and transitional housing facilities played a central role in implementing the state's neoliberal project to transform criminalized men into disciplined market actors. Drug treatment programs and anger management classes were designed to curb men's addictions and violent impulses, while workforce development programs and responsible fatherhood programs aimed to instill disciplined work habits and a sense of parental responsibility. Public funds flowed into these agencies to subsidize these efforts.

Interacting with these programs and facilities drew the state deeper into the lives of formerly incarcerated men, opening them up to further surveillance, behavior modification, and sanctions. Study participants' daily lives were constantly monitored through mandatory office appointments, home visits, and facility surveillance. They were required to actively search for work, participate in job training, and acquiesce in therapeutic interventions as conditions of receiving public aid or avoiding parole sanctions. And they were threatened with a cascade of sanctions if they failed to comply, including loss of public benefits, eviction from transitional housing, and reincarceration.

Yet this chapter also reveals how these forms of disciplinary social control were spread out across a decentralized and underfunded bureaucratic infrastructure. Each bureaucracy that study participants encountered had its own complex rules and procedures, unique paperwork requirements, strict eligibility criteria, and inflexible appointment schedules, leading study participants to experience a host of bureaucratic redundancies and irrationalities. Agency offices were often located on opposite ends of the city, sometimes requiring former prisoners to travel dozens of blocks or to multiple boroughs to attend appointments. What is more, these bureaucracies routinely failed to communicate or coordinate supervision. Formerly incarcerated men were constantly shuffling between various offices as they struggled to keep up with overlapping appointments or comply with complex paperwork requirements. Over time, formerly incarcerated men often found themselves churning through multiple housing facilities or participating in redundant rehabilitative programs to maintain service eligibility or satisfy parole requirements. Lack of oversight and regulation of transitional housing facilities left formerly incarcerated men vulnerable to predation by abusive housing operators looking to extract profits from residents' meager public assistance benefits.

In the end, former prisoners experience an institutional circuit that is both highly disciplinary and yet grossly fragmented. When former prisoners are not being controlled or punished by the institutional circuit, they are being neglected or displaced by it. This contradictory mixture of disciplinary social control and bureaucratic fragmentation creates the structural conditions for formerly incarcerated men to experience the runaround.

TWO

Jumping through Hoops

CALVIN SITS ACROSS FROM his career counselor at Second Chances. "I'm getting the runaround," he tells the counselor, Donald. Calvin begins explaining how a paperwork error at HRA, the New York City agency in charge of public assistance, is jeopardizing his access to food stamps. A few weeks earlier, Calvin had received a letter from HRA directing him to report to a mandated WEP assignment, where he would be required to participate in unpaid labor in exchange for his food stamps. A few days later, he received another letter from HRA stating that his WEP assignment had been canceled. Thinking the WEP assignment was canceled, Calvin did not show up. However, the letter canceling his WEP assignment had been sent in error, and when Calvin did not show up, he was automatically given an FTC sanction.[1] He is now in jeopardy of losing his food stamps permanently if he does not resolve the mix-up. Calvin says he has tried several times to explain the paperwork error to his HRA case manager, but he says that every time he goes to the HRA office he is shuffled around to different case managers, none of whom have been able to help him. He hopes that a letter and a phone call from Second Chances showing that he is participating in a job training program will help demonstrate his compliance with HRA work mandates and resolve the issue once and for all.

"Everyone's sending me back and forth.... I could cry," he tells Donald. Donald commiserates with Calvin but explains that in order to fix the problem Calvin needs to go back to the HRA office and present the letter of participation in person. Upset that he'll have to return once again to the HRA office, Calvin snaps back, "They were supposed to fix it! Now you're telling me I have to go back?!" Donald calmly shrugs and says, "Look, we don't have control over public assistance." Donald advises Calvin to call the welfare office before he goes. He explains, "You might have three different people working on your case who aren't on the same page.... The right hand doesn't know what the left hand is doing.... Whoever you're talking to, make sure you get a name and an ID number."

Calvin laments, "They mess up and then they blame it on you." "Exactly," Donald replies. "It's a win-win for them. If you fix the problem you fix the problem; if you don't, they can kick you off the rolls." Calvin begins gathering his things to make his way back to the HRA office. He stuffs a new set of paperwork from Second Chances into his backpack, which is already overflowing with a library of paperwork from his other bureaucratic entanglements. As he packs up, he says to himself, "Papers, papers, papers, I'm getting frustrated with all these papers.... This is all their fault." Donald replies, "It's always their fault.... The left hand doesn't know what the right hand is doing." As Calvin walks away, he grumbles, "I'm gonna spend my whole day dealing with this."

As Calvin's case illustrates, formerly incarcerated men experience the institutional circuit of reentry as a series of burdensome and degrading hassles. Calvin is facing the prospect of hunger because of an unexplained paperwork mix-up. He has been shuttling back and forth between HRA offices and Second Chances trying to demonstrate that his FTC sanction was a mistake and that he is in compliance with HRA rules, but he feels that no one will listen to him. He feels disempowered by a bureaucratic system that seems to care little for his material needs and is dismissive of his demands for accountability.

Calvin called this experience "getting the runaround." He must negotiate a series of administrative hassles, degrading experiences, and costs in his attempt to simply maintain access to food stamps. Almost all the men I met at Second Chances and Uplift described similar experiences when interacting with the institutional circuit of reentry. Although they did not always explicitly name their experience "getting the runaround," I use the phrase to describe the collection of hassles, costs, and degradations that returning citizens experience across their entanglements with the institutional circuit. As one study participant put it, the runaround encompasses the series of bureaucratic "hoops you gotta jump through" to avoid reincarceration and access public aid.

Formerly incarcerated men experience the runaround in both a literal and figurative sense. As we saw in the previous chapter, formerly incarcerated men circulate through a loop of facilities and programs in their attempts to access public aid and avoid reincarceration. This circulation of bodies across institutional space is the runaround in its most tangible and literal sense: the physical experience of *running around* the city to keep up with overlapping appointments and facility curfews, as well as the "ping pong housing" that returning citizens experience as they are shuffled between various facilities.[2]

But the runaround also encompasses a more intangible and impersonal experience of bureaucratic disempowerment. This is the runaround in its more figurative sense: the Kafkaesque experiences of feeling confused, misled, and controlled by a cold bureaucratic machine. This figurative runaround took the form of arbitrary and unresponsive treatment from institutional gatekeepers. Most commonly this involved being repeatedly delayed or redirected when attempting to communicate with frontline actors. It also included experiencing a host of bureaucratic irrationalities, such as having to wait for unspecified amounts of time, restart applications due to system errors, repeat programs to satisfy rigid eligibility requirements, or lose benefits due to minor rule violations. These types of experiences are not mutually exclusive. As we saw in Calvin's case, he was made to literally run around between HRA offices and Second Chances to resolve an unexplained paperwork error, and each time he attempted to communicate with HRA caseworkers they repeatedly deflected his questions.

The runaround is rooted in profoundly unequal power relationships between returning citizens and institutional gatekeepers. Parole officers, welfare caseworkers, and transitional housing staff wield power over returning citizens' access to community freedom and basic material necessities. They can obstruct returning citizens' access to material resources and community freedom by choosing to delay processes, reject applications, or require additional steps.[3] Their ability to regulate the lives of returning citizens in this way can have severely negative material consequences. By routinely subjecting returning citizens to the runaround, frontline actors can limit access to employment opportunities, undermine social relationships, and block access to public resources necessary for successful reintegration.

In this chapter I argue that the hassles of the runaround amount to more than just a series of inconveniences. Instead, their cumulative force creates *bureaucratic barriers* to reentry. The hassles associated with the runaround exact a series of financial and opportunity costs on returning citizens. These costs, in turn, obstruct returning citizens from accessing basic elements of social inclusion. For example, complying with the demands of the institutional circuit requires returning citizens to manage conflicting obligations, resolve clerical errors, and submit to various rules that limit free movement. These "compliance costs" are the price returning citizens must pay to avoid reincarceration and access basic material resources.[4] However, keeping up with these costs is a constant struggle. Returning citizens find themselves on a relentless treadmill of appointments, programs, and curfews. It requires so much time, energy, and financial resources to keep up with this grind that they are left without the resources necessary to pull themselves onto the road toward employment and economic independence.

THE DEMANDS OF CONFLICTING OBLIGATIONS

Navigating the institutional circuit of reentry required formerly incarcerated men to simultaneously manage multiple, overlapping bureaucratic obligations across a fragmented institutional circuit. These included mandatory appointments with POs and HRA case managers; BTW programs and WEP assignments; court dates for probation or family court; various therapeutic "groups" for drug treatment, anger management, or mental health; individual counseling appointments; and facility curfews. The demands of juggling these conflicting obligations was a significant source of stress and disruption in study participants' daily lives that undermined their efforts to achieve economic independence.

Curtis's experience was typical of how conflicting obligations create bureaucratic barriers to reentry. I met Curtis in July 2014. A 27-year-old Black man, Curtis had just been released from custody a month prior to our meeting after serving a 90-day sentence for a parole violation. Before that he had served three years in state prison for burglary and forgery. I told Curtis that I was interested in learning about his experiences with parole and HRA. Curtis told me, "They give you too much to do and not enough time to do it." For example, Curtis discussed how "frequently having to report to your parole officer" disrupted employment and family relationships. He explained:

> CURTIS: Now you can have a [job] interview lined up, you can have something positive going on for yourself, [but] if you have to report to your parole officer, it's mandatory. Forget whatever you're doing. If it's your daughter's birthday, if it's anything that's going on, if your family member just died—you gotta go and report to your parole officer.

He continued discussing how substance abuse treatment and HRA requirements created additional bureaucratic obstacles:

CURTIS: Um.... Drug and alcohol, substance abuse [treatment]. Even if your crime was not drug and alcohol related, or anything like that, you're mandated to take drug and alcohol substance abuse [treatment]. Even if you never drank in your life, smoked pot or anything, you have to take a mandatory drug and alcohol, substance abuse [program]. Now, drug and alcohol, substance abuse [treatment] can be anywhere from six months to eighteen months, and these are classes that go on for two hours a day, sometimes an hour a day, sometimes five days a week, sometimes three days a week, sometimes two days a week, depending on the discretion of the counselor, or the program that you're in. So, if you're trying to work, you're trying to do something positive with yourself, and your employer is actually giving you an opportunity to work, then you spring on him that these certain days you gotta go see parole and these certain days you gotta go to this mandatory drug program—even if you're sober—your employer looks at you like, "What time are you gonna have to actually work?" ...

And that's just dealing with parole and the stipulations they have, that's not even considering the stuff HRA, the public assistance department, is gonna be putting you through just to keep food stamps on your card or a little bit of cash or to get transportation. Because those things you're definitely going to need to survive. And they got their own process and things that you're mandated to do in order just to keep that.

Curtis also complained that the curfew at the shelter where he lived restricted his ability to attend to all his obligations throughout the day. The shelter has a strict 10:00 p.m. curfew, but Curtis had to be in by 9:00 p.m. as per his parole conditions. He wasn't allowed to leave until 7:00 a.m., leaving him just 14 hours a day to manage his various appointments, search for work, and spend time with his two-year-old daughter. Curtis was eager to leave the shelter, but he had to establish stable employment before he could be eligible for supportive housing. Otherwise, he would be continually "recycled" through the shelter system:

CURTIS: [The o]nly way you get out the shelter is if you work. You have to present them with pay stubs. You know, and that's how they get you subsidized housing ... or something you can afford, but if you're not working in the shelter ... the only thing a shelter does is just ... recycle clients. They'll send them from one shelter to another shelter to another shelter, and ultimately, they'll end up back at the first shelter that they left. You know what I'm saying?

However, Curtis's desire to establish economic independence was undermined by the runaround. Curtis felt that the constant grind of keeping up with parole appointments, HRA obligations, and shelter curfews created obstacles that prevented him from finding the kind of stable employment that would allow him to break free from the shelter system.

As Curtis's case illustrates, managing conflicting obligations creates a series of opportunity costs for returning citizens. They must forgo pursuing education or employment opportunities in favor of satisfying bureaucratic requirements necessary to avoid reincarceration and maintain access to basic material resources. For example, managing conflicting obligations was a major impediment to participating in the workforce development training programs at Second Chances and Uplift. Many men saw participating in these programs as an important step in achieving their goals of economic independence. However, the stress of managing competing appointments was a major roadblock to participating in workforce development training. Both programs required participants to attend class eight hours a day, five days a week for between two and four weeks. Missing class or leaving early meant having to return for makeup class. Too many absences resulted in having to restart the training all over again. Conflicting obligations often made it impossible for men to make this kind of time commitment.

While I was conducting recruitment activities with Selena at parole, a potential program participant told us that he wanted to enroll in the Workforce Development Program at Second Chances, but he was required to attend a mandated program. He explained, "Because it's mandated, they don't care about anything besides the program." He also told us that he had a pending WEP assignment that could get in the way of his attending the workshop. Freddie, a Black man in his forties, was also interested in enrolling in the Workforce Development Program. Selena asked Freddie if he was enrolled in any programs. Freddie said that he was currently enrolled in a parole-mandated outpatient program for drug treatment, anger management, and mental health treatment. Freddie had to attend daily one-hour group therapy sessions until either his counselors or his PO decided he could stop. Freddie was also the primary caregiver for his sick grandmother, whom he often took to doctor's appointments. In addition, Freddie suffered from a chronic health condition that required frequent doctor's appointments.

Staff members at Second Chances often complained that clients were "over-programmed" or "grouped-out" from having to attend too many mandatory appointments and group therapy sessions, leaving little time in their overpacked schedules to attend job-readiness training full-time. Eric, one of the job readiness facilitators, addresses the issue of conflicting appointments on the first day of class when discussing the rules of the workshop. He starts with the issue of attendance. He tells the class that he and other staff members recognize that the clients might have appointments with welfare, parole, drug treatment, halfway houses, or courts that conflict with the workshop. Eric explains that staff members will do their best to accommodate these obligations, either by allowing program participants to leave class early or by contacting the proper authorities to get them excused from the appointment. This is especially the case with parole. Eric explains, "We'll help you out with your parole officer. . . . We can work around appointments. . . . Being here is part of your requirements of parole: seeking and maintaining employment. . . . We'll call up your parole officer and explain that you're here doing the right thing and get your appointment rescheduled for after the workshop. . . . Don't worry, we'll help you without causing friction with them and their power trips."

Despite this support, managing conflicting obligations was difficult. Lack of transportation was a constant struggle for study participants. Without reliable cash income, returning citizens must scramble to cobble together enough money for carfare to travel to various appointments around the city. Tony, a 32-year-old Latino man, felt that without access to transportation, it was impossible to traverse the city to keep up with his litany of appointments. During a focus group at Second Chances he said:

TONY: They're supposed to help us, you know, get into society. But the way they make it is, they make certain deadlines even if they're gonna collide with each other. Because they know that there's no way that you're gonna make all these deadlines. Especially without having—they're not helping you with transportation. It's, it's their way of making a loophole for you to come back, you know? They make all these things mandatory, like this program, this program. And if you gotta deal with housing and a program at the same time, that's a lot to deal with. . . . And you still have to go to parole. On top of that . . . [i]f you're doing a program, that's three mandatory things they've got you doing at the same time. So how are you going to make three mandatory appointments?

Indeed, lack of transportation was a major impediment to accessing workforce development training. During my outreach work at parole, people routinely balked at participating in the Workforce Development Program at Second Chances due to lack of transportation. When I tried to get Ricky, a Black man in his twenties, to sign up for the Workforce Development Program, he replied, "I've done job readiness programs before. . . . At the end of the day between Metros [subway fare] and all that I'm losing money to attend this training." He went on: "I'm spending my last $2.50 to get to a job interview just to get turned down and then have no way of getting home."

To address this need, Second Chances and Uplift provided free Metro-Cards to incentivize program participation. In some cases, accessing a Metro-Card meant simply attending class. Men who participated in the Responsible Fatherhood class at Uplift received a free two-trip MetroCard at the end of every class to cover their travel costs for the day. But in other cases, program participants had to meet certain eligibility requirements to receive a Metro-Card. As we saw in the last chapter, Second Chances could only provide MetroCards to people receiving SNAP, which required program participants to produce an HRA budget letter to prove eligibility. For men not receiving SNAP, this meant that they would have to figure out transportation costs on their own. For men who were eligible but didn't have access to their budget letters, it meant having to find the time and subway fare to travel to an HRA office to track down a copy of the letter.

Even though many men were desperate to participate in workforce development training, participating in these classes created a series of financial and opportunity costs. They had to come up with subway fare to cover the transportation costs to and from programs or endure the hassles of HRA to obtain budget letters that would unlock travel subsidies. In either case, returning citizens incurred a series of "compliance costs" in their efforts to participate in these programs.

The stress of keeping up with these compliance costs led many study participants to view rehabilitative programs as barriers to reentry in and of themselves. For example, although many men saw participating in workforce development programs as a step toward economic independence, others thought that job-readiness classes were themselves obstacles to economic independence. Men who had already participated in workforce development programs felt that they were already "job ready." They had prior work experience, had a résumé, and knew how to interview; it was only their criminal record that was holding them back. They desperately wanted a job interview referral from Second Chances but refused to participate in yet another job readiness class. Unfortunately, Second Chances and Uplift would not provide a job interview referral to a formerly incarcerated jobseeker unless he completed the mandatory job-readiness class.[5]

For example, when I tried to get Jesse, a Black man in his twenties, to sign up for the Workforce Development Program at Second Chances, he explained to me that he didn't need any job readiness training, he just wanted an interview referral. "I have a résumé; I've gotten jobs since my release. I know how to interview," he told me. "Honestly my conviction is holding me back. I served two years for weapons possession. Right now, that's a liability because guns are everywhere in the news right now because of Sandy Hook [our conversation occurred in 2012 shortly after the mass shooting]. I honestly think that's what's holding me back right now." I tried to sympathize with Jesse but had to explain that there was no way around the program's rules. He would have to go through the organization's intake process, attend orientation, and complete the two-week workshop before he could be set up for a job interview. I gave him an orientation referral, we shook hands, and I sent him on his way, hoping that he would show up for orientation.

Another man I tried to recruit explained that he had already participated in a workforce development program. When I asked him if he'd be interested in participating in another job readiness class at Second Chances, he flatly told me, "That's a waste of time."

Some study participants also questioned the therapeutic value of substance abuse treatment programs. For these men, substance abuse treatment was not a meaningful form of rehabilitation. Instead, they saw it as a hollow bureaucratic exercise that undermined their ability to find work. This was especially the case for men who were mandated to attend substance abuse treatment by their POs. Men complained that these programs were redundant and a waste of time. They had already completed treatment while incarcerated and were being forced to repeat the same programs just for the sake of satisfying parole conditions, not because they needed help. During a class discussion at Second Chances, Darius, a Black man in his twenties, described how many of the things that parole was requiring him to do he had already completed in prison: "All the stuff you did in prison, you gotta do over again with parole." He said that he had participated in several drug treatment programs in prison, but his PO was requiring him to participate in another one as a parole condition. To him, these required drug treatment classes were just "hoops you gotta jump through" to satisfy parole requirements.

For men living in three-quarter houses, substance abuse treatment was not only unnecessary, it was exploitative. Recall that Andre took up residence in three-quarter housing to avoid the shelter system, despite claiming that he never had an addiction issue to begin with. As a former three-quarter house operator, Andre was well aware that mandated treatment is a means for operators to extract profits from Medicaid, not necessarily to provide therapeutic services to returning citizens. Andre explained, "So whether you have a[n] issue or not, you're gonna go to their program. . . . That's their bread and butter. . . . That's the business, that how it works . . . and they gotta make their money." Andre told me that after our interview was over, he was headed straight to a group meeting at his outpatient treatment clinic; otherwise he would have to attend a makeup session Saturday morning. "I mean, they have to police that, 'cause that's their structure," he explained.

Although Andre understood the profit motive behind the litany of drug treatment sessions he had to attend every week, he nonetheless saw them as barriers to accessing resources that could actually facilitate his economic independence, such as education or employment:

ANDRE: Because where are you going to go to school full-time, to get the sort of vocational [training] or degree, where you can actually have a career, if you have to take, not one, but three hours out of your day [to attend group]. 'Cause usually, it's about 45 minutes to an hour [of] traveling. Then it's an hour for group. It's 45 minutes traveling back to wherever you're gonna go. How you explain that to your professor? Or, now, what if you have a job? How do you explain that to your employer? "What do you mean you gotta leave for three hours a day?" Or "You gotta [come] in at 11 when I want you here at 9 or 8?" Or "You're leaving at 2, when it's a 9 to 5 position, because on three days out of the week, because you got group [therapy]? I have nothing to do with your gr—and you have to do a one-on-one once a week. So at least one time during the week, you're going to be gone four hours?"

Andre's experience again illustrates how the runaround creates a series of financial and opportunity costs in the daily lives of returning citizens. As these costs accumulate in the lives of returning citizens, they begin to function as bureaucratic barriers to reentry. Paying the compliance costs associated with the runaround forces returning citizens to choose between satisfying bureaucratic obligations and pursuing reintegrative projects like spending time with family or pursuing education or employment opportunities. The runaround of juggling conflicting appointments across the city derails stable routines and induces psychological stress, undermining the ability of returning citizens to plan ahead and make clear decisions.

"THEY MESS UP AND BLAME IT ON YOU": CLERICAL ERRORS AND BUREAUCRATIC OBSTRUCTION

Although HRA is meant to provide access to material support and a pathway to economic independence, its byzantine rules, overlapping appointments, and penchant for clerical errors created obstacles that perversely undermined economic independence. As we saw in Calvin's case, routine clerical errors play a significant role in undermining returning citizens' access to public assistance. A paperwork mix-up resulted in Calvin missing an appointment, which triggered an FTC sanction. Calvin now had to prove his compliance with HRA rules to reinstate his SNAP benefits. Unfortunately, Calvin's case is typical. Welfare rights advocates have found that "FTCs are widely used, not standardized, and wrought with errors."[6] One analysis found that "60% of FTC notices are found to be in error after HRA reviews the case at a conciliation hearing."[7]

Eddie's case is exemplary. When I interviewed him in 2014, Eddie was 45 years old. A short Puerto Rican man with a thin goatee, Eddie had been released from prison in 2002 after serving 15 years for manslaughter. With the help of a family friend, Eddie was able to find a job at an insurance company shortly after his release. He worked there for seven years, starting off performing office administration and then moving on to customer service. In 2009 he was laid off after his company restructured, and he has been unable to find work ever since. Eddie collected unemployment insurance for a year, but after his benefits ran out he moved in with his sister and applied for public assistance. During his time on public assistance Eddie has been FTC'd two times, both stemming from clerical errors. Eddie walks me through the process of being sanctioned. "The first time they FTC'd me because they said I was not at the Back-to-Work Program, but they forgot they had me at [a WEP]," he explained.[8] Eddie was required to report to his BTW program three days a week and his WEP assignment twice a week. He continues:

EDDIE: The day they said I was not at my Back-to-Work [program] I was at my WEP assignment. So, they FTC'd me. When I showed them, you know I'm at my [WEP assignment] they said, "Well, don't worry, just show 'em the documents," and I had to go through a process of actually staying home pretty much for almost a month 'cause you can't go to the Back-to-Work Program until they, I guess, take care of the problem by finding out why.

In order to get his benefits reinstated, Eddie had to attend a fair hearing. At the hearing, Eddie had to produce documentation proving that his sanction was the result of a bureaucratic error rather than his noncompliance. Eddie explains, "So you gotta bring the documents to these appointments proving . . . the information that you gave 'em is in fact . . . true [to] what you say." Eddie won his fair hearing and his benefits were reinstated. He was sent to another BTW program at a new location, but soon ran into the same problem again. He explains:

EDDIE: After a couple months, same thing happened. I had an appointment, um, I went to the appointment, told [BTW] about the appointment prior to [going to the appointment], came back the following week, they said I was FTC'd because I wasn't at the Back-to-Work. Told them I had the appointment, [they said] "Alright, um, don't worry, go to your same thing."

Once again, Eddie had to attend a fair hearing. However, Eddie had to wait several months before his hearing date. He tells me:

EDDIE: Couple months go by, I'm stayin' home 'cause I don't have carfare 'cause they stopped [my benefits], they don't give you nothin'. You don't get carfare, you don't get pretty much nothin' except food stamps until they see that, um, what you say is true is true. Then, once you start gettin' your carfare, your cash [benefits] back, then you could pretty much do what you need to do to look for work.

Like Eddie, Travis also routinely experienced bureaucratic errors that blocked his access to public assistance. Travis was a 33-year-old Puerto Rican man who lived with his 5-year-old autistic son in a homeless shelter. He was addicted to heroin for over a decade but has been sober since his release from prison six years before our interview. Travis complains that he constantly has to shuffle back and forth to HRA offices to deal with clerical errors. "It's like they're always closing out my case and telling me to go all the way there, to have me go back and forth," he tells me. Travis continues, "But usually I'm always there for no reason, they don't give me money to go over there, and when you do go, they don't give you money to go back, like transportation. . . . And um, I never see my social worker, and when I do call over there I never get in contact with no one."

Travis tells me about a time that his public assistance case was closed because a social worker forgot to file a piece of paperwork:

TRAVIS: I had got my case closed because they said I didn't put in a certificate from Puerto Rico, ok? So, they closed it and they told me I have to refile. So, I went downstairs and I'm telling the lady at [the] Information [desk] about it, because I had got back in line, and the lady said, "What certificate? This one right here?" because she pulled it up [on her computer]. And when she pulled up the certificate I said, "Whoa, how you got it in your system, and they don't have it upstairs?" So, she copied it to a file and clicked it to a stapler and told me, "Here, just take it back upstairs and refile and now you don't have to go through this process again." So, when I go back upstairs, the lady put it in. I waited three more weeks, and they sent me another letter saying they didn't receive that copy, and it was because that lady didn't put it in. And it just bothered me, it just bothered me. Because they make you go through the process all over again and once you go through the process all over again you gotta wait another 30 days in order for them to do an investigation to see if you're eligible, and then the person who suffers is me and my son. 'Cause now when you want the arrears for that [time] they don't give it to you. You gotta go to a fair hearing, to prove to them that this whole time I was [in need]. And when they give you a fair hearing date, you wait like another 30 days. So, you know the system is kinda set up that once they do open it, they'll find a way—not find a way. I blame the social workers. It's always something like that. They say they don't try to make it comfortable to wean you off, but that doesn't mean that the social workers shouldn't do their job properly. It's like [they think], "Alright, I didn't do my job. So what? It happens all the time. Cases get messed up."

Eddie's and Travis's experiences illustrate that routine bureaucratic errors aren't just inconveniences. Instead, they function as bureaucratic barriers that block access to crucial forms of material support. An erroneous FTC sanction doesn't just mean a few extra trips to the HRA office; it means that someone will go hungry and be without access to income and transportation for several weeks. The constant stress and disruption of trying to resolve these errors through office visits and fair hearings saps returning citizens' time and energy, disrupts daily routines, and generates opportunity costs that undermine reintegration.

In addition to clerical errors, men often encountered various forms of bureaucratic obstruction in the form of arbitrary, unresponsive, and evasive treatment from institutional gatekeepers. Men identified the child support system as a particularly capacious and incomprehensible system. Men with child support debt routinely complained that they didn't know how much they owed, where their payments went, or why their payments would change. This unresponsiveness from the child support system created financial and opportunity costs that undermined reintegration.

During the course of the fatherhood programs at both Second Chances and Uplift, an outreach worker from the Office of Child Support Enforcement named Sylvia, a Black woman who looked to be in her forties or fifties, would visit the classroom. She would explain how the child support system works and answer men's questions about their cases. Her presentation would usually begin by explaining that there are two types of child support orders. The first is private petitioner orders. These orders occur when the custodial parent (typically the mother) initiates a child support order through the family court, and the noncustodial parent (typically the father) makes a monthly payment directly to the custodial parent based on the noncustodial parent's reported income. The second is Department of Social Services (DSS) orders. These orders occur when the custodial parent receives public assistance, and the noncustodial parent is responsible for repaying the state for the costs of public assistance provided to the custodial parent and the child. In these cases, the custodial parent pays money directly to the state as repayment for the costs of public assistance, rather than as payment directly to the custodial parent.

During one evening at Uplift, Wesley, a 33-year-old Black man, raises his hand and tells Sylvia, "When I first found out about my child support case, I already owed $8,000!" Wesley's debt was owed to the state of Delaware, where the mother of his son was living at the time. Because Wesley was not in contact with her, he was unaware that she had enrolled in public assistance. By the time he found out about the order, he had already accrued significant arrears. Sylvia explains to Wesley how he can get his order modified to reduce his payment. Unsurprisingly, it involves shuffling between offices and producing paperwork.

Sylvia tells Wesley that he needs to go to the customer service window at the Office of Child Support Enforcement. He needs to bring an HRA budget letter, a benefits card, and a letter from Uplift showing that he is making a good faith effort to obtain employment and improve his parenting skills. She explains to Wesley that the people at the office will fill out the paperwork for him and lower the order to $25–$50 a month. However, the process is different if he owes arrears. If you owe arrears, you must produce documentation to prove that your income was below the poverty line at the time the arrears began to accrue.

Jonathan, a Black man in his thirties, raises his hand and begins asking Sylvia about his case. Jonathan thought he only owed money directly to his child's mother through a private petitioner order. However, he found out recently that DSS was somehow also involved in his case. He is frustrated because he doesn't know what amount he owes and to whom he is paying. "My order says one thing, and what they are taking out [of my paycheck] is totally different." Sylvia explains that part of this confusion may be due to the fact that Jonathan owes arrears. She explains that if you have arrears, child support will automatically tack that onto the weekly bill. For example, if you have a $100 a week order, they'll tack on an additional $50 to pay down the arrearage.

Jonathan says that he went down to the Office of Child Support Enforcement to ask for an account statement, but they couldn't produce one for him. The best they could do was print out an "audit" for him that contained a history of his payments. However, according to Jonathan the audit didn't say "What was paid to what and who owes it." Jonathan explains that he became frustrated at this meeting and had to be escorted out of the building by police officers when he attempted to make a recording of what was going on for his own reference. Jonathan continues to express confusion and frustration over his case. He says that the case was brought by a "private petitioner" and he had no arrears at the time of the incident at the child support office. He doesn't understand why DSS is involved in his case at all. Jonathan later complains that the demands of the child support system undermine his ability to maintain a relationship with his kid: "Going to court, going to programs, that's time you could spend with the kid!"

The child support system creates yet another layer of financial and opportunity costs for formerly incarcerated men. Men must navigate a complex and opaque system of child support that is unresponsive to their demands for accountability. The financial debts of child support undermine men's ability to establish economic independence. Men can lose up to 65 percent of their income to wage garnishment and have their unemployment benefits and tax returns intercepted.[9] When men are too poor to keep up with their debt, they can lose their driver's licenses or be jailed for nonpayment, pushing them even further toward the margins of mainstream social life. Moreover, as Jonathan points out, navigating the child support system undermines men's ability to fulfill their roles as engaged fathers.[10] Instead of actually spending time with their children, men with child support debt must spend their time traveling back and forth to court, attending various programs, and navigating the intricacies of the child support bureaucracy. Men spend so much time managing debt and avoiding sanctions, they are left with little time to attend to family relationships that are essential for reintegration.[11]

"YOU HAVE A TIME LIMIT ON EVERYTHING": CURFEWS AND FACILITY RULES AS BARRIERS

The rigid rules of transitional housing facilities also created obstacles to maintaining family relationships. These rules restricted the ability of formerly incarcerated men to freely move about the city and spend time with their children. For example, Ricardo discussed how the strict rules of the federal halfway house have negatively impacted his ability to spend time with his children.

I asked Ricardo to describe the rules and regulations of his halfway house. He explained that living there is "basically, [the] same thing it would be if you were in prison except that you have [a] little more freedoms." He explained that residents are required to obtain employment, must keep their space tidy, and are subject to search when they return to the facility. They are also allowed certain privileges, like owning a DVD player and a cell phone. But Ricardo's main issue with the halfway house was how it controlled his time:

> RICARDO: Well, the rules is to always be on time. You have to put in [requests for] passes. And these passes are either work passes, or they're passes to either go to your laundry or um, go to, you know, church. [They're] very limited, very limited on giving you time to spend with your family. Um, and if they do [give you a pass to visit family] . . . they're supposed to give you 12-hour passes, [but] they give you . . . eight-hour passes. They cut everything like down to, you know, the smallest minute. [. . .] [E]very—everything is based around you being on time. You can't be late coming in there . . . you have a time limit on everything.

Ricardo felt that because there is "a time limit on everything" he has been unable to spend time rebuilding relationships with his children. Ricardo's history of incarceration has taken a tremendous toll on his relationship with his two teenage children. He told me that the federal prison system is "built to destroy families." For example, Ricardo discussed how he was only allowed 300 minutes per month to call home. This amounts to about 10 minutes per day, which was never enough time for Ricardo. At the start of his sentence, he was receiving visits from his kids every other week, but as his sentence dragged on, he grew distant from his wife and they divorced, which put a stop to the visits with his kids.

I asked Ricardo if he was currently close to his kids. Ricardo said he felt attached to his children, but these feelings were not reciprocated. "At this point, the time [I spent in prison] for my teenage children has diminished our relationship. My youngest daughter right now doesn't speak to me. My oldest son, who's 17, doesn't have. . . . He doesn't speak to me a lot also because they're angry at the fact that I was away for so, so many years and at this point, I'm still in a halfway house, and I can't spend as much time as I want to with them. So, they're pretty upset."

Felipe similarly discussed how the curfew at his homeless shelter limited his ability to spend time with his kids. Like Ricardo, Felipe discussed how the shelter placed a time limit on his freedom: "Yeah, living in the shelter system is like, everything's on time. You know what I mean? You have to be there by a certain time. You gotta be there by 9 o'clock. You have to leave out by 8 o'clock in the morning. So, it's like, you know . . . it's like, if you working, you gotta come out of work, go, you know, see your kids maybe for, like, two or three hours and keep your curfew at the same time, if you in the shelter."

Finally, Dwight describes how the disciplinary rules of his residential treatment program limit his ability to see his kids. Dwight's residential treatment program exerts significant control over how he spends his time and where is able to go.[12] His ability to see his kids is subject to the whims of the facility's staff members, who hold the power to grant or deny weekend passes.[13]

For example, one of the facility's policies is called "Peter Pays for Paul." Under this policy, if staff discover that a rule has been broken (e.g., they discover that someone has been smoking indoors or find a stash of drugs) and no one confesses to having done it, the whole house is punished. If someone does confess to the rule violation, they are put on "contract." They lose all of their weekend passes, they must get up an hour early (at 5:00 a.m.) to perform menial labor like cleaning the bathrooms, and they must perform more cleaning duties at the end of the night (until 9:00 p.m.). What is more, they must go to the end of the line during mealtimes, when medications are passed out, and at any other time when the clients must wait in line for something.

Dwight lives in a poorly insulated room with eight other men. He suspects that one of his roommates stole $5 out of his wallet the other day.

However, he does not want to tell staff about it because of the "Peter Pays for Paul" rule. If he tells staff, and no one confesses, then the whole room is put on contract. Dwight is supposed to get a 12-hour pass this weekend to see his kids, and he doesn't want to risk it over $5. Right now, Dwight is only allowed a weekend pass every other weekend, so if he misses this weekend, it will be another two weeks before he'll be able to see his kids.

As these cases illustrate, keeping up with the compliance costs of housing facilities ultimately undermines family relationships. Families are crucial forms of social support that are necessary for reintegration, but men are forced to choose between rebuilding these relationships or maintaining a roof over their heads. Violating curfew to spend time rebuilding relationships with children can ironically lead to eviction, which pushes men further toward the margins of mainstream social life.

CONCLUSION

During a focus group at Second Chances, I asked the group how long they thought it would take to achieve economic independence. Tony initially estimated that it would take about six months. However, as he explained his answer, he began to realize just how challenging that would be:

TONY: In the beginning . . . first you have to fulfill their um . . . whatever requirements they want you to do to get public assistance. . . . You have to fulfill those first. So, to get full time employment, which is, you know, your first step to becoming independent after all that bullshit. You have to have a steady job. And you have to look at the market and the rooms out there. Like . . . cheapest you're ever going to find a room give or take is like $600, even in the shittiest area in Long Island or the city. It's like $600 . . . and it's hard to find. The average two-bedroom apartment is going for $1300 a month. Like, that's fucking ridiculous. So how am I going to be making, you know, $10, $10.50 an hour [or] even $11.50 an hour . . . for me to be able to afford that every month, pay that, um, transportation that it takes to keep the steady employment to break away from [welfare.] . . . That's going to take time. It's going to take a fair amount of time. . . .

But you're having me do all these damn classes and so much hours for this little chicken shit 200 dollars a month. It doesn't make no sense. That's like . . . how the hell am I supposed to, you know, get prepared for employment, or, or, or get this experience to do what I need to do, when you're having me do a ridiculous amounts of hour just for this little bit of assistance that I need. Because that's the whole reason you're in the office.

You need assistance, you need help. But, to give a little bit of help they ask, "Alright, I want you to do all this shit, I want you to walk, you know, this is . . . 10 miles to get this little bit of help." That's not helping. That's like a discouragement if anything.

Throughout this chapter, we have seen how the runaround exacts a series of compliance costs on returning citizens. Study participants had to constantly expend financial resources or forgo opportunities to comply with the mandates of the institutional circuit. In Tony's words, returning citizens must walk a metaphorical "10 miles" simply to maintain access to public aid and avoid reincarceration. But keeping up with the daily grind of these costs ultimately undermines reintegration. Formerly incarcerated men are constantly treading water to keep up with the litany of overlapping appointments and curfews necessary to maintain access to community freedom and basic material resources. Because they spend so much time and energy just keeping their heads above water, they are unable to pull themselves to the raft of employment, housing security, and family relationships necessary for full social inclusion.

In the next chapter we consider the subjective effects of the runaround, exploring the cognitive frames and emotional reactions that men develop in response to the experience of "getting the runaround" and examining how these subjective experiences shape patterns of noncompliance and resistance.

THREE

They Set You Up to Fail

WHEN I INTERVIEWED HIM IN 2015, Leon owed $17,000 in child support arrears. His debt was owed to the New York City Department of Social Services (DSS) to repay the state for public assistance benefits his ex-partner and sons had received in 2004.[1] Leon didn't find out about his child support order until about a year after it started. By that point, he already owed arrears. Leon was serving a jail sentence when he found out about the order. A letter had been sent to his home address, and his current wife had to relay the message to him. Leon was blindsided by the news. "I was incarcerated, and I'm like 'Wow man, I'm getting arrears? In prison? I'm in prison. Like, I can't help with nothing.'"[2] Upon his release from jail, Leon went to the family court to try to resolve the issue:

> LEON: I went down there, they let me speak to the judge one day. I told
> him "I don't have no job." He gave me 60 days to find a job. I'm like,
> "Like serious? Like, it's that easy in your world?" 'Cause sometimes you
> can't find a job in 60 days.

Leon said that he later returned to the family court to get his driver's license reinstated after it was suspended for nonpayment. He said he experienced the "runaround syndrome" and decided it wasn't worth his time:

> LEON: I wasn't . . . I'm not gonna say no body treated me bad or said
> anything negative to me, but it was just a whole lot of runaround red
> tape. Like, I'm—I don't know exactly where [to go] and then somebody
> will come [and tell me] "Oh, well you have to [go] over to this building,
> in this department." And I get there, it be the same thing. "You have to
> go over to this"—I'm like, "No this—does anybody know where I have
> to go?" Like, "You sending me here, they sent me to you, and you send

me back to them, but they just sent me back to you." And then, it's like a game, like, you know? Before I know it, I wasted two days. Getting nothing done.

He decided to go back to selling drugs in order to keep up with his child support payments. "Yeah, I was breaking my neck doing that. And, honestly, I was—I had to go back to slinging drugs to . . . get it down," he told me. Leon explained his decision to sell drugs to pay child support as a combination of resentment toward the state for the "hoopla" they had put him through as well as his identity as a "street dude" who eschews the degradation of low-wage work in favor of the fast money of the street economy:

> LEON: I went down there one time and they gave me so much hoopla where you got to go to this building and that building. To be honest, I got frustrated and I left. I was like, I'm a street dude, I ain't—I ain't gonna work no way, I'm going in the streets to get some money. 'Cause that was the thought I had then. They ain't gonna—[If] they gonna beat me one way, [then] I'll beat you another way. You know, I wasn't really . . . serious about just working then like that. You know, I was like every time I get something, they're gonna take it and do this and do that. Like, come on.

However, Leon's drug dealing eventually caught up with him. He wound up back in jail on gun charges in 2006. Upon his release in 2007, Leon decided to go straight, and he hasn't returned to jail or prison since. He feared that his wife would leave him and that he would be once again an absent father for his young daughter. Leon took a job working at a bread factory, but his wages were heavily garnished due to his child support arrears. "They snatched that up. They took that," he told me when discussing his paycheck from the bread factory. Leon and his wife's federal and state tax returns were also intercepted by child support. Despite losing a significant proportion of his income to child support, Leon continued to avoid the street economy and maintain his job at the bread factory. However, around 2010 Leon and his wife were both laid off from their jobs, and their landlord increased their rent by $400. Leon said that he and his wife "made an executive decision" to move to Pennsylvania with their daughter, where the cost of living was significantly cheaper.

Leon did not report his move to child support authorities and ultimately decided to stop paying child support altogether. He was tired of losing significant portions of his income and causing friction with his wife, all for an expense that wasn't even directly benefiting his children. He explained,

"[I]t's going into the system. My kids never saw a dime from it. And that was one of the reasons I stopped. I was like, they're not getting nothing out of it. I ain't with that."

Leon ultimately stopped complying with the child support system because he viewed it as an illegitimate institution. His view was shaped by repeated experiences of the runaround. Leon was initially denied information about his child support case and only found out about it after he was in arrears. When he attempted to address his various issues with child support, he was confronted by an opaque and convoluted bureaucracy. Rather than being provided an opportunity to express his concerns, Leon was shuffled between buildings and was left feeling confused and frustrated. Even when he was making payments, he felt that the state was illegitimately extracting resources from him, taking his meager income away from his family to fill state coffers.

However, Leon's resistance was ultimately self-defeating. When I spoke with Leon in 2015, he had not been paying child support for five years. During that time he had racked up $17,000 in arrears, and he was still unable to renew his driver's license. Leon said that he had missed out on "four or five job opportunities" because he didn't have his license. He told me, "Like I . . . could've been on my feet by now. 'Cause the driving jobs come up more than anything else. But, you know, I'm exiled from that because of the [suspended] license."

Leon's case provides a window into understanding the subjective effects of the runaround. The repeated hassles that Leon experienced with the child support system left him feeling confused, frustrated, and disempowered. He discussed how his decision to continue selling drugs to pay child support was rooted in his need to reassert his sense of masculine autonomy as a "street dude" in the face of this disempowerment. Even when he stopped selling drugs, Leon continued to resist paying child support. After being continually denied information about his case and having his wages heavily garnished, he viewed the child support system as being arbitrary, unaccountable, and extractive. These repeated experiences of "procedural injustice" fed into a long-standing distrust of state authorities, shaped by decades of harassment and abuse at the hands of police and corrections officers over the span of Leon's criminal career. This profound sense of distrust toward the state provided the reasons he needed to resist paying child support, even though this resistance was ultimately self-defeating.

This chapter take's Leon's experience as a jumping-off point for exploring how the runaround shapes men's perceptions of state power. I argue that the runaround exacerbates the physical and emotional strains of reentry and re-inforces men's distrust of state authorities. These negative experiences in turn feed into patterns of noncompliance and resistance. First, the chapter explores how the combined strains of reentry, severe deprivation, and bureaucratic pro-cessing leave men vulnerable to interpreting the runaround as a form of per-sonal disrespect. Men respond to these perceived slights with confrontation and verbal aggression toward institutional gatekeepers. These "compensatory manhood acts" allow men to momentarily reassert their sense of control but ultimately push them further away from their goals of reintegration.[3]

The chapter then turns to consider how men experience the runaround as a type of "procedural injustice." The runaround is a degrading experience that diminishes returning citizens' personal autonomy and reinforces their stig-matized status. These negative experiences teach men to expect arbitrary and abusive treatment from institutional gatekeepers, reinforcing an already dis-trustful relationship with the state formed through years of harassment and abuse at the hands of criminal legal actors. Men view the actions of frontline actors through this distrustful lens. They suspect that frontline actors are set-ting them up for failure by intentionally creating bureaucratic barriers. Men respond to this sense of distrust and disempowerment with noncompliance and system avoidance. In these ways, the runaround produces precisely the types of subjects the state seeks to govern. The stress and hassle of the run-around pushes men to be defiant and disengaged. Their resistance confirms negative stereotypes of criminalized men of color and provides legitimacy for the state's disciplinary regime of social control.[4]

THE SUBJECTIVE EFFECTS
OF INSTITUTIONAL PROCESSING

Policy scholars Pamela Herd and Donald P. Moynihan argue that when studying administrative burdens like the runaround, it is important to dis-tinguish the actions of the state from the experience of the individual: "The state can construct rules and processes that give rise to the experience of burden, but the individual experience of burden is distinct from rules and processes."[5] While it is often the case that policymakers intentionally de-sign administrative burdens to undermine access to rights and services, or that frontline actors behave in ways that are arbitrary and abusive, it is also the case that returning citizens might misinterpret or misremember their interactions with frontline actors in ways that don't necessarily align with the point of view of the state.

In focusing on men's subjective experience of the runaround, it is important to emphasize that we are not necessarily concerned with constructing an objective accounting of past events.[6] This chapter is mostly based on men's retrospective accounts of getting the runaround. These accounts are inherently partial retellings of what happened. They reflect men's selective, one-sided memories.[7]

For example, throughout our interview Leon had difficulty giving me a linear account of his involvement with the child support system. I had a hard time keeping track of how his case evolved over time and the exact timing of when he made visits to the family court. "I've been through so much, man, I can't give you accurate accounts on that," he explained to me when I tried to ask him a follow-up question about the timeline of events in his child support case. However, what is important here is not a forensic retelling of Leon's child support case. Instead, what is important for the purposes of this analysis is Leon's subjective experience of navigating the child support system: how he interpreted interactions with the child support system, how those interactions shaped his perceptions of the state, and how those perceptions provided a framework for future actions.[8] In this sense, Leon's difficulty remembering the exact details of his case are analytically important in their own right, illustrating how navigating the complex rules of the institutional circuit leaves returning citizens in a state of constant confusion, feeding into feelings of frustration and distrust that serve as justifications for noncompliance.

Even if returning citizens remember the sequence of events accurately, their negative reactions might be disproportionate to the actual hassles they experienced. They could be exaggerating, overreacting, or misinterpreting what may have been minor inconveniences from the point of view of frontline actors. While this indeed may be the case, it is important to understand why it is that returning citizens are prone to having such profoundly negative experiences with state actors in the first place.

Strain and the Runaround: Severe Deprivation, Cognitive Bias, and Compensatory Manhood Acts

Research from behavioral economics illustrates how the stress of poverty can reduce cognitive capacity and increase bias.[9] Under such conditions, the negative effects of the runaround are amplified. People who already feel threatened and exhausted by the stress of food insecurity and housing insta-bility are prone to interpreting what may seem to be "minor and defensible" bureaucratic inconveniences from the point of view of policy administrators as forms of intentional discrimination or abuse.[10]

Indeed, most of the people who came through the doors of Second Chances and Uplift were struggling with conditions of "severe deprivation" that made them vulnerable to interpreting interactions with frontline actors in dramatically negative ways.[11] Almost all study participants were experi-encing acute hardship, particularly food insecurity and residential instabil-ity. Most had incomes below the poverty line and were reliant on public assistance programs to meet their basic needs. Food stamps, food pantries, or free meals provided by Second Chances and Uplift were essential for study participants to meet their daily nutritional needs. Only three of the men I interviewed were independently housed. The rest lived either with family members or romantic partners or in a transitional housing facility, and in most cases these living arrangements were temporary.

These acute hardships were compounded by a variety of other factors. Study participants returned to some of New York City's most impoverished and racially segregated neighborhoods.[12] They all had difficulty finding stable employment. Owing to their criminal records, human capital deficits, and histories of addiction and mental illness, "employment was hard to find and easy to lose" for study participants.[13] They had also endured persistent hardship over their life courses. Most had grown up in disadvantaged neigh-borhoods in households with scarce resources. Many had family histories of substance abuse, which was passed on to them. And many had experienced violent trauma at an early age, either as a witness, victim, or perpetrator, and these traumatic experiences persisted throughout their lives.[14]

These conditions of severe deprivation further exacerbate the already stress-ful process of transitioning from prison to community. The time and energy it takes to secure basic material necessities, as well as the uncertainty and anxi-ety of not knowing where your next meal will come from or where you will lay your head at night, can "impair mental health, trigger relapse," and disrupt stable routines and social relationships that are necessary for long-term social reintegration.[15] Indeed, the daily grind of poverty survival has a corrosive ef-fect on the psychological well-being of returning citizens. Food scarcity and housing insecurity can make a person irritable, depressed, and anxious, fur-ther exacerbating preexisting vulnerabilities, such as histories of trauma, men-tal illness, and substance misuse. The recurrent experience of rejection and discrimination wears down returning citizens' self-confidence and stamina.[16] Constantly trying and failing to land a job or secure an apartment can leave formerly incarcerated people feeling depleted and discouraged. Such conditions of material and psychological stress can impair long-term decision-making and leave returning citizens vulnerable to relapse and recidivism.

For men, poverty can be an acutely psychologically distressing experience. Poverty is emasculating. Economic independence and self-sufficiency are core aspects of hegemonic masculinity in the United States.[17] Poor men of color are often blocked from achieving economic independence through participation in the mainstream labor market. For them, the illegal drug trade and the violence that comes with it have become ways to achieve not only economic self-sufficiency but also respect and power in neighborhood contexts devoid of other options for achieving hegemonic masculinity.[18]

Most study participants had become accustomed to being self-sufficient and respected in the contexts of the street economy. Suddenly being thrust into severe deprivation following release from prison was a blow to their masculine identities. For men who were fathers this was even more difficult. Many had fulfilled the role of family breadwinner through their forays into the street economy. Although most were absent from the lives of their children, they were able to use their earnings from drug dealing to provide regular cash support to the mothers of their children and shower their kids with gifts.

Leon took pride in being the breadwinner for his children through the money he earned in the street economy. However, now that he had put his drug dealing days behind him, he struggled to fulfill the breadwinner role. For example, Leon was at the grocery store with his two grandkids the previous weekend, and he couldn't afford to buy them what they wanted:

> LEON: I felt bad last weekend, like, taking some juices from them because they . . . just went to the counter with just too much. Like, I'm like, "Oh, put something back. You take two items; you take two items." You know, because I'm not . . . working . . . and I felt bad about that. Because I'm not used to that. I'm [usually] like, "Get what you want. Tear the ice cream truck up, you know, just don't make a mess," you know? But I had to limit them on what they get, so that really hurt.

Seeking aid compounded these feelings of emasculation for formerly incarcerated men. Having to rely on public assistance agencies, transitional housing facilities, and community-based service providers to meet their basic needs was an admission that they had failed to achieve masculine ideals of independence and self-sufficiency. What is more, receiving public aid meant that they had to submit to the demands of service providers in order to access resources, yet another admission that they were not fully in control of their lives and were dependent on others.

The runaround further exacerbates these stressors. Formerly incarcerated men feel disempowered by the demands of overlapping appointments, the degrading living conditions of transitional housing facilities, and the micromanagement of POs. In response to these pervasive feelings of emasculation, formerly incarcerated men engage in "compensatory manhood acts" to reclaim their masculine identities and signify "a capacity to exert control over one's self, the environment, and others."[19] In the context of navigating the institutional circuit, compensatory manhood acts involve resistance and noncompliance with the demands of frontline actors. This is expressed through verbal aggression, noncompliance with institutional rules, and absconding.

Verbal Aggression and Confrontations at Second Chances

The core mission of Second Chances was to alleviate the hardships associated with reentry. In addition to helping returning citizens overcome barriers to employment, the program provided a menu of "wraparound" rehabilitative services. Second Chances also made active efforts to alleviate the stress of hunger and housing instability through nutrition programs and supportive housing facilities. And it endeavored to treat program participants with dignity and respect by hiring almost all formerly incarcerated staff members and providing "culturally competent" services.

However, despite these efforts to be responsive to the needs of returning citizens, staff members nonetheless had to contend with the realities of operating a nonprofit organization. Second Chances was under constant pressure to produce performance metrics in order to ensure organization survival. Staff members had to enforce program rules and eligibility requirements in order to stay in compliance with funding mandates and ensure that future contracts would get renewed. Many study participants experienced the routine enforcement of these rules as yet another instance of being given the runaround. Struggling under the stress of poverty, social isolation, and the demands of completing bureaucratic obligations, they were prone to misinterpret the routine application of program rules as personal attacks.

This was especially the case for men, who were quick to respond to these perceived hassles with verbal aggression and confrontation.[20] These confrontations were most common when staff members had to enforce the rules of the Workforce Development Workshop at Second Chances. During the two-week workshop, participants were required to wear professional attire (i.e., slacks, collared shirt, dress shoes, and a tie) and behave in a "professional manner," which included showing up on time; actively participating in class; and avoiding practices associated with the "street," such as cursing, using slang, catcalling, drug use, fighting, and opposition to authority figures. These rules were designed to not only prepare program participants for the job market but also evaluate whether program participants could be trusted to positively represent Second Chances during job interviews with partner employers.[21]

The workshop was an important tool for filtering the client pool to ensure that the people they were sending on job interviews would get hired and could be counted toward job placement quotas that were essential for the program's survival. When program participants routinely violated the rules, they would be removed from the workshop and asked to restart the two-week program. Participants were allowed as many second chances as they needed to complete the program. However, if they engaged in overtly threatening or violent behavior, then they would not be allowed to return.

The policy of giving people multiple second chances to complete the program was rooted in the organization's recognition that reentry is an uneven process with multiple ups and downs. In contrast to parole's intolerance for rule violations and its quickness to send people back to prison for minor infractions, Second Chances's policy of allowing multiple attempts was meant to communicate that although people should be held accountable for violating the rules, the consequences should be nonpunitive and restorative.

Despite these good intentions, formerly incarcerated men nonetheless experienced having to repeat the program as an extension of the runaround. For men struggling under the weight of acute poverty, social isolation, and the hassles of other bureaucratic entanglements, having to repeat the workshop was a major inconvenience that compounded their already stressful circumstances. Repeating the workshop meant having to invest more time and resources to attend the next workshop. For men who were mandated to attend the program, it could also mean facing sanction for noncompliance with parole or HRA conditions.

Indeed, on one of my first days of fieldwork I met with Whitney, the senior director of the Workforce Development Program. She explained that there was a lot of "drama and tension" in the workshop between staff members and program participants. According to Whitney, program participants were under a great deal of stress, and the smallest perceived slight could set them off. "Some of these guys are like, tick . . . boom," she told me, meaning that they were ticking time bombs ready to go off. Enforcing the workshop's rules and removing participants from the program were significant sources of this "drama and tension." Formerly incarcerated men sometimes interpreted the application of these rules as forms of disrespect and affronts to their masculinity and responded through aggressive confrontations with staff members, which sometimes escalated into threats of violence.

Bernard, a Black man in his thirties, was removed from the workshop on a Friday afternoon during the first week of class. Eric, who was the workshop facilitator that week, had caught Bernard sleeping in class on several occasions throughout the week. Bernard said that he hadn't been getting much sleep lately and that he was on new medication that made him sleepy. After catching him sleeping again on Friday, Eric decided that he would have to be removed from the workshop and start it over. While Eric and I were conducting mock job interviews with the other program participants, Bernard was pulled out of class by his career counselor and given the news. After a few minutes, Bernard returned to the classroom. He interrupted a mock job interview that Eric and I were conducting and tossed a Second Chances button on the desk. As Bernard walked away, he turned and pointed at Eric, using his index finger and thumb to make a gun, and said coldly, "I'll be seeing you," while he wiggled his thumb, as if to suggest he was shooting the gun.

Shortly after this incident Eric sent the class on break. Before they left, however, Eric addressed what had just happened: "I've said this since day one. It's all business in here. Nothing is personal. This workshop is run this way for a reason. I don't come to your house and rearrange the furniture. If you can't stay awake or fulfill the requirements of this workshop, then maybe you need to do it another time."

After everyone left the classroom, Eric pulled me aside to vent about what had just happened. He was upset that Bernard's career counselor didn't escort him out of the building and instead let him come back to the classroom. "I didn't want him to come back into my class. . . . This guy has an attitude. . . . He thinks he's a killer. But I never let it get to me. . . . The way he said "I'll be seeing you" that was aggressive, that was threatening. . . . I've had guys waiting for me outside my last job. . . . I had a coworker who had her face cut by a client who didn't like her."

As class wrapped up for that day, Donnell, a Black man in his thirties, approached Eric and me about the incident. He asked Eric if he had noticed that Bernard had made a gun gesture at him. Eric told Donnell, "It doesn't bother me. . . . You can't let other people occupy space in your mind." Eric thought that it was mostly an empty gesture, reassuring Donnell that Bernard "doesn't want to go back [to prison]." If it was a legitimate threat, Eric would have let law enforcement deal with it: "I'm a productive community member now. . . . I'll just call the cops." Later on in the day Eric had to write up an official incident report, since it had involved threatening behavior.

Bernard responded to the perceived hassles of the workshop with an exaggerated display of manhood, in this case a threat of violence. Bernard had invested a full week in attending the workshop. Having to start over meant that he had wasted nearly 40 hours of his week attending class with nothing to show for it, and he'd have to go through the hassle of reenrolling in the workshop to get access to an interview referral. Bernard took his frustration out on Eric, whom he blamed for exacerbating his hardship by blocking his access to a job interview referral. Eric ultimately viewed Bernard's threat as an empty gesture, an act of bravado made by a man trying to save face by acting tough. At the same time, Eric also recognized that these kinds of threats can escalate into real acts of violence, as he had experienced in his previous job.

While formerly incarcerated men can become overwhelmed by frustration with the runaround and misinterpret the actions of frontline actors, so too can frontline actors become burned out by the stress of administering this rigid and convoluted system of bureaucratic rules and misinterpret the actions of returning citizens. When both sides of the service transaction are experiencing burnout, the likelihood of a dispute dramatically increases.

We can see this tension arise in disputes over the eligibility rules surrounding access to MetroCards. Access to a free MetroCard was a lifeline for men with meager cash incomes who couldn't afford to pay for subway fare to travel to various appointments around the city. Disputes were not uncommon when men were blocked from accessing MetroCards because they did not meet rigid eligibility requirements. I experienced one such dispute firsthand.

It was the first day of the workshop. Forty new participants were starting the two-week program that day. In addition to delivering the first day of curriculum, the major task of the day was to distribute MetroCards to eligible participants, as well as to issue official letters of participation for those who needed to be excused from other bureaucratic obligations.

Program participants receiving SNAP benefits were eligible to receive a free 10-trip MetroCard to attend class. However, they needed to produce an HRA budget letter to prove their eligibility for a MetroCard. Many participants said that they were receiving SNAP benefits, but they didn't have a budget letter with them that day. Because of the workshop's strict attendance policy, they didn't have time to go to HRA to get their paperwork that day. Eric promised to accommodate their schedules and would let people leave early so they could pick up budget letters from HRA.

Many participants also needed official letters of participation from Second Chances to get them excused from WEP assignments and BTW programs. If program participants did not submit these letters to HRA promptly, then they could be sanctioned for noncompliance and have their benefits suspended or cut off. Eric also promised to let these participants leave early so they could travel to the HRA office to submit their letters in person.

Throughout the day there was a great deal of confusion about budget letters and letters of participation. Many program participants were confused about whether they needed a budget letter, a letter of participation, or both. Some participants had already turned in their budget letters to Second Chances. Others needed to leave early to make it to an HRA office to get their budget letter before the office closed. Other participants didn't need to get budget letters, but they needed letters of participation from Second Chances. They also needed to leave early to submit their participation letters to an HRA office to avoid getting sanctioned.

I was running around all morning trying to help staff members sort out the confusion. I attempted to make a list of all of the people who needed letters of participation from Second Chances so that career counselors could get a head start on drafting the letters. I sent a sign-up sheet around the classroom, asking that anyone who needed a letter of participation (not a budget letter) write their name on the sheet. However, some people who put down their names needed to travel to an HRA office for a budget letter and did not need a letter of participation from Second Chances. I reminded the class that the list was only for people who needed letters of participation, not budget letters.

I took the list to Tina and Donald, who were the career counselors in charge of distributing letters of participation. They started scheduling meetings with participants who needed letters of participation beginning at 2:30 p.m. that day. I headed back to the classroom to read out the schedule of appointments for the afternoon. As I started going down the list, confusion ensued. There were still people on the list who needed budget letters and not letters of participation. I crossed these names off the list, but my frustration started to build. I thought I had been clear with my instructions. *Why isn't the class listening to me?* I thought.

My frustration continued into the afternoon. At 2:30 p.m. participants who needed letters of participation began heading over to Tina's desk. Around this time Eric began excusing people from the class to go get their budget letters from HRA. About half the 40-person class either left to go to HRA for a budget letter or waited by Tina's desk to receive a letter of participation.

I took a seat at an empty desk adjacent to Tina. While I was sitting there, Gustavo, a Latino man in his forties, approached me. Gustavo needed to get his budget letter from HRA, but he had no way of getting to an HRA office that day. He was under the impression that Second Chances would give him a MetroCard to travel to the HRA office. I explained to Gustavo that he was mistaken. Second Chances could only authorize a MetroCard if he presented an HRA budget letter showing he was receiving SNAP benefits.

I told him that I understood that this whole situation was "bananas": he needed to travel to an HRA office to get a copy of his budget letter so he could receive a free MetroCard, but he couldn't afford subway fare to travel to the HRA office in the first place. Even though I tried to sympathize with Gustavo's situation, I also tried to be firm and clear about the program's rules. I explained that there was nothing I could do to give him a Metro-Card unless he had a budget letter from HRA.

Gustavo began to get agitated. "What do you expect me to do?" he asked me, his voice getting louder and angrier. "Jump the turnstile? Can you give me a letter from you saying that it's OK for me to violate my parole?"

I began to get defensive. My sympathy quickly turned into frustration. I remember thinking to myself, *We told you last week at orientation to bring your budget letter on Monday. Why didn't you go to HRA last week? You should have been more responsible and planned ahead. This isn't my fault.*

I told Gustavo that we didn't want him to violate his parole. If he couldn't make it to the HRA office on his own that day, then there was no point in his leaving class early. He should go back to the classroom and finish the lesson for that day. My response frustrated Gustavo even further. He said that he was going to leave class anyway because "you're not telling me positive things" and that he was "gonna do what I gotta do" to get to HRA.

Realizing that my shortness with Gustavo had escalated the situation, I pleaded with him to stay so we could work something out and he wouldn't have to potentially violate his parole by jumping the turnstile. Whitney had heard our argument escalate from her office a few feet away and stepped in to intervene. She took Gustavo into her office to calm him down, explaining to him that I was "only an intern" as she walked him over.

I took a seat back at my desk and tried to gather myself. Vanessa, one of the career counselors, asked me what had just happened. Whitney's office door was open just a few feet away, so I leaned forward and recounted the argument to Vanessa in a low whisper. Vanessa said that she had met Gustavo the previous week during orientation and that he had a "sassy" attitude. "We're just trying to help you. You don't have to be like that," she whispered. I began talking to Eric about what had just happened. "He's an old dope fiend. He's trying to manipulate," Eric said under his breath.

A few minutes later Gustavo emerged from Whitney's office. He walked over to me and shook my hand, apologizing for getting frustrated. I apologized too, saying that I was frustrated that there wasn't more I could do to help out. Whitney arranged for Gustavo to get a roundtrip MetroCard for that day, and Tina printed out a letter of participation for Gustavo to take to the HRA office. Before he left, we shook hands again and I wished him good luck.

Even though Gustavo ended up getting the resources that he needed, this incident taught me just how quickly and easily tensions between frontline actors and returning citizens can escalate, especially when both parties are experiencing cognitive overload and emotional burnout. Formerly incarcerated men become burned out from the stress of poverty and the disempowerment of bureaucratic processing, leading them to misinterpret minor hassles as intentional forms of disrespect and to respond with verbal aggression. At the same time, frontline actors experience burnout from the stress of administering the convoluted rules of the institutional circuit, leading them to misinterpret returning citizens' frustrations and resentments as character flaws rather than as symptoms of deeper social vulnerabilities.

Gustavo was frustrated by a rigid set of eligibility rules that were preventing him from accessing a MetroCard. He was desperate for material aid. He was so broke that he couldn't afford the $4.50 roundtrip subway fare to travel to an HRA office. He needed help, but a rigid set of eligibility rules stood in the way of his accessing the material aid he desperately needed. He took his frustration out on me, whom he blamed for enforcing a set of rules that were blocking his access to crucial material resources.

At the same time, I was cognitively and emotionally burned out from a long day of trying to disentangle the confusing mess of budget letters and letters of participation. I lost my patience with Gustavo. In the moment, I dismissed his legitimate frustration as a character flaw and interpreted his resentment as a sign of his personal irresponsibility. Luckily, Whitney stepped in to resolve the problem, but the situation very easily could have ended differently. Gustavo could have left that day and decided that dealing with HRA and Second Chances wasn't worth the hassle, that front-line actors like me were indifferent to his problems, that complying with the institutional circuit wasn't worth his time. He may have decided that he could reclaim some semblance of self-respect and control by returning to the street economy. Or he could have left that day, jumped the subway turnstile to get to an HRA office, gotten arrested, and been in violation of his parole.

"WE'RE STILL JUST A NUMBER": PROCEDURAL PUNISHMENT, PROCEDURAL INJUSTICE, AND RESISTANCE

One evening after the Workforce Development Workshop at Second Chances, I ran into Todd, Victor, and Manny waiting next to their career counselor's desk. At the orientation session the previous week, all three men were told that they were eligible to receive MetroCards for attending class. However, because of a paperwork mix-up earlier that day, their career counselor, Deanna, could not issue them their MetroCards. All three men were evidently frustrated. They had been promised a free MetroCard and had no other way of getting home that day. Deanna was running around the office frantically trying to sort out the mix-up. As the men waited, Todd complained that he felt exploited by social service agencies. He told Victor and Manny, "You got all these programs coming around trying to make money off of us. . . . We're still just a number. . . . We're just in a bigger prison, full of con men."

All three men lived in transitional housing facilities, and the waiting was threatening to make them late for curfew. After a half hour of waiting,

Victor had had enough. He got up from his chair and walked toward the exit with a look of anger and frustration on his face. A few minutes later Deanna emerged with the approved MetroCards. She noticed that Victor had left, and she asked Manny and Todd where he went. Todd replied, "He left. He's gonna find his own way home and try to make his way back tomorrow, hopefully."

This vignette captures how returning citizens interpret the runaround as a dehumanizing experience. Constantly being shuffled around to offices, being told to wait, and having their complaints go unheard made formerly incarcerated men feel like frontline actors did not recognize their humanity. Instead, they felt like "just a number" lost in a cold bureaucratic machine. These feelings of degradation exacerbate the stress of poverty and reinforce distrust of state authority. As we saw in Victor's case, men respond to this sense of disempowerment with noncompliance. Victor's actions suggest that he had lost trust in Deanna's ability to address his needs. Instead, he chose to go it alone rather than rely on Deanna's help. Although Victor was able to assert a sense of autonomy in the face of bureaucratic disempowerment, his resistance was ultimately self-defeating. Had he just endured a few more minutes of waiting, he would have been able to access a MetroCard. Instead, he decided to "find his own way home."

The feelings of degradation that returning citizens experience reflect how the runaround is the outcome of profound power imbalances between returning citizens and institutional gatekeepers.[22] Returning citizens are often powerless over their material circumstances. They are excluded from mainstream social and economic life by "thousands of laws and policies that make it nearly impossible for them to meet their basic human needs without the help of others."[23] Because of these vulnerabilities, institutional gatekeepers wield enormous power over the lives of returning citizens. Parole officers can decide whether returning citizens remain in the community or go back to prison. Welfare case managers, transitional housing facility staff, and assorted social service providers have the power to decide whether returning citizens can access food, shelter, and rehabilitative services.

Institutional gatekeepers also have the power to restrict the social and civil rights of returning citizens.[24] They can invade returning citizens' privacy through home visits, facility surveillance, and gathering of personal data; they can restrict free movement through curfews, mandatory appointments, and facility rules; and they can impose behavioral mandates such as substance abuse treatment or job training as conditions of receiving aid. They also have the power to punish returning citizens for failing to comply with these restrictions. They can send returning citizens back to prison, mandate them to residential programs, or restrict their access to food and shelter for failing to comply with their mandates.

In these ways, returning citizens experience the runaround as a kind of procedural punishment. Like other forms of punishment, the runaround diminishes returning citizens' autonomy and reinforces their stigmatized status. However, unlike formal criminal sanctions, the runaround operates through a series of informal bureaucratic hassles.[25] By forcing formerly incarcerated men to constantly wait for appointments; withholding information; dictating their movements throughout the day; and extracting resources from them in the form of fines, fees, and opportunity costs, the runaround extends the state's power to punish.[26]

But, unlike more direct and coercive forms of state punishment, like arrest and incarceration, the runaround is a more diffuse and impersonal experience. Because returning citizens experience hassles across multiple institutional settings, they are often unable to pinpoint the exact source of their frustration. The sheer complexity and opacity of the institutional circuit makes it difficult to communicate with officials and hold them accountable for their actions. This lack of transparency keeps returning citizens in a state of "enforced ignorance" about why they experience bureaucratic hassles in the first place.[27]

Taken together, these experiences constitute a form of procedural injustice. If procedural *justice* encompasses "treating people with dignity and respect, voice (which can include citizen participation and allowing individuals to express their concerns), neutrality (freedom from bias), and conveying trustworthy motives (explaining how the police are helping reach an important social goal)," then procedural *in*justice is the inverse.[28]

Procedural punishments, like the runaround, are inherently procedurally unjust. Because they operate outside the bounds of formal criminal sentencing, procedural punishments are not subject to due process safeguards that can protect returning citizens from bias and abuse. Moreover, because the runaround operates through a diffuse network of institutions and actors, returning citizens have a diminished ability to exercise voice or understand the motives of institutional gatekeepers.

In the context of the institutional circuit, returning citizens experience procedural injustice when they feel treated as "just a number" rather than as a human being in need of help. They experience it as a denial of rights without explanation or due process. It manifests when they feel silenced by a bureaucratic system that seems unwilling to hear their complaints of unfairness. And they experience it when they perceive bias in the actions of frontline actors, who seem motivated by animus or self-interest rather than by promoting the social good. The recurrent experience of procedural injustice erodes returning citizens' trust in state authority and leads to patterns of resistance and noncompliance.[29]

Waiting

Waiting is emblematic of how returning citizens experience the runaround as a form of procedural injustice. Waiting is a ubiquitous aspect of the criminal legal process. As sociologist Javier Auyero observed, waiting is not just an inconvenience; it is an expression of unequal power relations.[30] To make someone else wait is to exert control over how that person spends their time; it is a way of communicating to that person that their time, and therefore their social worth, is less important than the person's making them wait. In the context of the criminal legal system, waiting is an expression of state power; it is a means by which the state deprives freedom and communicates stigma by exerting control over how criminalized populations spend their time.

From the moment a person is placed in handcuffs, the state usurps control over how that person will spend their time. People under arrest wait for hours in squad cars, police transports, and holding cells as they are processed into the criminal legal system and await bail hearings.[31] Those who can't make bail can wait months and even years in jail for a trial date. At criminal court, people are subjected to routine "procedural hassles" that require them to wait in security lines and sit quietly in court for hours as they wait for their cases to be called.[32] Once incarcerated in the total institution of the prison, a person loses complete control over time.[33] Incarcerated people are told when to wake up, when to eat, and when to go outside. They wait for visits, for phone calls, for letters, for an appeal to be heard, for family members to send money, for the day they will be released.[34] And formerly incarcerated people do not fully regain control over their time upon release from prison.

Waiting is a pervasive aspect of the institutional circuit of prisoner reentry. For example, applying for public assistance requires a 45-day wait before benefits are dispersed. Men living in transitional housing facilities must wait for months or even years for permanent housing placements. Here, I focus on shorter but no less consequential forms of waiting: the hours that formerly incarcerated men recurrently spend in waiting rooms at parole and

HRA offices as they wait for mandatory appointments. These forms of waiting diminish returning citizens' autonomy, communicate stigma, and exacerbate material poverty.

Study participants identified parole offices as the place where they were most frequently made to wait. In addition to controlling where they can go, how late they can stay out, and with whom they can interact, parole also controls how returning citizens spend their time through mandatory office appointments.[35] Waiting at a parole office begins before a person even enters the building. People reporting to parole are required to pass through a metal detector and have their bags searched, which means long lines on heavy reporting days. On one occasion I saw the line stretched out into the street, with people waiting outside in the rain. Once inside, people with appointments check in with the receptionist, who sits behind bullet-proof Plexiglas, and then they take a seat in the waiting area, which consists of four or five rows of cold metal benches in a brightly fluorescent-lit concrete room surrounded by security cameras. Once they are called for their appointment, they are buzzed through a series of locked metal doors to the back office and escorted by their PO to a cubicle.

The room is patrolled by a security guard, who enforces the room's rules of conduct. Among the dozen or so rules listed on signs throughout the room are the following: No loud talking, no headphones, no visitors without PO's permission, no handheld games, no cell phones, no pets, no eating or drinking. I would see POs enforcing these rules throughout the day, telling people in the waiting area, "No cell phones, guys—Sir. Put the cell phone away. No cell phones." People under parole supervision wait in these conditions for hours on end. Study participants reported that it was not uncommon to wait there for two to five hours for a routine 20-minute parole appointment. When conducting outreach work at parole I observed people under parole supervision entering the building with me at 8:00 a.m. and still waiting there when I left at noon.

HRA offices were also routinely discussed as sites where study participants were made to wait for interminable amounts of time. The initial process of applying for benefits was especially harrowing. Miguel, a Latino man in his midtwenties, describes a Kafkaesque ordeal of arbitrary waiting and paperwork. After serving a 90-day sentence at Rikers Island jail, Miguel was released to a residential treatment program as a condition of his drug court plea. On his first outing from the facility, a peer chaperone took Miguel to enroll in public assistance.

They arrived at the office at 8:30 a.m., and there was already a line to get into the building when it opened at 9:00 a.m.[36] Once inside, they took an elevator a few floors up and waited in another line. Eventually he was given a packet of paperwork to fill out and was finally allowed to sit down. Then he waited again. "*And we waited*," Miguel tells me. "The first time I got called [in for a meeting with a case manager], it was like probably 1:30, 2:00 p.m. Then they told me I had to wait for another [meeting]. In total there [were] three people I had to see in order for the day to be done and the whole thing to be processed. So, I ended up coming out of there almost quarter to five. It was a whole day. No food, nothing to eat, no money. So, it was aggravating."[37]

The experience of waiting reinforced returning citizens' perception that frontline actors were lazy, indifferent, and abusive. When discussing waits at HRA officers during a focus group, Eduardo, a 41-year-old Latino man, told the group:

> EDUARDO: Because like, I guess [HRA caseworkers] want a line, then they [can] keep 'em there for all day. You ain't got no money, you ain't got nothing to do, so they don't really care, you know? 'Cause my wife's daughter works for HRA, she works for Public Assistance, so I know how that works. They really don't care; you know what I mean?

Ramon, a 47-year-old Latino man, echoed this sentiment:

> RAMON: They're back there . . . there [are] so many people back there [and] the only thing they're doing is shooting the shit with each other. You know, instead of grabbing your paper and saying look, this guy been here at eight o'clock in the morning and it's now 12 o'clock. And we still not, he still not seen not one person.

Eduardo argued that it wasn't just laziness; he felt that HRA caseworkers were actively discriminatory toward formerly incarcerated men:

> EDUARDO: I also believe that there's a difference if you're male, female, when it comes to those kind of services and dealing with those kind of people. I also believe that those people, they um, are a little harder on the males 'cause there's a lot of stereotypical people in HRA who live in your neighborhood and what have you. And they have their predetermined notions about this person. You know, they feel like they know. . . . And so they might judge you bad and determine how they're gonna run your case. You know, because they got the power to do it. Just because you in a

position of power. So, a lot of them I feel abuse their authority. That's why they got, you know, metal detectors now. Because they tend to be very brash and disrespectful at times.

And just because they got the position of power. So, they feel that they can talk to you and treat you in any way, form or fashion. The stereotypic is always on some like you're a bum, you're poor, you're a crackhead, you're . . . you understand? And all of us, or many, you know they're not gonna tell it to you visually but they gonna sit there and stare on people like if you're under. . . . That, you know, you're underprivileged. . . .

Especially like, and I also feel like if you're coming home from jail, they feel that as though they have the right to treat you in such fashion. You understand? Because there's just . . . discriminatory, you understand, it's a discriminatory . . . stereotypical system. You know, "Oh he just came home from jail, so he was out here committin' crimes, so you know, I'm gonna make him do this, that, the third, da-da-da-da-da . . . and as soon as you don't. . . ."

'Cause I told you, my wife's daughter works for HRA as we speak. And she's real crazy with it. . . . If you miss anything or you late for anything or anything, she's—it's just a body. For her it's just a body. And, and it'll mess your whole case up and you know, things of that nature. Those things can get frustratin' 'cause it's like you're being treated like less than a human.

You understand? No matter what education level you're at, no matter what experience you have, the people just talk to you, "You need our assistance, you need me to request your assistance, then you're gonna do what I say do and if you don't, I'm gonna press the red button."

Eduardo's case illustrates the experience of procedural injustice that formerly incarcerated men feel when interacting with the institutional circuit. Returning citizens are desperate for aid and must submit to the whims of institutional gatekeepers, who have the power to press a metaphorical "red button" and cut returning citizens off from material resources they desperately need. They feel dehumanized and disempowered at the hands of discriminatory caseworkers, who view returning citizens as "just a body" instead of as a human being in need.

Resisting Procedural Injustice

Waiting and other bureaucratic hassles reinforced men's distrust of state authority, especially parole. Indeed, many men believed that parole supervision was intentionally designed to ensure that they wound up back in prison. A common refrain was that parole "sets you up to fail." Some study participants thought that POs deliberately created obstacles to reintegration just for the sake of being vindictive. They believed that POs enjoyed their position of authority and relished abusing their power. Another common interpretation was that POs created obstacles to reintegration to protect their jobs. Participants believed that POs have quotas for issuing revocations, so they impose arbitrary rules and obligations to ensure they "make the numbers" and climb the career ladder.

Stephan is emblematic of this worldview. Stephan was a 53-year-old White man who had been home for about a year and half when I interviewed him in 2012.[38] He had served just under two years for grand larceny. He described a contentious relationship with his PO. "I think she's mean . . . just to be mean," he told me. "She's young. She's by the book. I can't stand her." Stephan felt that his PO imposed unreasonable restrictions on him just for the sake of being spiteful. For example, Stephan's driver's license had expired earlier that year, and his PO blocked his attempt to renew his license.[39] "They wouldn't renew it. And I think that was to be spiteful," Stephan told me. "There was no reason for it." I asked Stephan if he thought his PO was looking out for his best interests. "No. No. It's a joke," Stephan replied. "Who do you think she's looking out for?" I asked. "Herself. Her job. It's a numbers game. The whole system's a numbers game," Stephan told me.

Later in the interview I again asked Stephan if he thought parole was in any way helpful. Stephan replied, "No, it's not helpful. Why take away my driver's license? What is that doing to me?" Stephan had also been denied merit release from parole earlier that year. Stephan felt that his level of supervision was entirely unreasonable given his criminal history and social class. He had a nonviolent conviction, no prior criminal history, no history of substance abuse, and a clean disciplinary record from prison. He was college educated and owned his own apartment. "Do you really think I'm gonna go back to prison?" he asked rhetorically. "It's not going to happen."

Thus, in Stephan's view, parole is an inherently procedurally unjust institution. Parole officers are self-serving and vindictive. They intentionally create obstacles to reintegration to serve their personal interests rather than to protect public safety. Although Stephan grudgingly complied with his parole conditions, other men who had similar experiences reacted by resisting and subverting parole rules.

For example, Tony, a 32-year-old Latino man, believed that his PO was intentionally piling on obligations so that he would become overwhelmed with stress and violate his parole.[40] Tony's distrust of state authorities was rooted in a decades-long history of experiencing the runaround. Tony narrated that from the moment of his arrest he was repeatedly obstructed, delayed, and degraded by state authorities. Tony struggled with the trauma of incarceration and the stress of reentry, and he blamed his hardship on what he perceived to be the procedurally unjust actions of state authorities.

Tony pled guilty to involuntary manslaughter in 2003 after a fight turned deadly and Tony stabbed a man to death. He served 10½ years of a 12-year sentence in California state prison. Tony was initially paroled in California in 2014. A year and a half later he was allowed to transfer his parole to New York because his parents and extended family lived there.[41]

Tony felt that he never should have gone to prison in the first place. According to Tony, he and his then pregnant wife were attending a parade when "this guy attacked me for no reason." In the scuffle, Tony brandished a knife, hoping to scare the man away, but it didn't work. Tony wound up stabbing the man to death. Tony says that he waited at the scene for the police to arrive. He was 19 at the time, a ninth-grade dropout who worked as a landscaper and hadn't had any previous contact with the criminal legal system.

Tony felt that he had a clear-cut case of self-defense and shouldn't have been charged with anything at all, but the district attorney didn't believe his story. "They washed me up," he tells me. Tony was charged with first-degree murder and was facing a 25-to-life prison sentence. His public defender initially supported Tony's desire to go to trial but over time began encouraging him to take a plea deal. Tony felt that at the time he was young and didn't know any better, so he took the deal, pleading guilty to involuntary manslaughter and receiving a 12-year sentence.

During his incarceration Tony's relationship with his wife and newborn son deteriorated. Initially, Tony's wife visited him once a week with their son. But after about two years, the visits started to become less frequent. She started to come only once a month. And then not at all. He eventually contacted his wife's mother and found out that she was dating other people. Tony's wife eventually served him with divorce papers. Tony nonetheless attempted to establish visitation rights with his son.[42] He petitioned the family court, but Tony says they never responded to his paperwork. He told me:

TONY: [T]rying to obtain visitations while you're in prison, it's just a futile effort. Because they don't look at it. . . . Like, you're legally entitled to see your kid. They supposed to, even if they don't want to, they supposed to give you days to where you visit. Um, the courts agree upon it, make a schedule. But out there, once you're incarcerated, that's how the system looks at incarcerated parents. They don't give them no right; they don't even answer their paperwork. Unless you have a private attorney, they will not answer your paperwork. . . .

'Cause they look at you as the . . . ultimately, they just look at you as scum. And if you go into prison you're scum, and you're better off, it's better off that you're not in the child's life. That's how they see it, so that's why they allow it.

Cut off from his family and surrounded by the violence and degradation of the prison, Tony's mental health suffered. He described feeling "mentally broken" by the trauma of incarceration. When I asked him what he thought was the hardest part of prison, he replied:

TONY: You're in a place where there's a lot of, uh, just hostile people. There's a lot of violence going on. There's a lot of danger going on. There's a lot of mental breakdowns going on because there's always a power struggle between the cops [corrections officers] and the people on the prison. And, um, [corrections officers], they're wantin' to feel superior, they're wantin' to feel that they have control. And they don't talk to you like a human being, pretty much. You're, you're not treated like a person, like a human being. . . .

Every day it feels like something that you're never gonna get out of. Like, time goes by, like, really, really, really, really slow 'cause all you're doin' is waiting. You're just waiting to get out and waiting. And when you're looking at the clock and waiting for things to happen over years, it, it, it really wears you out. It does something to you.

To cope with the "stress, pain, and anxiety" of incarceration, Tony focused on a regimen of vigorous exercise and studying in the law library. Tony says his devotion to exercise and studying kept him out of trouble and earned him good behavior points, leading to his release from prison in 2014. He served his first 20 months of parole in California. During this time, Tony tried to rekindle things with his ex-wife, but things fell apart once again. After that, Tony decided to move back to Long Island, where he was born, to be closer to his parents, siblings, and extended family. He applied for a parole transfer and after three months of good behavior, he was granted the transfer.

Tony arrived in Long Island in September 2015. He moved in with his aunt and within a week he found a job working in a manufacturing plant. Tony says that parole in California is relatively lenient compared to what he experienced in New York. "Out here, like, they're pretty much trying to break you mentally," he told me. "That's what they do here. They got so much crazy goin' on, I mean, it's, it's, it's ridiculous the amount of restraints they're allowed to put on a person that they trying to say they're helping."

He tried to push the rules with his PO. He said that on the weekend he would take the money he earned from work and go out to bars, meet girls, and stay in hotels. Tony wanted to visit his mom, who lived about 45 minutes away from his aunt in another county, but his PO wouldn't let him leave the county. Tony felt that this restriction was unreasonable. "I'm working, you know, I'm not a gang member, I'm not selling drugs, so I started getting really frustrated because that's what I came out here for [to see my family]," he told me. In response, Tony took on a second job working nights. He explained: "[S]o I'm like, 'Screw it.' I got another job. So, I'm, like, 'If I'm not gonna have no time to myself or visit family, I might as well just make more money.'" Because Tony was now working two jobs, he would often sleep at his sister's house, which was just 10 minutes away from one of his jobs. As a result, he often was not home at his aunt's house when his PO would come to visit.

Tony was arrested for violating curfew (because he was at work after curfew) and for changing his address and not notifying his PO (because he was sleeping at his sister's house off and on). He served 25 days in jail for the violations. In addition to the jail sentence, Tony's PO placed him under increased surveillance and mandated that he attend a variety of rehabilitative programs. Tony had to attend anger management and enroll in the Workforce Development Program at Second Chances. His PO also placed an ankle bracelet on him, restricted him from living with his aunt or sister, and put him on a 7:00 p.m. curfew. Tony lost both of his jobs and was forced into a homeless shelter, where he shares a room with one other person. Because of his circumstances, Tony had to apply for public assistance through the DSS, the agency in Long Island that administers public assistance programs. At the time of our interview, Tony was receiving a rental subsidy, which is paid directly to the shelter, and was waiting for his application for $200 a month in cash assistance to be processed.

He felt frustrated that his pursuit of economic independence had been derailed by parole and felt overwhelmed by the new set of bureaucratic obligations he had to navigate. "[I]t's like everybody's chopping you in half at the same time" he told me. Indeed, Tony felt that parole is intentionally designed to cause people under supervision to have a "nervous breakdown" and revert back to criminal behavior, thus ensuring the job security of POs:

> TONY: So when these people get out of prison and they come . . . into society and they [put] parole on them, talking to [them] in this certain way and giving them all these things they have . . . million things they have to do when they don't even have housing, they are, like, literally, causing these people into a freakin' nervous breakdown, or to crash. . . . They want to get you depressed to the point where, like, you feel you have no control, you feel you're not gonna be able to make nothin' of yourself so you lean back to drugs. So, you go back to this or go back to that. So then [the POs] could go back to making their annual $50,000 . . . a year for locking you up. I mean, that's their goal, that's . . . to meet their quota. Um, and that's, ultimately what it boils down to. They're not out to help you.

To Tony, these experiences were part and parcel of the punitive logic of the institutional circuit. He believed it was a system designed to keep people trapped in cycles of recidivism rather than to provide support to facilitate reintegration:

> TONY: It's like . . . the way . . . the system goes at a person once they mess up. It, it's ridiculous. There's, like, no kind of [common] human decency towards trying to help this person get his brain . . . even straight so he could think things through to start. You know, to help the other parent or to get a job or to make something of themselves. To [them] just, it's, everything is sanctioned, sanctioned, sanctioned, sanctioned, sanctioned, sanctioned. Or fines, sanctions, rule this, rule that, rule this. I mean, it's all the same system. You know, parole, DSS, family court, it's all the same system.

Tony's cynicism toward parole, DSS, and the family court was rooted in a decades-long history of experiencing procedural injustice. From the moment he came into contact with the criminal legal system, Tony felt routinely degraded and disempowered by frontline actors. Tony felt that the district attorney in his case denied his due process rights by railroading him into a plea deal after unfairly charging him with first-degree murder. While in prison he felt constantly dehumanized by corrections officers, who imposed their authority through constant degradation. His petitions to gain visitation rights with his son were ignored by a family court system that treated Tony "like scum." The recurrent hassles of parole fed into his perception that state actors were biased and untrustworthy, more motivated to protect their jobs and prop up an unjust system than they were to help formerly incarcerated people reintegrate into society.

These feelings of distrust toward the state have concrete material effects. People are less likely to cooperate with legal authorities when they view the law as illegitimate.[43] For formerly incarcerated men like Tony, this sense of distrust animates how they experience the institutional circuit. They become prone to interpreting the actions of frontline actors as being intentionally discriminatory or abusive, regardless of actors' intentions. These interpretive frames are amplified by the stress of poverty and social isolation. Tony's hostility toward parole and his selective compliance with parole rules were a way for him to assert his autonomy amid the degradation of parole and the stress of unemployment, housing insecurity, and social isolation.

Rather than reflecting a rejection of the law or a return to criminality, this reflected Tony's desire to achieve economic independence on his own terms. But Tony's case illustrates how asserting too much autonomy too soon can be met by repression from parole. Because Tony sought independence outside the boundaries of formal parole rules, his PO determined that he wasn't ready for the full freedoms of citizenship. These sanctions, ironically, have pushed Tony further toward the margins of mainstream social and economic life. He is now unemployed, lives in a homeless shelter, and is receiving public assistance instead of working and living with family. These experiences only serve to reinforce Tony's social isolation and his sense that his PO was setting him up to fail.[44]

Tony's case illustrates how feelings of disempowerment and frustration can translate into resistance and noncompliance. Regardless of whether Tony's PO was intentionally creating obstacles to reintegration, Tony *believed* that parole was setting him up to fail. Tony was not alone in this belief. The notion that frontline actors intentionally create obstacles to reintegration in order to "make the numbers" was part of a powerful narrative that circulated among formerly incarcerated men at Second Chances and Uplift. This narrative reinforced returning citizens' long-standing distrust of the state and undermined their willingness to comply with the mandates of the institutional circuit.

The runaround is a frustrating and degrading experience for returning citizens. The constant stress of running around the city to keep up with conflicting appointments, combined with the indignities of being made to wait and having complaints go unheard, generated feelings of anger, resentment, and distrust toward state authorities. The stress of severe deprivation amplified these negative feelings. The strains of loneliness, hunger, and housing insecurity made formerly incarcerated men vulnerable to interpreting what might have been minor inconveniences as forms of intentional abuse or disrespect. This was especially the case for men with histories of experiencing procedural injustice. Their experience of the runaround reinforced their distrust of the state and their belief that frontline actors were setting them up to fail.

Men responded to these feelings of disempowerment by attempting to reclaim their sense of autonomy and self-respect through aggressive confrontations with frontline actors and noncompliance with institutional rules. Although these "compensatory manhood acts" allowed men to reassert a sense of control over their lives, they ultimately pushed the men further toward the margins of mainstream life. Noncompliance resulted in losing access to material resources and invited further repression from state authorities, who imposed tighter surveillance and sanctions in response to resistance.

More broadly, these acts of resistance reinforced negative stereotypes about criminalized men and provided legitimacy for the state's disciplinary regime of poverty governance. When men become argumentative, disengaged from service providers, or disobedient to institutional rules, they confirm cultural expectations that criminalized men are aggressive, lazy, and oppositional to authority. Thus, by repeatedly subjecting men to procedurally unjust treatment, the institutional circuit pushes men to be the kinds of subjects the system is designed to govern: defiant and disengaged men in need of discipline and punishment.[45]

However, not everyone who experiences the runaround responds with resistance and noncompliance. As we explore in the next chapter, men's relationship to the state shifted as they aged out of crime and embraced identities as fathers. Drawing on cultural narratives of individualism, they learned to reinterpret the stress of the runaround as a short-term inconvenience that can be overcome through tenacity and a positive attitude.

FOUR

In Search of Respectability

EDUARDO HAS SPENT MOST OF HIS LIFE on his own. His mother died when he was in the tenth grade. He never knew his father and had no siblings or extended family. He dropped out of school soon after his mother's death and began selling drugs to support himself. Between 1995 and 2008, Eduardo was embroiled in the drug economy and cycled in and out of prison.

In his young adulthood, Eduardo was defiant of state authorities. In 1995, when he was 20, he was convicted of selling drugs for the first time. He took a plea deal to avoid incarceration if he completed an alternative-to-incarceration program. However, Eduardo "messed up the program" and wound up serving his full sentence. "I was young at the time," Eduardo explained. In 1998, Eduardo was again convicted of selling drugs and was incarcerated. Upon his release a year later, he absconded from parole and went "on the run." During that time Eduardo was in a volatile relationship with the mother of his son. During an argument, Eduardo hit her in the face. She took out an order of protection against him. In 2000, Eduardo was arrested for violating the order of protection during an "incident" at the woman's apartment. Eduardo was sentenced to three years for violating the order of protection and another five years for absconding from parole.

When he began his sentence, Eduardo had a lot of resentment toward his son's mother for having him arrested. "I had a lot of hate and anger towards her," Eduardo tells me. However, as time went on Eduardo came to realize that his son's mother was justified in calling the cops on him, and he decided to spend his time in prison focusing on bettering himself. He committed himself to a project of self-improvement. "I did my time. I got my GED. I did my programming. And I kinda got into myself," he told me. In 2008, Eduardo came home ready to change. Rather than selling drugs to get by, he took up residence in a homeless shelter and applied for public assistance. As a condition of his public assistance, he was required to participate in a 90-day outpatient drug treatment program. During his time at the program he met the woman who would eventually become his long-term partner. After Eduardo completed drug treatment, he and his partner enrolled in a culinary arts training program. Eduardo found his calling as a cook and was able to transition out of the shelter system into an apartment with his partner.

Eduardo was steadily employed as a cook for five years, but in 2014 he began selling drugs again and was arrested. He served a 15-month prison sentence and was released in 2015. When I interviewed Eduardo in June 2016, he had just been released from jail a month before after serving 90 days for a parole violation. He had applied for public assistance upon release but was waiting for his application to be processed, which takes 45 days. Eduardo says that he is committed to staying out of jail for good this time:

> EDUARDO: I can't sell drugs no more. 'Cause, if I catch another felony for substance abuse, I get 25 to life without the possibility of parole. So, being the fact that I'm used to having money every day and now I gotta wait a month.... It's a little more difficult, you know? Because, before, I'd just get up and go to the block and go commit a crime. You know what I mean? Make ends meet. Today I'm more susceptible to just go home and go to sleep. If I ain't got it, I ain't got it. You know, and I'll... I'll sacrifice. You know? I don't care. I don't trip off ego. Like, before, I was a ego, kind of like, you know? "I'm this kind of drug dealer. And I get this money. And you can't tell me nothing." Me being on public assistance today, it's really helping. It's helping me stay home and helping me stay free.
>
> But the process, it doesn't make me feel any smaller, because I don't have the image. Like I broke [my] image. 'Cause you know, some people. You know, you'll be on public assistance and you feel like it's a ... It's a ... How do I wanna say the word? It'll discourage you from wanting to, you know, do things, 'cause you'll start to feel that you're under, you know, like you're a bum or something like that. I don't wanna feel like I'm a bum.

In addition to avoiding old habits and complying with HRA mandates, Eduardo is also trying to make things right with his 16-year-old son. Although their relationship is frayed, Eduardo is trying to make amends for the damage he has caused to their relationship. Eduardo's history of recovery and relapse was common among study participants. Like Eduardo, most study participants were in the process of aging-out of crime and embracing their identities as fathers. These men were committed to leaving behind the aggressive and self-destructive "street" lifestyle of their youth and instead embracing a more mature and domesticated sense of manhood rooted in work, fatherhood, and compliance with state authorities.

Eduardo's case illustrates how men's relationship with the state changes over the life course. In his youth, Eduardo defined his masculine identity through his opposition to state authority. He saw himself as an entrepreneurial drug dealer, who made money on his own terms and didn't have to answer to anyone. However, now that he's older he sees himself differently. Fearing that another drug conviction will result in a life sentence, Eduardo has learned to humble himself and forgo the instant gratification of the drug economy. Instead, he is embracing the help he is receiving from public assistance, viewing it as a stabilizing force in his life. Although Eduardo acknowledges that navigating HRA can be a degrading experience (see chapter 2), he casts himself as someone with the emotional strength to rise above the denigration of the runaround.

This chapter explores how men like Eduardo learn to cope with the stress of the runaround. Middle-aged study participants yearned for the trappings of a respectable, middle-class lifestyle, characterized by steady employment, stable housing, and fulfilling family relationships. They viewed complying with the mandates of the institutional circuit as central to achieving their goals of economic independence and involved fatherhood.

Drawing on cultural narratives of individualism and resilience, they developed a set of interpretive frames to recast themselves as masters of their own destiny, able to overcome the hardships of the runaround through grit and determination.[1] But these identity transitions did not occur in isolation. The institutional circuit played a central role in shaping and reinforcing these expressions of reformed masculinity.[2] Inside prison and throughout the institutional circuit, men were bombarded with the message that they alone are responsible for changing their lives, that they alone could rise above their circumstances and attain reentry success by simply choosing to remain positive and tenacious. At Second Chances and Uplift, frontline staff acted as "recovery sponsors" to program participants, offering self-help sermons and peer mentorship to cultivate returning citizens' ability to remain resilient when faced with the hardships of the runaround.[3] At the same time, there was ambivalence about these institutional scripts. Staff members and program participants were constantly negotiating tensions between cultural narratives of personal responsibility and the realities of structural inequality and procedural injustice.

When I began my fieldwork in 2011, most of the men I met were transitioning into middle age. They had come to the end of their criminal careers and were looking to settle into a more quiet, domestic life. This collective life-course transition reflected a broader demographic shift. These men are part of the generation of men whose "collective coming of age" was defined by mass incarceration. Sociologist Bruce Western calls this generation of men the "mass imprisonment generation." For the cohort of non-college-educated Black and Latino men born after 1965, incarceration became a normalized life event, more common than marriage, military service, union membership, or college attendance.[4] Unlike other birth cohorts of the twentieth century, such as the "Greatest Generation" or the "Civil Rights Generation," whose collective coming of age occurred in the context of "great programs in social improvement," such as the GI Bill, the Civil Rights Act, and the War on Poverty, the collective biographies of the "Mass Imprisonment Generation" were defined by the unprecedented expansion of the carceral state.

Most of the men I met at Second Chances and Uplift were born in the late 1960s and 1970s. They had spent their adolescence and young adulthood growing up in some of New York City's most disadvantaged neighborhoods during the 1980s and 1990s, when open air drug markets and gun violence proliferated in the city's poorest neighborhoods. Most had dropped out of high school and had spent their youth embroiled in the drug economy, becoming the primary targets of America's grand experiment in mass incarceration. Many had experienced decades of contact with the criminal legal system, either through repeated cycles of incarceration and reentry or by serving decades-long prison sentences for serious crimes.

By the time I met them in the 2010s, they were in their late thirties, forties, and fifties and were in the process of aging out of crime. They were struggling to navigate what sociologist Reuben Jonathan Miller calls the "afterlife" of mass incarceration: the ways in which "prison lives on through the people who've been convicted and long after they complete their sentences."[5] As they emerged from decades of incarceration, these men struggled to reintegrate into mainstream social life under the weight of criminal records and histories of violence, trauma, and substance abuse. They sought to atone for their self-destructive pasts and rebuild their lives as respectable citizens through projects of self-transformation.

To craft reformed identities, study participants had to reconcile their histories of violent and self-destructive behaviors with their current attempts to become law-abiding community members.[6] This meant repudiating their past actions and taking accountability for the harm they caused. Gender ideologies—"normative understandings of what it means to be a 'good' or 'real' man"—played an important role in shaping these practices of identity work.[7] Men redefined their sense of manhood not only through internal processes of self-discovery but also by actively rebuilding relationships with family members and complying with state authorities. Indeed, men marked their identity transitions through their ability to withstand the stress and degradation of the runaround.

"If I Could Get a Do-Over, I'd Do It All Different"

Leon was a 45-year-old Black man whom I interviewed in 2015. In his youth, Leon defined his manhood in terms of his identity as a violent drug dealer. He was able to accumulate money, respect, and power through his entrepreneurial initiative and his willingness to engage in violence. Leon had spent much of his life in environments defined by profound economic and physical insecurity. During his adolescence and early adulthood, he turned to street entrepreneurship and violence to assert control over his life and resist exploitation amid this chaos. This "street" lifestyle became a way for Leon to construct a masculine identity.

However, now that he's older, Leon expresses regret for spending his youth embroiled in the violence of the drug economy:

> LEON: I've been shot up, stabbed, I can show you wounds, man. I've been
> hurt, man. And, I've done some things to some people. It's no fun . . . and,
> at the end of the day, it doesn't help in life. You're destroying your life.
> You don't get it as a kid, but when you grow up, when you say, "Wow, look
> at this situation I'm in." You know?

Looking back on his life, Leon wishes he could do it all over again:

> LEON: I'm just gonna say, if I could get a do-over, I'd do it all different.
> There would be no prison, there would be no gangs, no street thug
> bullshit. . . . I would just go to school and fly straight and take care of my
> kids the right way. Early bird get that worm, you know? Hard work pays
> off. I'm learning that later in life.

Rather than seeking "respect" through violence or the accumulation of material status symbols, as he did in his youth, Leon is now in search of "respectability."[8] He yearns to align his masculine identity with conventional markers of middle-class status, especially full-time employment and breadwinning.

As we see in Leon's case, growing older played an important role in shaping men's desistance narrative. It was only through the passage of time that Leon was able to recognize the damage he had caused through his drug dealing and violence. Some men tried to pass on the wisdom of age to younger men with the hopes of saving them from a similar fate. Ronald, a Black man in his forties, and Curtis, a Black man in his twenties, had worked together as interns in the building maintenance department at Second Chances. The two became close over the course of their internship, and Ronald took on a mentorship role. He would call and text Curtis outside of work, trying to give him advice and mentor him through the reentry process. However, despite Ronald's efforts, Curtis was rearrested and sent back to prison for a parole violation. After finding out about Curtis's arrest, Ronald lamented, "I tried to coach him, but if you don't listen to your parents, how you gonna listen to a stranger?"

Ronald felt that Curtis got rearrested because he was still too young and impulsive to understand that the costs of crime always outweigh the benefits. In discussing Curtis's arrest, Ronald began reflecting on his own impulsive behavior during his youth. When Ronald was 19 years old, he participated in a robbery. At the time, he felt that the money and respect he would gain from the robbery outweighed the potential cost of five years in prison. Now that he is older, however, Ronald's calculus has changed. Ronald says that he was recently offered the opportunity to rob someone for $60,000. When he was 19, he probably would have taken the job. But now as a middle-aged man in his forties, he doesn't have as much life ahead of him to waste in prison. Moreover, he has already been convicted of robbery twice, and a third conviction means life in prison. At this point in his life, $60,000 is not worth spending the rest of his life in prison. According to Ronald, Curtis will have to come to this realization in his own time.

Embracing Fatherhood by Complying with the State

In addition to growing older, atoning for their failures as fathers was also a central aspect of constructing a reformed masculine identity. Previous literature suggests that becoming a father for the first time is a "turning point" in the lives of criminalized young men that leads them down a path of desistance.[9] However, this wasn't the case for many of the men I interviewed. When they became fathers in their late teens and early twenties, it didn't change much about their lives. They continued to earn money through the street economy and cycle in and out of prison and were largely absent from the lives of their children.[10] But in middle age these men began to embrace their identities as fathers as part of a broader life course transition. In embracing this role, they had to come to terms with the damage that their self-destructive behavior and absence had caused in the lives of their children. The men expressed reformed masculinity not only through a changing relationship with their children but also through a changing relationship with the state, particularly parole, the child support system, and family courts.

Rickey is a 50-year-old Black man. He is the father of three children: a 31-year-old son, a 19-year-old daughter, and a 16-year-old son. Rickey's oldest son was born in 1984 while Rickey was incarcerated. He got to see his son for the first time two years later during a visit. Looking back, Rickey discusses how he was scared to be a father. "I sabotaged my own freedom, because it was very, very overwhelming. . . . Being 18, 19. I didn't have a clue . . . what being a father was," he tells me.

Between 1984 and 2012 Rickey was in and out of the lives of his children. He cycled between prison and the streets on a series of charges for robbery, theft, and parole violations. During that time Rickey was constantly "on the run" from legal authorities. He had very little contact with his children while he was incarcerated. Rickey says that he blocked out thoughts of his children when he was incarcerated, as a survival mechanism. Thinking about his kids would be too painful and would make him vulnerable in prison. He spoke with them over the phone and through letters, but he avoided visits because he didn't want to put his kids and himself through the emotional trauma of a prison visit.

But even when Rickey was out of prison, he avoided his responsibilities as a father. Rickey struggled with anxiety over whether he was capable of being a father. "How am I gonna provide for them, you know, without no job, without, you know, no education, you know? Would they even accept me in their life?" Rickey dealt with those emotions through avoidance. He self-medicated with alcohol and spent his time "just being in the streets. Just not dealing with it."

Rickey says he "started a new life" in 2012. He was released from prison, completed his first full term of parole supervision in 20 years, and committed himself to leading a law-abiding lifestyle. Rickey spent 20 years dodging POs, but looking back he blames himself for not accepting the help they were offering him. He says his POs were "pretty much helpful . . . but it was up to me if I wanted to be helped. You know what I mean? They'd point me in the right direction as far as resources and what have you, but it was up to me, you know?"

Part of Rickey's process of constructing a reformed identity was confronting his guilt over being absent from his children's lives. "I wasted a lot of time," he tells me. "And I had opportunities to make sound decisions when I made bad decisions, which in turn took me away from my kids. My actions, my decisions did that. Not nobody else."

Rickey is now working to establish relationships with his kids. I asked Rickey about how often he now sees his 16-year-old son. Rickey says that he sees his son every weekend. "He damn near lives with me!" he says with a chuckle. "Every weekend he comes over and stays with me." Spending this much time with his son is a big deal for Rickey. He has never spent this much time with any of his kids. Saying it out loud in that moment makes Rickey realize just how much he has missed by being absent.

"You know, for the summer I had him [stay with me]. You know, which is major." Rickey stops midsentence. He takes a deep breath and begins tapping his hand on the desk as he becomes overwhelmed with emotions. He takes a deep breath. His voice quivers as tears begin rolling down his cheek. "Like, sometimes it could be overwhelming," he says through tears. There is a long pause as Rickey tries to gather himself. To break the silence, I ask Rickey what he likes to do with his son. "Play games, go to movies, play basketball, have cookouts, invite family over, you know. Go to the library. Sometimes we just go to Manhattan and hang out," he tells me, his voice still trembling. He tries to laugh his way through the crying. "Although at 16, you know, he's got his own set of friends," he says with a laugh. "So, I'm probably too old to be hanging out!" The laughter is short lived. "We do spend a lot of quality time together," he says softly. "You can't get back . . . You can't get back [the] time you lost. But you can just deal with the moment and move forward."

Part of Rickey's efforts to rectify his past mistakes as a father was complying with the child support system. Rickey owed substantial child support arrears. The mother of his 16-year-old son opened a child support case against Rickey in 2001. At the time, Rickey had just been sent back to prison for a parole violation. In his absence, the court set his order at $1,072 per month.

Rickey found out about the order when he was released, but he avoided dealing with it for over a decade. Rickey explains:

RICKEY: You know, [the order] was high as hell and I just, I . . . Like I said, I was in the streets. I wasn't even stable. So, to go back down there and try to get it modified, I . . . That was not the least of my worries, but I wasn't really worried about that. I was trying to worry about where I'm gonna lay my head. Where . . . 'cause I was all over the place.

During the next decade Rickey spent "in the streets" and in prison he accrued $50,000 in arrears. Rickey lost his driver's license and was arrested once for failing to pay child support. In 2013, with the help of family counselors at Second Chances, Rickey got his order modified down to $50 a month because he was unemployed and receiving public assistance. Although his payments are lower, he still owes $50,000 in arrears. He's working with a legal aid lawyer to help him get some of the debt reduced so he can get his driver's license reinstated.

Rickey expressed reformed masculinity not only through a changing relationship with his children, but also through a changing relationship with the state. Once Rickey decided to desist from crime, he became actively compliant with parole, completing his parole sentence for the first time in his life. Looking back on his time being on parole, he doesn't discuss onerous parole conditions or abusive POs. Instead, he blames himself for not taking advantage of the help his POs were offering him. Likewise, although Rickey resents the fact that his driver's license is suspended due to his outstanding child support arrears, he is nonetheless actively complying with his child support order. Rather than defying or avoiding state authorities, as he did in his youth, Rickey is actively in compliance with them.

Indeed, complying with state authorities was a central aspect of how participants marked their transition from street life to domestic life. Chris provides a clear example of how men's relationship with the state changes as they grow older and embrace fatherhood. When I interviewed Chris in 2015, he was 44 years old and had not had any criminal legal contact for over a decade. But Chris says that during his early twenties, he was living a "wild life." He was "stealing, selling drugs" and embroiled in violent disputes with neighborhood rivals. Between 1989 and 2001, Chris cycled in and out of prison for a series of drug- and gun-related charges.

When recounting that period of his life, Chris describes himself as immature and oppositional to authority. When he experienced the runaround at parole, he simply decided to abscond. "I just stopped goin'. I just got tired of goin' to my parole officer all the time," Chris tells me. "I was on the run, I ran from parole. . . . I basically ran for like 14 months, and they caught up with me," Chris adds.

Chris explains that his decision to abscond was motivated by his anger and frustration with his over-demanding PO and the arbitrary waiting he had to endure at routine parole appointments. Chris recalls:

CHRIS: Yea, I [would] wait for about 2 hours, sometimes longer than
that. . . . I remember quite a few times I sat there all day just to find
out that my parole officer didn't even come. He didn't even show up,
and they're like "Come back tomorrow." And I'm like, "I'm not comin
back tomorrow. I'm not coming back. I sat here all day, from 9 o'clock in
the morning 'til 4 o'clock in the afternoon for y'all to tell me, 'Oh, your
parole officer didn't come in today.'" Like, you could've told me that a
while ago.

Chris also felt that his PO made him attend too many appointments and placed unrealistic demands on him that he felt were impossible to meet. He tells me:

CHRIS: [There] was a lot of things that angered me with parole. My parole
officer too, I didn't like him. . . . He was a real a-hole, you know? He was
too demanding, he didn't reason at all, you know? I just felt like he put
stipulations on me that I couldn't meet.

JOHN: Like what?

CHRIS: Get a job in two weeks. Like, how you gonna get a job in two weeks?
You expect that to happen? Sometimes it does happen, but really, most of
the time, no, it's not gonna happen like that. . . . Report to him every week.
And you know, at that time I was young, I was really bullheaded. I didn't
really respect authority that much. Actually, I hated authority. So, coming
to report to you was like, [sarcastically] "Pssh, yea okay. You wait for me, I'll
be there." [Chuckles]. That's how I felt about it. [So], yea, I'll make the first
visit or the second visit, [then] I'm not coming any more.

JOHN: Did he ever require you to do any kind of programs?

CHRIS: Yea. I didn't get a job one time, so he said I'm gonna give you
another chance and put you in a drug program. He said you have to stay
there for a year. I was like, "Alright." I agreed to [do] it so I wouldn't have
to go back to jail. But I knew I wasn't staying there. I was like, "As soon
as I see that door open, I'm going right out of it." So, I went there . . . and
I was there for about 4 days, and as soon as they gave me a pass to go out,
I went out and I never came back.[11]

Chris was "on the run" from parole for 14 months. He was eventually arrested and served the remaining 10 months of his sentence in upstate prison.

The last time Chris was incarcerated was in 1998. When he was released in 2001, he had just turned thirty and was beginning to grow tired of "ripping and running" from the police and constantly cycling in and out of prison. Recounting his last bout of incarceration, Chris tells me, "It made me think a lot about where my life was going and what I wanted to do, and I just didn't want to waste my life. I just got tired of that stuff." He realized that he wanted to be a positive role model in his son's life, and he couldn't do that from prison: "My son definitely . . . made me think about what I wanted to do with my life. I didn't want him to grow up with me in jail. I wanted to be in his life. I just made a conscious decision to change my life."[12]

Chris's son was three years old when Chris was incarcerated in 1998 and was seven years old by the time of his release in 2001. Chris discusses how missing important milestones, like teaching his son to throw a football and ride a bike, motivated him to change his life. He discusses making a deliberate decision to abandon his past identity as a street entrepreneur and craft a new identity as a law-abiding citizen. He stopped making impulsive decisions, quit smoking weed, and sought legal employment. He started hanging out with prosocial peers and avoided "people, places, and things" associated with his criminal past. In 2005 he had a second son. He embraced his role as a father and played an active role in his kids' lives, despite his relationship with the mother of his two sons eventually deteriorating.

Chris expressed reformed masculinity not only through a renewed sense of self and a commitment to work and family life but also through his changing relationship to the state. In 2007, Chris began a two-year odyssey to establish custody of his two sons.[13] Although Chris saw his sons often, he had never formally established paternity or custody. This was hugely consequential when his sons were taken into foster care after their mother was arrested on drug charges in 2007. Because Chris had never formally established custody or paternity, the Administration of Children's Services (ACS), the New York City agency in charge of child welfare cases, would not release his sons to him until he could prove paternity. His sons were placed in the care of Chris's mom for the time being.[14]

Chris was determined to establish formal custody of his sons. In order to do so, he had to comply with a series of mandates from the family court. "They put me through the wringer [but] I just kept showing up. Whatever they wanted me to do, I did it," Chris tells me. Over the course of about a year and a half, Chris attended a series of family court hearings, during which he established paternity and completed a court-ordered substance abuse treatment program after he admitted to occasional drinking.

After Chris finished the program, he had to find a job and establish independent housing. By this point it was 2009, almost two years since Chris started his quest to get custody of his sons. The judge granted Chris temporary custody of his sons, but only on the condition that Chris moved out of his girlfriend's apartment and into a scatter-site housing program.[15] "That's no problem. Whatever you want me to do, I'll do it," Chris recalls telling the judge.

Chris and his sons lived in a supportive housing facility for 10 months. During this time, Chris once again had to comply with a series of bureaucratic mandates to maintain his housing and work toward permanent custody. He had to attend regular appointments with his case manager to update her on his apartment and employment search. Chris was receiving public assistance, so he had to complete WEP assignments and BTW programs. He also had to show that he was a competent father by making sure his sons regularly attended school and medical appointments. Chris's oldest son had difficulty coping with the ordeal of foster care and the sudden absence of his mother. With the help of his case manager, Chris found him a therapist and made sure he attended regular appointments. Eventually Chris landed a job with the Parks Department and moved into a subsidized one-bedroom apartment with his sons. Although at the time of our interview in 2015 he was unemployed and collecting public assistance, he still lives in the apartment with his sons.

For two years, Chris was given the runaround by the family court. He had to repeatedly show up to court hearings, where he waited in security lines and court waiting areas. He had to acquiesce to a drug treatment program, which he had to attend five days a week for a year. He was forced out of his girlfriend's apartment and into a scatter-site housing program, where he had to submit to the ongoing surveillance and behavioral mandates of case managers. But Chris didn't view the runaround he experienced with the family court as that much of a hassle. When I asked him what he thought about his experience with the family court he told me, "It was easy; I just did what they told me to do."

Chris's case also illustrates how formerly incarcerated men express reformed masculinity through compliance with state authorities. In his twenties, Chris's sense of manhood was rooted in an oppositional relationship to the state. He expressed an unwillingness to submit to the demands of state authorities and responded to the frustration of the runaround by absconding from parole. In his thirties, however, Chris's perspective on manhood changed. He embraced his role as a father and was willing to do whatever it took to be there for his kids. He actively complied with the demands of state authorities and developed positive relationships with state actors. Rather than viewing the runaround as an affront to his sense of masculine pride, he learned to view it as a short-term inconvenience, something that was "easy" to deal with if you just show up and do what you are told.

It's the Person, Not the System: Reentry, Individualism, and the Hustler Mentality

Viewing the runaround as a short-term inconvenience was bound up with a broader individualistic worldview. In interviews, conversations, and informal focus groups, study participants routinely discussed how individual willpower and personal responsibility were the most important factors in determining reentry success. According to this framework, unemployment and recidivism were the result of individual weakness, not structural inequality or institutional failures.

This worldview is undoubtedly shaped by the broader American ethos of individualism.[16] Indeed, as former drug entrepreneurs or "hustlers," many of the men ascribed to an exaggerated version of American individualism. Surviving in the hypercompetitive and violent context of drug markets required study participants to develop what Chris called a "hustler mentality" characterized by a lifestyle of aggressive and relentless entrepreneurship. By adopting the hustler mentality, men like Chris had pulled themselves out of poverty and achieved the American Dream of financial success—at least until they got caught and went to prison.

Chris and others learned to take the lessons of the hustler mentality, such as the importance of hard work, taking initiative, and self-reliance, and apply them to reentry. The hustler mentality provided formerly incarcerated men with a set of interpretive frames to cope with the stress and hardship of reentry. Rather than succumbing to the bleak realities of poverty, racism, and social exclusion, study participants recast themselves as the masters of their own destiny: men who would define their own fate and not let society define it for them.

This individualistic outlook was also rooted in a fundamental distrust of the state. As we saw in the last chapter, study participants narrated long histories of harassment and abuse at the hands of state authorities. Experiencing the runaround was yet another reason to distrust the state. Men expressed little faith that parole, public assistance agencies, or transitional housing facilities would offer any meaningful help. Instead, men would have to learn to help themselves.

If these men were to define their own destinies, it meant that they couldn't blame the runaround for their problems; they would have to accept personal responsibility for their own success or failure. During a focus group at Second Chances, I asked the group if they thought the hassles of the runaround were just short-term inconveniences. Michael responded:

MICHAEL: [W]hen I came out of prison I had done all the necessary footwork to secure a three-quarter house ... [a]nd the facility had jumbled up my paperwork and sent me to Bellevue [Men's Shelter]. I had to go to that place. I went there just to fulfill the requirement from parole, so I don't you know ... do anything I wasn't supposed to do. And then from there I, you know, I took it step-by-step paces, and then transitioned over. But, you know, it's all about your attitude, perspective, you know what I mean? How ambitious you are, and how much you want to survive, and how much you want to be successful; you know what I mean?

Everybody, whether you've been incarcerated or not, everybody has shitty days, everybody has problems, everybody has obstacles, you know what I mean? Most times in life ... it's not the things that you have in your view that you can see, it's the things that come from the side. So, you know, it's just a matter of your attitude and how you want to move forward.

Michael experienced the literal runaround of being shuffled between housing facilities due to an unexplained paperwork error, despite having done the necessary work to secure a spot in a three-quarter house. But according to Michael, there is nothing exceptional about the hassles of the runaround. Everyone has problems in their lives; overcoming those problems is simply a matter of having a positive attitude. Indeed, Michael seemed to accept the fact that the institutional circuit was a dysfunctional and procedurally unjust system. If he wanted to succeed, he'd have to muster the tenacity to endure the runaround.

Dwight felt the same way. Dwight is a recovering heroin user and had recently relapsed after losing his job as a janitor. He dropped dirty urine at a parole appointment and was mandated to a residential program (see chapter 1). Dwight blamed himself for his failure to stay clean:

DWIGHT: A lot of people do come home and do good. You know like, I did a couple of bids. Each time I come home, I come home, I did a good job, am able to be on my own, but I always mess it up. So, I can't really blame it on the system. A lot of time, it's the person. You know what I mean? Like both times I came home, like this last . . . the one I'm on parole for now . . . I had a damn good job. And I fucked it up. Now I got to deal with it and that's why I'm here, you know what I mean? So, I'm really, I'm not bitter, I can't blame nobody because if you work hard, you can make it. Period.

According to Dwight, reentry success boils down to individual hard work. It means taking personal responsibility for your life rather than blaming the system for your problems.

INSTITUTIONALIZING REDEMPTION

However, formerly incarcerated men do not develop reformed identities in a vacuum. While study participants drew on their previous life experiences as street hustlers to construct reformed masculine identities, cultural narratives of individualism and resilience are also institutionalized in the curriculum of rehabilitation programs inside prisons and throughout the institutional circuit of reentry.[17]

Cultivating Redemption inside Prison

For some men, their reformed identities were incubated in prison-based rehabilitation programs. Participation in these programs helped men develop positive relationships with state authorities. Once released, they carried over these positive experiences into interactions with POs and service providers, which helped them to interpret the runaround as a short-term inconvenience rather than as a form of harassment or abuse. Oscar's case illustrates how men's positive experiences in prison-based rehabilitation programs carry over to the outside.[18]

Oscar was a 40-year-old Puerto Rican man. When I interviewed him in 2016, he had been out of prison for four months. Oscar had served 21 years in New York State prison for murder. In 1995, when he was just 19, Oscar got into an "altercation" with a man from his neighborhood. Oscar said that "out of anger" he went and got "an illegal firearm" and "approached him and we began to fight." According to Oscar, the other man also had a gun, and a shootout ensued. "I shot and killed him," Oscar told me. Oscar was sentenced to 20 years to life in prison. "However, after 21 years of incarceration, rehabilitating myself and good behavior, I was released," he told me.

Oscar's redemption narrative centered around finding "reason and purpose" through fatherhood and peer mentorship. During his incarceration, he was a model inmate who took on active leadership roles in self-help and educational programs. Oscar poured himself into these programs as a way to cope with the pain of imprisonment and find hope amid the despair of a life sentence.[19] He also viewed this as a way to be a role model for his daughter.

Indeed, Oscar's most important relationship in his life was with his daughter. Oscar's girlfriend was pregnant at the time of his arrest in 1995, and his daughter was born while he was incarcerated. Over the years, Oscar was able to form a strong relationship with his daughter through visits, letters, and phone calls. However, Oscar initially struggled with the fact that he wasn't physically present in his daughter's life:

OSCAR: [N]ot being able to be there for my daughter was probably my biggest struggle and my biggest heartache. The feeling of hopelessness that tries to just take over you, disappointment with yourself, feeling, you know, like a failure. Those feelings, they tried to invade my mind and tried to destroy me, but thankfully I found, I summoned up the courage and the ability to ask for help, and was able to take those feelings and redirect them and tell myself, "I'm not going to give up. Even though I'm here, I want to be a role model. I want to be the type of person that can show my daughter that even if you fall you could be resilient, and you can get back up and you can make a way for yourself."

Oscar enrolled in several parenting workshops to cope with these feelings. He stood out as a model student and came to the attention of the workshop facilitators. He was eventually asked to take on the role of a peer facilitator for the workshops and became a mentor to other incarcerated fathers, helping them navigate child support, custody, and visitation issues. Oscar took on other leadership roles in the facility. He was placed in charge of orientations for new inmates. He also led a program that allowed incarcerated fathers to record themselves reading a children's book to their kids. In addition to his work in peer support groups, Oscar also earned a college degree while he was incarcerated and was the student speaker at his graduation ceremony.

Oscar's active participation in educational and self-help programs cultivated a positive view of state authorities. Oscar had developed many positive relationships with prison staff, particularly counselors and "civilian" non-profit workers who facilitated fatherhood workshops. He carried over these positive interactions with state authorities to his relationship with his PO once he was released. He described a "very good relationship" with his PO. Oscar has been actively compliant with all of his parole conditions. Within his first two weeks of release he was able to find a job doing construction labor. He has diligently attended all of his parole appointments as well as his mandated anger management classes.

Because of his active compliance with his parole conditions, Oscar's PO has lowered his risk classification. When he was initially released, Oscar had to report to parole every week. Now he only has to report once every four months. Oscar feels that his lower risk classification is closely related to his consistent payment of parole fees, which are $30 for every parole appointment. Oscar explained that POs typically do not enforce these legal financial obligations, but paying them looks favorable:

OSCAR: They don't force you to pay those dues, but those dues play a role in how your transition unfolds.... When they see that you're paying your dues, it's like an incentive where they give you permission, like let's say if I want to visit family members outside the State of New York. Right now, [one] ... of my ... restrictions on parole is that I can't leave a geographical location, so I need permission. So, what those dues do is they usually open the door for that...

If you don't pay it, they don't really make a big deal of it, but it lessens the chances of you getting off parole sooner. And I don't want to be a cynic, but the reality is sort of like a unspoken pressure, like ... I don't want to call it extortion, but it's like, you know, you've got to pay in order for you to get what you want.

Oscar viewed paying parole fees as inherently extractive: he was paying money to the state in exchange for his freedom. However, despite this cynicism, Oscar was actively compliant with paying his fees. He saw paying the fees as a short-term inconvenience, a small price he would have to pay on his journey toward full community freedom.

Oscar experienced the runaround in other aspects of his parole, but he nonetheless remained compliant. Oscar was initially paroled to a three-quarter house. As in other residential treatment programs, he was subject to a strict 10:00 p.m. curfew, had to be out of the house by 8:30 a.m., and was regularly drug tested. But beyond the surveillance, "the living conditions were not good," Oscar told me. The building was overcrowded. "They were putting four or five, sometimes six, people to live in a very small quarter," Oscar said. He was assigned to "a very small room that had four bunk beds and eight people living in it and it was . . . there was no space for anything." He continued, "It was so packed with people; they had people living in the kitchen. So, you couldn't even utilize the kitchen, because they had beds in there." The three-quarter house was not a safe environment either. "There was a lot of drugs, there was a lot of gang activity," Oscar explained.

Despite living in this crowded and unsafe environment, Oscar kept his head down and kept moving toward his goal of community reintegration. He drew a clear boundary between himself and the other residents of the three-quarter house. Oscar felt that he was a member of "a small remnant of men and women who really take advantage of those programs offered by [the] Department of Corrections and . . . manage to change themselves and move toward progression and continue to thrive despite whatever the situation was. . . . I'm blessed enough to say that I was one of them while I was in there. I educated myself, pursued a degree. I worked hard. And so, my mentality coming home into this transitional home was not to really make any friends or to socialize, just to use it as a place to lay my head and then continue to move on with my life."

After two months, Oscar's PO allowed him to move out of the three-quarter house and into his niece's apartment because of the facility's unsafe conditions. Oscar was given permission to move after a fight broke out between two men in Oscar's room while Oscar was at work. According to Oscar, during the fight "one of them got hit with something in the head and was cut and was bleeding profusely and bled all over my bed, bled all over my property and all of my things, and as a result of that I was given permission to move from there to my niece's house, by parole."

At the time of our interview, Oscar was still living with his niece, but he hoped that by continuing to actively comply with parole conditions, he'd be able to move in with his wife, who lived upstate, within a few years. Oscar also continues to "make good" on the outside. He is volunteering with a violence interruption program. "You know, I work with youth now," Oscar told me. He works with a team that goes "out to the street and reach[es] out to kids who are at risk of either getting shot or shooting someone. . . . I've been able to take all those skills that I learnt and that experience and translate it and transfer it out here to help the community."

Oscar's case illustrates how participation in prison-based rehabilitation programs plays an important role in shaping men's reformed identities and providing them with the tools to cope with the stress of the runaround. Oscar internalized the cultural narratives of individualism and resilience he had learned in prison. He crafted a redemption narrative in which he was able to overcome the bleakest of circumstances through tenacity and a positive attitude and find newfound purpose in his mission to help others. This identity work also involved boundary work. He cast himself as being different from other formerly incarcerated people. Unlike men who just do their time, Oscar had worked hard to take advantage of the rehabilitative and educational programs offered by the Department of Corrections. He distanced himself from other residents of his three-quarter house and maintained his focus on his mission to "make good."

Oscar's case also illustrates the importance of peer and family support in shaping men's ability to cope with the runaround. Recall Tony from the last chapter. Tony was also convicted of a serious violent felony and served over a decade in state prison. However, unlike Oscar, Tony developed a deeply cynical view of state authorities. He described antagonistic relationships with corrections officers, family courts, and POs, marked by repeated experiences of procedural injustice. But Tony served most of his prison sentence in a state of social isolation. In contrast to Oscar, who received frequent visits from his daughter and extended family, Tony was cut off from his family and rarely received visits. Tony coped with his isolation by withdrawing further into himself, devoting his time to exercising and studying in the law library alone. Contrast this with Oscar, who coped with the pain of imprisonment by developing a network of peer support and forging connections with prison staff.

While Tony navigated the institutional circuit mostly on his own, Oscar was able to rely on a large extended family upon his release, which allowed him to tap into a financial and emotional support system that cushioned the hardships of the runaround. For example, when Oscar's three-quarter house became too dangerous, he was able to quickly move in with his niece rather than being shuffled into another transitional housing facility. This support provided a vital safety net for Oscar that helped him to remain resilient amid the hardships of reentry. It was easier for him to interpret the runaround as a short-term inconvenience when he knew he had family support to fall back on.

Recovery and Respectability on the Institutional Circuit

The reformed identities that men formed inside prison are reinforced on the institutional circuit of reentry. Narratives of individualism and resilience form the ideological backbone of the institutional circuit.[20] In parole offices, BTW programs, substance abuse treatment facilities, and responsible fatherhood programs, institutional authorities repeatedly tell formerly incarcerated men that they are personally responsible for their own rehabilitation and reintegration.

This ideology of personal responsibility is heavily influenced by the rhetoric of twelve-step recovery programs. Indeed, for formerly incarcerated men in New York City, contact with twelve-step programs is nearly unavoidable.[21] Residential substance abuse treatment programs are a significant juncture of the institutional circuit of reentry. Men flow into these facilities not only seeking treatment, but also to satisfy conditions of parole, probation, and drug courts or to avoid the moral and physical dangers of homeless shelters. Inside these facilities, men are subjected to a totalizing regimen of addiction recovery therapy, consisting of a strict schedule of chores, therapy sessions, and group meetings.[22] Movement is restricted in and out of the facility, and residents must demonstrate progress toward sobriety by reaching treatment milestones in order to earn various privileges, such as access to a cell phone, visits, or passes to leave the facility. The therapeutic content of these programs tends to focus on correcting the individual character flaws and moral failings that underlie residents' addictions. The goal is to take criminal-addicts who are "deceitful, manipulative, impulsive, and openly defiant of authority" and transform them into self-disciplined and personally responsible citizens.[23]

Men are also exposed to twelve-step programming through mandated outpatient treatment programs tied to parole or welfare conditions. Even for men who somehow avoid contact with substance abuse treatment altogether, twelve-step rhetoric circulates in spaces beyond support groups and treatment facilities. Indeed, twelve-step rhetoric played a significant role in the curriculum of job readiness classes at Second Chances and Uplift.

Frontline staff at Second Chances and Uplift constructed job-readiness workshops as spaces of recovery akin to self-help groups like Alcoholics Anonymous.[24] Second Chances and Uplift promoted themselves as being "culturally competent" organizations that employed staff made up primarily of people with histories of incarceration, addiction, homelessness, and welfare receipt. Frontline staff took on the role of "recovery sponsors": older, wiser peers who possess a special kind of expertise based on their lived experience rather than formalized credentials.[25] Because frontline staff shared similar life experiences as clients, they could make claims to having an authentic perspective on navigating reentry processes. Much like AA meetings, formerly incarcerated staff would share stories of how their self-destructive behaviors had led them to "rock bottom." Only after taking personal responsibility for their actions and accepting the help of others were they able to recover and "make good."[26]

For example, during the first day of the Workforce Development Workshop at Second Chances, the class discussed the barriers to employment. Eric asked the class, "Give me an example of a barrier to employment." Eric then wrote their answers on the whiteboard. One class came up with the following list:

Interviewing skills
Convictions
Substance abuse
Age
Housing
Transportation
Food
Clothing
Legal issues—open cases, warrants, parole, probation, stop and frisk
Financial situation

After the class was done listing barriers to employment, Eric added one more item to the list. "I see this as one of the main barriers," he told the class. He wrote S-E-L-F on the whiteboard in large capital letters.

Eric then began narrating his own struggle to find employment after incarceration. When he first got out of prison, Eric thought that no one would want to hire him because of his extensive criminal record. He told the class, "When I was out looking for work I didn't realize that I already shut myself out before they did.... I've been arrested 72 times, so I felt like employers wouldn't ever want to hire a person like me in the first place." But over time, Eric began to realize that it was his own self-doubt, not his conviction, that was holding him back. He told the class, "I had to take an honest inventory: was it my conviction or was it me? Am I holding myself down? I used to say that opportunity doesn't knock on my door.... But it was me who was holding me back.... Opportunity don't knock on my door because I didn't have a door to knock on. I had to build a door. I went back to school.... I learned how to interact with people.... I learned the difference between being aggressive and being assertive."[27] Eric repeated similar inspirational mottos throughout the two-week class:

> "Your conviction can be a barrier . . . but you can be a barrier too."
> "I lived the majority of my life blaming other people for my choices. . . . If I want my world to change, it starts with me."
> "It starts and ends with you. You can go to 100 programs. The bottom line is you, you, you."[28]

Even though the workshop was not explicitly orientated toward substance abuse treatment, the rhetoric of twelve-step programs nonetheless played a significant role in shaping how frontline staff constructed the barriers to reentry. Eric had extensive experience participating in twelve-step programs and saw himself as a recovery sponsor for program participants. He even explicitly referenced step four: "Make a searching and fearless moral inventory of ourselves" when discussing how he came to realize that his bad attitude was holding him back from employment.

Eric acknowledged that external barriers, such as labor market discrimination, housing insecurity, and lack of transportation, hold people back from employment. But he emphasized that even if those external barriers are addressed, there are still internal barriers that prevent people from getting jobs, such as having a defeatist attitude or blaming other people for your problems. This institutional narrative constructs a world where the barriers to reentry, including the runaround, can be overcome through tenacity and a positive attitude. Indeed, rather than allowing participants to use the runaround as an excuse for relapsing, frontline staff focused on cultivating participants' capacity to remain resilient and emotionally composed when faced with the hardships of the runaround.

While workforce development programs drew heavily on twelve-step rhetoric, responsible fatherhood programs were influenced by the rhetoric of respectability politics. Indeed, efforts to transform formerly incarcerated men into "responsible fathers" were reminiscent of turn-of-the-century "racial uplift" projects in which members of the "Black bourgeoisie" sought to "uplift the race" by correcting the "bad" customs and habits of poor Black people through charity and moral education.[29]

Today, respectability politics tends to focus on fixing the "culture of poverty" in low-income communities of color. According to contemporary social commentary in this vein, social problems like unemployment, violence, drug abuse, and low educational attainment are rooted in a morally deficient culture that pervades poor communities of color. This culture of poverty encourages immediate gratification and condones irresponsible behavior, such as drinking, drug use, violence, sexual promiscuity, and out of wedlock childbirth. Black men in particular are singled out for their failure to "step up" and be respectable men by "taking control, being the man of the house, or showing boys how to be 'real men.'"[30] According to this narrative, if men of color were more present in the lives of their children, there would be fewer social problems in these communities.

The rhetoric of respectability is central to the curriculum of responsible fatherhood programs. Indeed, the entire premise of federally funded responsible fatherhood programs is that noncustodial fathers—a population that is disproportionately composed of poor men of color—lack a sense of personal responsibility and need to be cajoled into working and paying child support.[31] Take the following scene from a back-to-school event hosted by Uplift's Responsible Fatherhood Program.

It's a late summer day, and about 50 people are gathered in the classroom at Uplift. The audience is made up of Black and Latinx program participants, community members, and their kids. Before lunch is served and school supplies are passed out, the event features a speaker to promote an upcoming event called Dads Take Your Child to School Day. The speaker is Tim, a Black man in his forties who works for the ACS and the Office of Child Support Enforcement. Dads Take Your Child to School Day is designed to encourage noncustodial fathers, particularly Black fathers, to become actively involved in their children's education.[32] By having fathers show up to schools en masse with their children, the event is intended to be a symbolic display to raise awareness about the importance of fathers being present in the lives of their children. Tim begins his presentation by telling the audience, "This message is for the men. . . . Women have held us up for generations. And now we're asking the men to step up."

Tim begins by telling the fathers in the classroom, "You represent a significant developmental element in your child's life." Tim explains that a variety of studies have shown that children walk and talk at an earlier age and are more likely to go to college if they have a father involved in their lives.[33] Tim argues that mothers parent through emotions and nurturing, and this can sometimes lead to children becoming dependent and spoiled adults who lack self-control. In contrast, fathers parent through logic and discipline, which leads children to become independent, rational, and self-controlled adults.

Tim argues that many of the problems in the Black community stem from the absence of fathers in the lives of children. He points to the crack epidemic as one of the primary factors that has led to the deterioration of the Black family. "Crack hurt us as a generation," he tells the audience. He continues, "There were 50,000 kids a day in foster care for nine years because of crack." Many of the at-risk youth growing up today are the direct product of absent parents lost to the crack era. "We have an opportunity to get back into the race," Tim tells the audience. "We have to teach each other and challenge each other to be there for our children."

We can also see respectability politics play out in the formal and informal curriculum of responsible fatherhood classes. Take the following scene from a Responsible Fatherhood class at Second Chances. Louis, a Latino family counselor in his fifties, is teaching a class on the importance of complying with child support orders. Louis asks the class, "So what's the point of child support?" Keith, a Black man in his forties, answers bluntly, "To steal money from people." Louis seems to be a bit taken aback by Keith's response. "Why is it that you think that?" Louis asks. Keith replies, "Because the money doesn't go to the mother." Keith owes money to the DSS to repay the cost of public assistance his son's mother received. Keith continues, "The money they take from you don't go to the child; it go to them [DSS]." Keith sees this policy as being fundamentally unjust. He explains to the class: "Let's say I give you $100 to give to my son, but you keep some of it and only give some of the rest to my son. . . . That's not right."

"OK let's think about this," Louis says to the class. "How much do you think it costs a month to raise a child? Let's just say $500 for the sake of argument." He goes on, "So now mom has all these costs of raising the baby, but she doesn't have enough income, so she goes on welfare. And when she goes down to the welfare office, they ask her to name the father of her child and she names "Joe" or whoever as the father. Now welfare is gonna go and find Joe. Now Joe works a minimum wage job, so they set his order at about $50 a month. Now Joe is bitching and complaining about having to pay $50 a month because he's only making minimum wage, but he's really getting over."[34] Louis points out that "Joe" is only paying about one-tenth of the entire cost of raising a child per month (i.e., $50 out of $500).[35] Louis continues, "Now why Joe feels the need to bitch and complain even though he's getting over, that goes to a different area. . . . That goes to the area of personal responsibility."

Louis keeps the lesson moving along. "Now let's talk about the conse-quences of not paying child support." Louis discusses how your driver's li-cense and other professional licenses can get suspended for not paying child support. Your wages can also be garnished for not paying child support. One participant points out that some men work off the books to avoid having their wages garnished. Louis replies, "That goes back to the issue of personal responsibility." Louis points out that men who work off the books in order to avoid paying child support could eventually wind up getting arrested for non-payment. Keith replies, "You think that helps the kid?" Louis replies, "No. They shouldn't be arrested, but they should pay." "But what if he can't pay?" Keith replies. "There are mechanisms to reduce the order," Louis answers.

Louis says that he once had a client on his caseload who owed $50,000 in arrears. This man wanted to pay his child support, but he couldn't possibly afford to pay that amount in arrears. Louis helped him make arrangements with the Office of Child Support Enforcement to reduce the order to $500. Louis differentiates men like this, men who want to pay child support but are "dead broke," from the men who deserve to be arrested for nonpayment —the "deadbeats" who have the ability to pay child support but refuse to. He explains, "But guys who just don't care, who don't want to pay, who want to run around and just do them, then the court says you gotta sit in jail."

Louis then gives an example of an "irresponsible" father who was on his caseload a few years ago. During their first meeting, the man claimed that he was participating in the Parents in Transition Program because he wanted to "take care of his kid" by paying child support. The man got placed in an internship and started earning a modest income. During their weekly case management meetings, Louis would ask the man if he had started making any child support payments, but the man would claim that he still needed to "get back on his feet" before he could start making payments. How-ever, Louis says that the man once showed up to a case management meet-ing wearing a brand-new pair of Nike Foamposites, a pair of sneakers that can cost upward of $250. Despite wearing this expensive pair of sneakers, the man continued to claim that he still needed to "get on his feet" before he could start making child support payments. "He was trying to get over," Louis asserts. "And it's his kid that's the one who pays the price. He hap-pened to be born to a father who doesn't give a shit."

In each of these scenes, we see how Responsible Fatherhood Programs reinforce the cultural narrative that the social problems plaguing poor communities of color are rooted in the moral pathologies of individual men, particularly their devaluation of education, their valorization of drug dealing and materialism, and their general lack of personal responsibility. According to this narrative, if formerly incarcerated men are struggling with unemployment or child support debt, they alone are to blame for their current predicament, and they alone are responsible for making better choices to change their circumstances.

Challenging Redemption Scripts

For many men these cultural narratives of individualism resonated with their identities as "hustlers" and reinforced their commitment to leading a reformed lifestyle. However, these institutional scripts did not go unchallenged. Indeed, program participants were constantly pushing against narratives of personal responsibility during the classes I observed. To them, platitudes about personal responsibility were incongruent with their ongoing experiences of disempowerment and exclusion. Staff members also had nuanced views about the relationship between reentry, personal responsibility, and structural inequality.

We see these tensions play out in an informal focus group at Second Chances. Stanley, a Black man in his late forties, raises his hand and begins discussing how staying out of prison is a matter of personal choice and individual willpower. He discusses how even before a person is released from prison, "You have to come to the realization that you won't go back, and that freedom is the most important thing to you in your life." Stanley vehemently asserts that he will not go back to prison because he has made the choice that his personal freedom is the most important thing in his life and that nothing will get in the way of that.

Ron, a Black in forties, raises his hand and challenges Stanley's point: "You can value your freedom all you like, but if you can't eat and you have nowhere to sleep, how long is that gonna last?" He continues, "I'm just trying to introduce some realism here."

Stanley replies that you have to be "mentally, emotionally, and spiritually ready" before you can confront the barriers to reentry. He discusses how 20 years ago "during Reaganomics" there weren't any programs available for returning citizens. Today, "there's programs out there," and if people don't take advantage of them then they're "just making excuses'" Stanley reiterates that he will do whatever it takes to remain out of prison, "If I can't get a job, I'll be the best mutha fuckin 5 cent can collector there is."

Other men had a more systemic view of the barriers to reentry. Charles, a Black man in his forties, discusses how "these politicians" create laws that make reentry harder, such as questions about criminal history on job applications. He also discusses how programs in prison are "just people staying employed." He goes on, "You gotta do all of these programs when you're inside, and then you gotta do more programs when you get out just to survive."

Ron chimes in, "Let's not forget, prison is a multibillion-dollar business." He continues, "You used to be able to get a PhD in prison, but you can't have that because people stopped coming back to prison.... You gotta keep making money." Marvin, returning to the issue of the prison-industrial complex, brings up the 13th Amendment: "You're a slave when you're in prison. I mean read the law; it says that." Mark chimes in, saying that he was surprised to learn that individuals from New Jersey convicted of drug offenses are barred from receiving public benefits. He comments, "You put a CEO, anyone in our situation, and he's gonna start breaking the law.... A man will do whatever he needs to do to survive." Marvin raises his hand and discusses how he can't get public housing because he has a drug conviction. He discusses how he was caught with "a bag of herb" in his apartment and now cannot get access to public housing even though he has "money in the bank." He says that housing authorities look at his housing application and say, "Oh well you have a drug conviction, I don't know if you can live in a building with single women and young children."

Despite these systemic critiques, others continue to return to the narrative of personal responsibility. Shaun, a Black man in his late thirties, tells the class, "I made the decision to do what I did.... My decisions hurt my family and myself.... I can't expect family to pat me on the back when I came home after all of the hurt I put them through." He continues, "Everything boils down to me.... I hurt my family, so I have to take responsibility.... I can't expect them to send me packages every week, put $150 in my commissary every two weeks, take the 8-hour train ride to Attica to visit me because of the decisions that I made.... I made the decision to put my family to the side.... It's on me, not them.... I can't fault them ... It's my responsibility to turn them back around."

For staff members, cultural narratives of individualism were central to their identities as "recovery sponsors." At the same time, staff members relied on these narratives because they were aware of how deeply limited they were in their ability to address the structural conditions that circumscribed program participants' lives. Because staff could do little to address systemic racism and poverty, they focused on teaching participants cognitive and emotional tools to cope with these harsh realities.

This is not to say that these organizations were apolitical. Both organizations emphasized the shared destiny of communities of color, highlighting the need for collective action to combat police violence and mass incarceration. Indeed, personal responsibility was often linked to collective action: it was only when formerly incarcerated men took personal responsibility for their lives that they would be able to take part in broader efforts to effect social change in their communities. Second Chances in particular organized a variety of advocacy and fundraising campaigns for progressive causes. The organization provided legal workshops about citizens' rights during "stop and frisk" encounters and the rights of formerly incarcerated people to pursue antidiscrimination litigation against employers. They also organized trips to the state capital in Albany to stage protests for progressive criminal justice reform, such as expanding access to prison education and implementing "ban the box" legislation.

At the same time, these narratives of individualism reflected a sense of cynicism about the ability of the state to address the needs of formerly incarcerated people. Indeed, staff members often expressed distrust that the state was capable of helping formerly incarcerated people at all. Eric tells the class: "The DOC [Department of Corrections] is not designed to rehabilitate us. It's up to you. . . . You can navigate your way through the system, do what they ask you to do, but it's up to us to make the change."

Indeed, this individualistic approach was often rooted in a fundamental distrust of the institutional circuit. Because the institutional circuit was so punitive and dysfunctional, it was up to formerly incarcerated men to take charge of their own rehabilitation. No one would be there to do it for them. Parole wouldn't help. The job of POs is to catch rulebreakers and protect public safety, not act as a social service provider. "If parole actually rehabilitated people, they'd be out of a job," Eric tells the class. Public assistance programs couldn't lift people out of poverty. Between the frequent appointments, behavioral mandates, and meager benefits, public assistance programs were more hassle than help. Transitional housing facilities were "prisons without bars," rife with moral and physical danger. And no community-based rehabilitation program, no matter how well intentioned, could undo the structural conditions that kept poor men of color trapped at the margins of society. These men were on their own. The best staff at Second Chances and Uplift could do was teach them the psychological tools to remain resilient amid this bleak reality.

CONCLUSION

Formerly incarcerated men develop a variety of psychological tools to cope with the stress of the runaround. They draw on cultural narratives of individualism and resilience to construct reformed masculine identities, casting themselves as men capable of rising above the stress and degradation of procedural injustice through grit and self-reliance. The institutional circuit plays an important role in shaping these practices of identity work. Cultural narratives of individualism and resilience are institutionalized in the formal and informal curriculum of rehabilitation programs inside prisons and throughout the institutional circuit of reentry, playing a central role in shaping and reinforcing these expressions of reformed masculinity. However, successfully navigating the institutional circuit requires more than just identity work. Formerly incarcerated men also had to learn practical skills to navigate the complex and convoluted bureaucratic systems that governed their daily lives. In the next chapter we explore the bureaucratic labor of systems navigation, illustrating how traversing the institutional circuit is itself a full-time job.

FIVE

Becoming Professionally Poor

AS WE HAVE SEEN throughout the book, formerly incarcerated men expend a significant amount of time and energy navigating the institutional circuit of reentry. They must engage in the day-to-day labor of managing multiple, overlapping bureaucratic entanglements across a fragmented institutional circuit. They must traverse the city to keep up with overstuffed appointment schedules, participate in redundant rehabilitation programs, and arrive back before facility curfews. And they must endure the indignities of interminable waits, evasive and unresponsive frontline actors, and unexplained bureaucratic errors that block access to resources. Andre discussed how the amount of time and energy he spent running around the city to attend various appointments was equivalent to having a full-time job. "This is what I do for a living," he told me.[1] He explained:

> ANDRE: I gotta do group [therapy], three, four times a week. I gotta do this WEP program, um, three or four times a week, usually five days a week. And now that I've done all of that, I have at most, the ability to have $189 a month in food stamps, and $223 every two weeks in cash. This is basically, for all of those efforts . . . I get to stay here [in the three-quarter house], in basically, a prison without bars. And I get to do that, all day, every day, and from here, unless I do something else, it can only get worse. Because after a while, I get kicked out of here. Unless I find another place for myself, I'm going to an actual shelter. . . . So what the hell do I do? I find myself another situation, I tell another program, that, you know, I have a substance abuse issue, and I go there. Because, obviously, I know this system now. But now you've made me professionally poor. This is what I do for a living. And there's nothing else that I can do, because you haven't given me the time to go and find a job.

As Andre described it, his current "job" was complying with the litany of mandates required to access public assistance and transitional housing. He complained that rather than having an actual job, his full-time job was navigating the institutional circuit, what he called being "professionally poor."

This chapter uses Andre's notion of being "professionally poor" as a jumping-off point to explore the hidden forms of bureaucratic labor formerly incarcerated men undertake to comply with the mandates of the institutional circuit.[2] In order to avoid reincarceration and access public aid, formerly incarcerated men had to constantly prove their status as deserving citizens. In the words of sociologist Paige Sweet, formerly incarcerated men had to make themselves "institutionally legible."[3] That is, they had to translate their complex experiences of reentry and recovery into coherent bureaucratic narratives that resonated with dominant institutional understandings of rehabilitation. To do so, men learned to see themselves through the eyes of frontline actors. This helped them to develop strategies of self-presentation to convince institutional gatekeepers that they were citizens worthy of community freedom and public aid.

Gaining recognition as worthy citizens required a significant amount of bureaucratic labor. First, formerly incarcerated men had to "get on paper." It was not enough for men to claim that they had been rehabilitated; they had to prove it through formal paperwork. They also learned the importance of "performing rehabilitation" by demonstrating capacity for emotional control, remorse, and respectability during interactions with institutional gatekeepers. By making themselves institutionally legible, men mold themselves into the kinds of masculine citizens the state seeks to produce: men who are sober, docile, and willing to take any available work. But in doing so, they reinforce symbolic boundaries between the deserving and undeserving poor and reaffirm the notion that only formerly incarcerated men who devote themselves fully to the bureaucratic labor of systems navigation deserve community freedom and public aid.

SEEING LIKE A STREET-LEVEL BUREAUCRAT AND BECOMING INSTITUTIONALLY LEGIBLE

By taking on systems navigation as a temporary, full-time occupation, study participants acquired a set of skills and sensibilities that facilitated interactions with the institutional circuit. Through recurrent experiences with the runaround, they began to learn the quirks of the system: when to arrive for appointments, what paperwork to bring, how to develop rapport with front-line actors, what to say and how to say it to get the services they needed.[4] By doing so, men developed strategies to make the institutional circuit work in their interest. For example, Andre discussed how he learned that if he wants to avoid living in a homeless shelter, he'll have to claim that he has a substance abuse issue to gain access to another residential program, even though, as Andre claimed, he's never had a substance abuse issue to begin with.

Men were able to develop shortcuts through the institutional circuit by learning to "see like a street-level bureaucrat, to borrow a phrase from sociologist Forrest Stuart."[5] Much like residents of LA's Skid Row neighborhood in Stuart's study, who learn to "see like a cop" through repeated encounters with the police, formerly incarcerated men in New York City learned to "see like a street-level bureaucrat" through repeated encounters with the institutional circuit.[6] Through these experiences, they developed a set of cognitive schemas to interpret the runaround from the point of view of frontline actors. They developed folk theories to explain why actors behaved the way they did. They then used these theories to read and decode interactions with institutional gatekeepers, strategize about future interactions, and align their actions with institutional rules and expectations.

For example, study participants were aware that as men of color with criminal records, street-level bureaucrats likely viewed them with suspicion or contempt. In response, formerly incarcerated men learned to adjust their behavior to avoid evoking negative stereotypes associated with their status as criminalized men of color. Men were constantly trying to prove that they were members of the deserving poor who had genuine needs and were willing to follow the rules, not the stereotypical "gangbangers," "deadbeat dads," and welfare cheats who haunt the public imagination. Indeed, men organized their reformed identities around a set of symbolic boundaries between themselves and "undeserving" others. By drawing these distinctions, the men could validate their deserving self-image and distance themselves from negative stereotypes of criminalized men of color.[7]

For example, men living in transitional housing facilities routinely differentiated themselves from other residents. Indeed, transitional housing facilities were regularly discussed as sites of moral danger, with other residents being the primary threat. Jorge discussed how living alongside other addicts in his three-quarter house was putting him at risk for relapse. He told me:

JORGE: In the three-quarter house, you got guys stealing your property, stealing your food. . . . It's an environment not conducive to staying clean. . . . You go into the day room and everyone is nodding off. It makes guys think, "If they're getting high, I can get high too." It's discouraging to be in that environment. . . . You leave for the weekend to see your family and someone stole all your shit. It's discouraging. . . . You can't leave anything in the icebox because people will steal your food. . . . It's crazy. You got guys smoking that K2 [synthetic marijuana].[8]

Similarly, men on parole who were actively compliant with their parole conditions would contrast themselves with less deserving men who had run afoul of their POs. For example, Roland, who had been convicted of murder, boasted that he only has to report to parole every two months, in contrast to men convicted of less serious crimes who have to report more often. He told me:

ROLAND: Yeah, matter of fact, uh, my parole officer . . . I see her, every two months. Like now, you got guys that have been home five or six years, still have to go every month, you know? Every two weeks, something like that. That's because they still using. They been coming in, getting violated, they got a dirty urine or whatever. When I go there, I have clean urine. My PO . . . she know that . . . I ain't trying to get in no type of trouble.

Gender ideologies also played an important role in this boundary work. Men were constantly drawing distinctions between themselves—real men involved in their children's lives—and "deadbeat dads"—men who abandon their children and fail to take financial responsibility for them. Almost all of the men who owed child support complained that they were unfairly pegged as deadbeat dads by child support authorities. Although they all thought that the child support system was unfair in some way, they also felt that the system, in theory, serves a legitimate purpose. They all agreed that the state should force "deadbeat dads" to take financial responsibility for their kids. The problem, in their eyes, was that they were not deadbeat dads; they were involved fathers whom the child support system was unfairly targeting.

Justin, a 26-year-old Black man and father of three, exemplifies this experience.[9] Justin lived with his three sons and their mother. He had served a few jail sentences for drug and gun possession as a teen, but by the time of our interview in 2015, Justin had transitioned out of the street lifestyle and had settled into a domestic life with his family. He was currently unemployed and owed $1,350 in child support arrears to the DSS to repay the state for the cost of benefits his family had received. Justin had been working for a time and keeping up with his payments, but he had lost his job a few months earlier and been accruing debt ever since. During our interview, I asked Justin if he thought the child support system was fair. Justin replied:

JUSTIN: Yes [it's fair]. People shouldn't make kids and not take care of them. . . . I think [child support is] only for the people that . . . like have kids and abandon them. I think they should have to pay. But for the people that's doing for their kids, I don't think they should be so hard on them.

JOHN: [Do] you think they're treating you like you were the type of dad who just runs out?

JUSTIN: Yeah, you know that's how they looking at it. I can't blame them for that, but they don't really know my situation.

JOHN: Right, right. And so, when you go to court, you're hoping to kind of maybe make that clear?

JUSTIN: Yes, make it clear and let them know that. Listen, I'm in my kid's life, and I would do anything for them. I'm in the process of looking for work. The order is way too high. I can't pay.

JOHN: So, if you were a policy maker, someone in charge of the child support system, what would you do to help relieve child support debt. Like [for] people in your situation, how would you maybe change the system?

JUSTIN: I would have rules.

JOHN: What kind of rules?

JUSTIN: For people that's living with their kids and trying, I would work with them. I would . . . I'd still probably have to put a order, but I'd work with them. For the people that just make kids and run away, then they going to have to pay. They going to have to pay. Well, if not, everybody going to do it. Everybody be running wild just having kids and leaving them everywhere. And not taking care of them.

JOHN: Right, so you think they should, they should make that distinction more?

JUSTIN: Yeah, for the fathers that's actually there . . . 'cause sometimes it's not the father's fault too at the same time. It'd be the mothers at the same time too. They don't want them around the kids. For whatever reason, I don't know. They don't want them there.

JOHN: Do you think there's other ways that fathers can help their children? Like other than paying child support?

JUSTIN: Well it's not about money all the time. It's about time. Time you spend 'cause kids don't care about money, they care . . . they not going to remember that. They going to remember "Oh my God he took me outside every day to play." Or you know, "My daddy tells me life stories. He's teaching me things." It don't take money to make your kids happy. Takes time.

Throughout our exchange Justin distinguished himself as a "real" man who was involved in the lives of his children. He was not a lazy deadbeat dad who had kids and ran out on them. These men deserve the state's discipline and punishment, not men like Justin, who take the time to nurture their children and are doing their best they can to find work and pay child support. In this exchange we can see how men's reformed identities rest on distinctions between themselves and undeserving others. Justin's claim to being a reformed father, and thus his deservingness of leniency from the child support system, is derived from the symbolic boundary he constructs between himself and deadbeat dads. By constructing this boundary, Justin upholds the fundamental legitimacy of the child support system and reinforces distinctions between the deserving and undeserving poor.

Indeed, study participants felt that the institutional circuit was so punitive and disciplinary because members of the "undeserving poor" had abused the system in the past. For example, Dwight thinks that public assistance is so difficult to access because women have abused the system in the past. During a focus group at Second Chances, Orlando, a Black man in his twenties, complains that workfare is "like slavery" because you have to work 30 hours per week for a measly $200-a-month food stamp check. Dwight replies, "That's what happens when people abuse the welfare system. It makes it bad for everybody else. You know, back in the day, people, you had girls just having nine and ten kids because they can get $500 worth of food stamps. Know what I mean? And this is why they was having them [kids]. So, the system is so messed up now."

Later, Eduardo complains that his Social Security Disability Insurance (SSDI) application has been denied, even though he has a documented heart condition. Dwight chimes in, "They're making sure you're serious about it." He continues:

DWIGHT: That goes back to, again, people abusing the system. I seen countless people . . . people was just lazy. They'd rather than work, and try to work hard to find a job, people want to get on social security. They don't want to work. And that's again what's fucking it up for everybody else that really needs it, you know what I'm saying?

As we see in this exchange, Eduardo positions himself as a deserving aid recipient who wants to work but can't because of his heart condition. According to Dwight, the reason Eduardo's SSDI application was denied is that manipulative welfare cheats have made it harder for deserving aid recipients like Eduardo to access SSDI. Through their laziness and grift, the undeserving poor are "fucking it up for everybody that really needs it."

Men engaged in a significant amount of bureaucratic labor to distance themselves from these stereotypes of the undeserving poor and prove their status as deserving citizens. In the words of sociologist Paige Sweet, formerly incarcerated men had to make themselves "institutionally legible."[10]

In her study of domestic violence survivors, Sweet illustrates how women seeking domestic violence services must become legible as "good survivors." They have to contort their "complex and confusing experiences of violence" into coherent narratives of trauma and psychological recovery in order to access shelters, obtain legal protection, or comply with child welfare authorities. Sweet shows how institutional performances are imbued with social expectations around gender, race, class, and sexuality.[11] To perform the role of a "good" survivor, women's institutional performances must draw on dominant cultural narratives about respectable motherhood, sexual virtue, and female empowerment that align with institutional categories of how a "worthy" domestic violence survivor should behave.[12]

Formerly incarcerated men must engage in similar kinds of institutional performances in order to maintain community freedom and access public aid.[13] While women seeking domestic violence service must prove that they are "good survivors" engaged in ongoing projects of psychological recovery, formerly incarcerated men must prove that they are "good" ex-prisoners engaged in ongoing projects of rehabilitation and redemption.

As is the case in the field of domestic violence, institutional performances in the reentry field are suffused with social expectations around gender, race, class, and sexuality. Formerly incarcerated men, especially men of color, must contend with dominant institutional expectations that they are violent "gangbangers" and irresponsible "deadbeat dads." They must engage in bureaucratic labor to dispel these negative stereotypes and prove they are worthy citizens deserving of inclusion. To become "legible" as rehabilitated men, study participants had to show that they were capable of following rules, controlling their emotions, taking accountability for their crimes, and fulfilling their roles as wage workers and family breadwinners. Formerly incarcerated men accomplished the task of becoming institutionally legible through two interrelated processes: getting on paper and performing rehabilitation.

GETTING ON PAPER

"This class is the blind leading the blind," Paul tells me. We are sitting in a classroom at Uplift waiting for the evening's Responsible Fatherhood class to start. Paul is a White man in his late thirties. He grew up poor in an Irish Italian family in Philadelphia and was a successful independent contractor before serving seven years in prison for aggravated assault. Paul is brash and loud, and he is vocal about his criticisms of Uplift. Paul thinks the class facilitator, Ray, a Black formerly incarcerated man in his fifties, is "ignorant" and unqualified to teach a parenting class. "I came from nothing," Paul tells me. "I built a million-dollar company from the ground up. There is *nothing* [Ray] can teach me."

Before I can ask Paul why he is attending class when he feels that the instructor is incompetent and that the class is a waste of his time, he tells me, "I'm having trouble seeing my kids. That's why I'm here." Paul had a rocky relationship with his son's mother prior to his incarceration. "I was sinful," Paul tells me, explaining that he slept with multiple women while he was living with his son's mother. Around the time of his arrest, Paul had moved out and they were in the process of breaking up. Paul feels that his son's mother withholds visitations with his son as a way to retaliate against him for his unfaithfulness. Paul says that he has an upcoming family court date, and he's been gathering official documentation to support his case for visitation or possibly joint custody. He says that he's joined the Guardian Angels, an urban vigilante group, and has gathered letters from pastors and other community leaders. "I'm trying to get everything on paper to show the judge that I'm not a bad, violent, threatening person."

Paul's case illustrates the significance that formerly incarcerated men attach to formal paperwork. Formerly incarcerated men are largely defined by who they are "on paper." Institutional gatekeepers, like family court judges, make decisions about the character and deservingness of formerly incarcerated men based on the profile created by their criminal records and other official documents.

Formerly incarcerated men like Paul try to counteract the "negative credential" of a criminal record by accumulating "positive credentials."[14] A certificate of completion from the Responsible Fatherhood program at Uplift is one such credential. Even though Paul feels like the class is beneath him, he nonetheless participates in the class to gain official recognition of rehabilitation. Paul has already developed a redemption narrative and is making progress toward reintegration. But in order for this redemption arc to be "legible" to institutional authorities, he must translate it into a form of official documentation that can be "seen" by the state.[15] The family court judge won't just take Paul's word for it. He must prove it by "getting on paper."

Indeed, one of the most common reasons for enrolling in the Responsible Fatherhood program was to "get on paper." Men believed formal paperwork was the most powerful form of currency in family court.[16] During another fatherhood class, Lawrence tells his peers, "You have to bring your paperwork to court. The judge don't want nothin from us besides, 'Hello, good morning your honor.' Everything else is just paper." Later in class Lawrence discusses how talking too much in court will only work against them. He tells his peers, "Yeah, they'll give you enough rope to hang yourself." He goes on, "It's all about the paperwork. It doesn't matter what comes out your mouth. They're not assholes, they just want you to prove it."

Formal paperwork, such as certificates of program completion and letters of recommendation, represent the accumulation of bureaucratic labor. The time and effort of participating in rehabilitation programs and building social relationships with institutional authorities becomes distilled into official paperwork that formerly incarcerated men can use as currency in various bureaucratic venues, such as parole boards and family court hearings. In this way, they function as forms of cultural capital.[17]

Men learned the importance of formal paperwork while they were incarcerated. Compiling certificates of program completion and letters of recommendation were important steps to prove rehabilitation to parole boards and earn early release. "Getting on paper" was also symbolically significant to constructing a redemption narrative.

Indeed, formal certificates of rehabilitation were significant anchor points for men's reformed identities. As criminologist Shadd Maruna observes, "Reformation is not something that is visible or objective in the sense it can be 'proven.' It is, instead, a construct that is negotiated through interaction between an individual and significant others in a process of 'looking-glass rehabilitation.' Until ex-offenders are formally and symbolically recognized as 'success stories,' their conversion may remain suspect to significant others, and most importantly to themselves."[18]

We see this process of "looking-glass rehabilitation" in Oscar's story from the last chapter. Recall that Oscar devoted himself to rehabilitation programs while incarcerated, completing several programs and becoming a group facilitator and peer mentor. By participating in these programs, Oscar was able to gain formal recognition of his reformed identity, allowing him to prove to himself, his family, and the parole board that he was sincere about the remorse he felt for taking another man's life.

Indeed, a significant part of Oscar's redemption narrative was the fact that his daughter was present at his various graduation ceremonies so she could see Oscar receive formal recognition for his rehabilitation. "And so, it was so important to me, every certificate, every graduation, every success that I had I made arrangements for my daughter to be there," Oscar tells me.

Oscar's case illustrates how "getting on paper" has both symbolic and material effects. Graduation ceremonies, letters of recommendation, and certificates of program completion were symbols of official institutional recognition that validated Oscar's reformed identity. At the same time, "getting on paper" had helped Oscar earn early release from prison. The dozens of certificates of program completion Oscar had earned provided official proof to the parole board that corroborated Oscar's claims of rehabilitation and remorse.

Outside of prison, the most common avenue for getting on paper was completing various community-based rehabilitation programs. These included programs for substance abuse treatment, job readiness and vocational skills training, anger management, mental health counseling, and responsible fatherhood. Formerly incarcerated men must earn these certificates by engaging in bureaucratic labor. They must spend the time finding a program, either through a referral or on their own, and then travel to a facility for intake. Intake procedures typically require men to fill out paperwork, sit for an intake interview, and attend an orientation session before they can begin formal classes. Programs can last several weeks or even months, requiring program participants to attend class multiple times a week, for several hours at a time, often during normal business hours. Factoring in travel and class time, the time it takes to earn rehabilitation certificates can amount to roughly 10–20 hours per week, the equivalent of a part-time job. This is in addition to other bureaucratic obligations that men must simultaneously manage, such as parole appointments, BTW programs, mandated treatment programs, and facility curfews.

Given the amount of time and effort it can take to complete a rehabilitation program, formerly incarcerated men took great pride in the certificates they had earned. For example, Kareem, a 56-year-old Black man, carried around a binder in his backpack with all of his laminated certificates. During our interview he pulled it out and proudly showed it to me. When I asked Kareem why he carried all these certificates around with him, he told me he does it to remind himself of all the things he was able to accomplish while incarcerated. "I did time, time didn't do me," he said.

Staff members at Second Chances reinforced the importance of getting on paper. During the Workforce Development Workshop at Second Chances, Eric told the class his own story about how getting on paper had helped him reenroll in college classes, despite owing thousands of dollars in outstanding fees. "You shouldn't underestimate the power of a letter from the right person," he said. Eric explained that he had completed two years of college courses but was reincarcerated and couldn't finish his degree. After he got out, he wanted to continue his education, but he couldn't register for classes because he owed thousands of dollars in outstanding fees. Eric said that he wrote a letter to the college president asking for the fees to be waived. Along with his letter, he attached a letter of recommendation from one of his counselors and a certificate of completion from a drug treatment program. Eric said that a few days later his balance was zero and he was able to register for classes.

Eric told this story as part of a broader curriculum at Second Chances designed to teach former prisoners how to navigate formal legal channels to lower criminal record barriers. Indeed, Eric's story about the importance of getting on paper was part of an information session on how to obtain certificates of relief from disabilities and certificates of good conduct. These certificates are issued by New York State and can remove statutory bars to obtaining occupational licenses and employment. These certificates can also restore rights and privileges lost due to a conviction, such as serving on a jury, owning a firearm, or residing in public housing.[19]

Both certificates officially demonstrate a person's rehabilitation and restore almost all of the same rights. However, only a certificate of good conduct can restore a person's right to hold "public offices," which in New York include not only elected positions but also occupations like police officer and firefighter.[20] The certificates also differ in terms of the eligibility and application procedures. A person is eligible for a certificate of relief from disabilities if they have only one felony conviction. They may apply for this certificate while they are still incarcerated or any time after their release.[21] By contrast, a person with two or more felony convictions can only apply for a certificate of good conduct, and they must wait three to five years after their release before they are eligible to apply.[22]

Applying for either certificate requires a significant amount of paperwork. In addition to the application itself, which must be signed and notarized, applicants must also submit a number of supporting documents. They must provide copies of federal tax returns, proof of income (W-2 or 1099 tax forms), and proof of payment of fines and restitution. If the applicant received any public benefits, they must provide a printout from the agency showing the benefits they received. If the applicant has no reportable income for the last two years, they must provide a notarized document explaining how they supported themselves.[23] In addition to accounting for their employment and income, applicants are also encouraged (but not required) to submit other evidence of rehabilitation, including school transcripts; certificates of completion for job training and other rehabilitation programs; and letters of support from institutional authorities, such as teachers, school administrators, employers, coworkers, counselors, therapists, POs, and clergy.[24]

While these certificates can restore rights and remove statutory bars to licensure and employment, they are not pardons or expungements. A person must still list their convictions when asked on job applications, and their convictions will still appear on rap sheets and background checks. Moreover, although employers and licensing agencies must take certificates into account when deciding to hire or license a person with a criminal record, "the law still allows an employer or licensing agency to refuse to hire or license [a person with a criminal record] if they have a basis for finding that [their] convictions are 'job related' or that hiring or licensing [them] would create an unreasonable risk."[25]

Given the significant amount of bureaucratic labor involved in obtaining one of these certificates, as well as the lack of guarantee that they will even work to remove criminal record barriers, program participants questioned whether it was even worth it to pursue them. During class, a man asked Eric if it was really necessary for him to obtain one of these certificates. Eric replied, "It's like having a revolver. Those certificates are your bullets and you want to load up every chamber." However, given the complicated and convoluted application process, in addition to the inability of these certificates to fully erase a person's criminal history or prevent disqualification, I did not encounter anyone in my fieldwork who went to the trouble of obtaining one.

In addition to gaining institutional recognition for rehabilitation through formal paperwork, men also had to embody rehabilitation during interactions with institutional gatekeepers. In the last chapter we explored how men constructed reformed identities by drawing on cultural narratives of individualism and resilience. But to successfully navigate the institutional circuit of reentry, it was not enough for men to simply construct new identity narratives for themselves. Formerly incarcerated men also had to *perform* these redemption narratives during interactions with institutional gatekeepers.

Men's ability to "see like a street-level bureaucrat" was central to this process. By learning to see themselves from the point of view of frontline actors, men were able to modulate their performance of self to align with dominant institutional expectations of how "good" ex-prisoners should behave. For example, study participants discussed how they learned to control their emotions and remain calm when they experienced arbitrary or degrading treatment. As we saw in previous chapters, the runaround can be incredibly frustrating. This is especially the case for men experiencing conditions of severe deprivation. The stress of food scarcity and housing insecurity, coupled with the hassles of the runaround, can leave men feeling anxious and irritable. Being made to wait or experiencing a bureaucratic snafu—a system glitch or a misplaced document—can lead to an emotional outburst at a welfare or parole office.[26]

However, study participants knew that as men of color with criminal records, they could face a cascade of sanctions for losing control of their emotions. An argument with a welfare case worker could lead to an FTC sanction and result in a loss of benefits; a spat with residential treatment staff could lead to being "put on contract" and might eventually result in an eviction; an angry outburst at a parole office could result in an arrest and a return to custody.

For example, Peter, a 34-year-old Black man, said he was arrested for a parole violation after he cussed out his PO during a curfew check. Peter was living in a homeless shelter at the time. He was participating in a job training program and complying with his parole conditions, but his PO repeatedly woke him up at 3:00 a.m. to make sure he was in his bed. He told me:

PETER: So, at any time she could have just [seen] my name on the [sign-in] list, [or] she could have came up and, you know, physically viewed me in the bed. She didn't have to wake me up. And I was askin' her, you know, stop wakin' me up. It's not conducive. . . .

And I'm tellin' her, listen, like, okay, you know, I'm compliant with all the rules, so why are you waking me up in the middle of the night like somebody that's . . . showin' a disregard for the rules? And she blew it off. She came back and she woke me up again after I asked her not to do it. I went off. I cussed her out. Um, in the process of me cussin' her out she says I threatened her.

Peter was sent back to prison for a year on a parole violation for allegedly threatening his PO.

To avoid such outcomes, formerly incarcerated men learned to be silent and smile on the outside when they felt frustrated. Duane says that he is constantly frustrated by the waiting he experiences at parole. For example, "One time, like, for my parole she left at like 3:00, went on her lunch, came back at 5:00. And said we still had to wait because she didn't eat lunch. And I'm like, 'Who's paying for this?'" But despite these frustrating experiences, Duane explains that he's learned to accept waiting as something that's unavoidable. Rather than getting upset and walking out of his parole appointment, he's learned to just smile and laugh it off. He tells me, "Like . . . it is what it is. . . . I just, I've been frustrated enough every time I go there where I expect to wait, and I just smile. Like it's just. . . . It's just funny."

When I ask Duane why his weekly parole appointments took so long, he takes the point of view of his PO. He explains, "I don't know, man, maybe it's some type of method they have where they get to look through the camera in the back and just to see who gets frustrated." Duane theorizes that his PO makes him wait to test his capacity for rule compliance. By viewing waiting in this way, Duane is able to adjust his actions to align with his PO's expectations of deservingness. Even though being made to wait is a degrading experience, Duane understands that he needs to keep his cool during these frustrating situations in order to prove to his PO that he is someone deserving of community freedom.

Other study participants similarly viewed waiting through the eyes of their POs. During a focus group at Second Chances, Oscar discusses how he interprets waiting as a compliance test intentionally designed by his PO to evaluate how he responds under stress. According to Oscar, POs make people wait to "try to break your spirit and will. . . . They're playing psychological games with you." According to Oscar, parolees must learn to play by the rules of this "psychological game."[27] When men get frustrated, they only confirm POs' preconceived notions that men on parole are immature and in need of discipline.[28] However, if men learn to submit to the indignities and hassles of waiting, if they can show that they are patient and docile subjects, they will earn leniency from their POs and will experience fewer hassles. Indeed, Oscar was rewarded with a lower risk classification and less frequent parole appointments after he proved his status as a reformed man by being patient and compliant at his parole appointments.

During the Workforce Development Workshop at Second Chances, Eric related a similar story about how facility staff at his halfway house would engage in the same types of compliance tests. Eric said that facility staff would arbitrarily revoke weekend passes to see how residents would react. Some men reacted violently and assaulted staff, while others simply walked out of the facility without permission. When Eric's pass was revoked for no reason, he learned to keep his cool. He had seen how the men who reacted negatively to the staff's provocation received new charges and were sent back to prison. Eric remained calm, avoiding reincarceration and proving to facility staff that he was deserving of community freedom.

Men also learned to view child support hearings from the point of view of the judge. For example, one night at Uplift, Sylvia, an outreach worker from the Office of Child Support Enforcement, was visiting the class for an information session about how men can obtain order modifications. During the discussion Lawrence, a Black man in his thirties, gives his peers some advice about appearing before a family court judge. He begins by telling his peers that they need to remain calm and composed throughout the hearing. He tells them, "The judge is gonna listen to both sides, unless you have a chip on your shoulder." Sylvia agrees, "That's right. If you've got a record and you get agitated in court, they're gonna make you do a program, like anger management."

Lawrence continues, telling his peers that they need to avoid evoking negative stereotypes associated with poor men of color. He tells them, "When you go to family court, you gotta be mindful." He explains that they need to avoid using African American Vernacular English (AAVE) when addressing the judge. "You can't be in there with the 'Nah-what-I-mean [you know what I mean]?" Silvia responds in agreement, "That's right." Lawrence emphasizes that if they want an order modification, they need to make a good impression on the judge because the judge holds all the power. "Once you go to court, that decision is in the judge's hands," Lawrence explains.

Lawrence and Sylvia's advice illustrates that men must behave in ways that align with the judge's preconceived notions of how a rehabilitated and respectable man should behave. They need to control their emotions and remain calm, lest they confirm the negative stereotypes that criminalized men are aggressive and dangerous. And they must modulate their speech patterns to align with the dominant White middle-class linguistic standards of the court to avoid evoking negative stereotypes associated with the ghetto poor.[29] Men's efforts to perform rehabilitation—to remain emotionally composed during frustrating situations and to align their interaction styles with dominant middle-class cultural expectations—were designed to distance themselves from negative stereotypes of the "undeserving" poor and demonstrate that they were members of the "deserving" poor who were worthy of social inclusion.[30]

WORK WISDOM

For men, a significant aspect of performing rehabilitation was showing that they could fulfill economic roles as wage workers and family breadwinners. While the imperative to work cuts across gender lines in the era of neoliberal paternalism, criminalized men face unique pressures to engage in wage work.[31] Indeed, state actors construct men's rehabilitation as being synonymous with labor market activity.[32] While criminalized men also experience therapeutic interventions, such as anger management, substance abuse treatment, and responsible fatherhood classes, workforce development training is central to the state's efforts to transform criminalized men into the "average Joe taxpayer."[33] In her ethnography of POs, sociologist Jessica Wyse finds that enforcing rule compliance, particularly showing up to appointments on time, obtaining employment, and paying child support, is central to how POs manage criminalized men. Discussions of employment dominate parole meetings with men. Other concerns, such as housing insecurity, emotional traumas, and family relationships, are of secondary concern, if at all. Instead, POs' rehabilitative efforts focus primarily on pushing men to assume markers of conventional, adult masculinity, viewing "a rehabilitated man as having exchanged criminality for a role in the marketplace."[34]

The pressure for criminalized men to find work is amplified by their entanglements with the child support system. Child support authorities define "parental obligation in strictly financial terms that value monetary contributions above all else."[35] Child support authorities give little credence to men's roles as caregivers or moral guides. If men are not paying child support, even if they are fulfilling parental obligations in other ways, the state considers them to be parental failures deserving of punishment. Men are under constant pressure to find work and pay their debts or face a cascade of sanctions, including fines, loss of driver's licenses, and jail sentences.

But the pressure for men to find work is not isolated to parole or the child support system. The imperative to work is a core ideology that cuts across the institutional circuit. Men face work mandates at virtually every juncture of the institutional circuit of reentry. In addition to parole and child support, men must find work to satisfy work mandates from public assistance programs, shelters, halfway houses, and residential treatment programs. Failing to find work in any one of these venues can trigger a cascade of sanctions ranging from loss of benefits to eviction to incarceration.

Men were often desperate to find work in order to satisfy bureaucratic obligations and turned to Second Chances and Uplift for help. At Second Chances and Uplift, they learned how to perform the role of a rehabilitated and respectable worker during interactions with employers and other institutional gatekeepers. These lessons focused on teaching formerly incarcerated men strategies of self-presentation to convince employers that they were remorseful, nonthreatening, and respectable, a curriculum I call "work wisdom."[36] While there are certainly aspects of work wisdom that apply to both men and women, significant portions of the curriculum center on teaching men of color specific strategies for allaying the anxieties of White, middle-class employers fearful of the stereotypical "criminalblackman."[37]

The centerpiece of the Workforce Development Workshop at Second Chances was teaching returning citizens how to discuss their convictions during job interviews. These lessons focused on teaching program participants how to manage discrediting information, convey remorse, and appear nonthreatening. The facilitators begin the lesson by writing the following script on the board:

In _____ I was convicted of _____ where I was sentenced to _____. After serving _____ I was released on good behavior. While incarcerated _____, _____, _____. Since my release I have _____. Given this opportunity would keep me on the right track.

Next, one of the facilitators acts out the script. Here is one of Walter's performances:

WALTER: In 1998 I was convicted of selling drugs. I was sentenced to 15 years but was released after 12 years for good behavior. While I was incarcerated, I realized that I had made some poor choices in my life and decided to make a change. I enrolled in a GED program and received my high school diploma because I think education is important. I also complete various life skills classes. Since my release I have taken time to volunteer and mentor at-risk youth in my community, and I am currently seeking employment.

After his performance, Walter breaks down the script line by line. According to Walter, the most important aspect of performing rehabilitation is showing remorse by taking personal responsibility for the past. He emphasizes that men must frame their criminal history as a willful choice and not downplay it as a mistake or something that was out of their control. He tells the class:

WALTER: I took responsibility for my actions. There are no mistakes, only choices. You made choices. You don't mistakenly rob someone. You made choices. It don't matter that you were innocent. You were convicted, and that's all that people see. You gotta take ownership. Take responsibility so people don't ask questions. I don't have to tell you all the details because I took responsibility.

For Walter, taking personal responsibility was not just an issue of morality; it was also strategic. Walter is trying to teach the class to "see like an employer." The person conducting the job interview doesn't care that the person in front of them was wrongfully convicted or that they were pushed into crime because they grew up in an impoverished and violent neighborhood. All the interviewer can see is that the person sitting across from them has been convicted of a crime, and the interviewer needs to decide whether they are willing to take a risk on hiring a person who may be deceitful, thieving, or violent.

Indeed, staff members often point out that (White) middle-class employers likely have never in their lives interacted with someone who has been to prison. Eric tells the class, "For a lot of these employers, the only thing they know about prison comes from that TV show *Oz*. You can't come in confirming those stereotypes." By conveying remorse through the language of personal responsibility, formerly incarcerated men can counter negative stereotypes that depict criminalized men of color as predatory and dangerous. Instead, they can tap into broader cultural narratives about redemption and forgiveness and show that they are penitent men looking for a second chance.

Although staff members emphasized the moral dimensions of remorse, they acknowledged that these displays of remorse were performances that needed to be practiced. Mastering the art of performing rehabilitation required a significant amount of dramaturgical labor. Inside the class, the facilitators ran through drills in which they cold called program participants and had them answer the conviction question in front of the class. There were multiple rounds of mock job interviews in which staff reviewed and critiqued participants' performances in front of the class. Outside of class, men practiced their performances as homework. All in all, formerly incarcerated men spent nearly half of the two-week class strategizing about and practicing for job interviews. But these lessons were just the start of men's employment journeys. It could take months or even years for the men to fully perfect their performance of rehabilitation, and even then, they might still feel out of place. Eric told the class about his own experience of learning to perform remorse for employers:

> ERIC: I'm not used to being a nice guy. I had to learn how to talk to people. I used to get so nervous before job interviews. I would smoke like two 200 [extra-long] cigarettes before an interview because I was so nervous. One day I thought, "Why am I so scared to talk to these people?" . . . In my old world I didn't fear no fear. Didn't matter where I was. I would go out looking for what I was trying to get, knowing full well that someone could ambush me and rob me at any second. I had to learn that the people sitting across from you in that interview are just people. They have problems of their own. They could have committed just as many crimes as you, they just never got caught.

Eric discussed how he got over his anxiety by learning to treat job interviews as a performance. He told the class, "I act. I put it on. You gotta show remorse." Eric pretended that he was just asked about his conviction. He looked down and took a deep breath. He looked up and began speaking, but his voice sounded sheepish and repentant, "Oh, I'm glad you brought this up because it's the hardest part of the interview and I want to get this off my chest. Well, my last conviction was in 2007." Eric stopped midsentence and switched back to his normal voice to illustrate the performative nature of job interviews. Walter also emphasized the performative aspects of job interviews:

WALTER: You gotta be an actor for 15 minutes. . . . It's not like acting, but to get the job you have to rehearse. . . . It's like a fair hearing at HRA. . . . You get everything together. You get that letter from someone vouching for you, you get yourself together for the hearing. . . . You were moving. . . . You strategically planned all that, and you got it done. . . . That's the same effort you have to put into this.

Part of crafting an effective performance was learning to frame discrediting information in the least threatening way possible. Walter described this as "a language game." He told the class, "The little words make people think certain things. Say sale of controlled substances instead of *criminal* sale of controlled substances. Just say larceny. You don't have to specify grand or petty. Just say robbery, you don't have to say if it was armed or not." Later in the lesson he told the class, "When talking about your sentence, always state the back number. If you were sentenced to 12–18 years, say 18. If you say 12–18, and then it took you 14 years to get out, people are going to be wondering why it took you an extra two years. But if you say 18 and you got out in 14, it looks better."

Facilitators also encouraged program participants to discuss how they were rehabilitated inside prison, even if that wasn't their experience. Eric told the class, "We've all been incarcerated. We know that there's no rehabilitation or correction going on in there." Nonetheless, facilitators encouraged program participants to discuss their time in prison as a period of reflection and reform. They coached program participants to emphasize that the reason for their release was for good behavior. Walter explained, "The key thing is to highlight good behavior. That you was rehabilitated. It's all a language game."

At the same time, Walter encouraged program participants to be vague about their rehabilitative programming. "Don't say substance abuse or anger management classes. Say Life Skills Program instead. That way you're just learning about life and you don't have to label it. Don't get back into details." By avoiding the details, program participants could discuss having taken active steps to atone for their criminal pasts without further stigmatizing themselves by revealing a history of addiction or violence.

Although staff members acknowledged that program participants were engaged in a strategic performance, they nonetheless emphasized that the most effective performances were the ones that were sincere. As Walter wrapped up the lesson, he told the class, "Sometimes people only hear the crime. You gotta have a voice. You gotta make someone believe in you. But if you don't believe in you, it's all for nothing." He later compared showing remorse during a job interview to giving an allocution statement in court, "It's like copping out," he told the class. "You gotta believe in the remorse."

. . .

These lessons in performing rehabilitation illustrate how becoming "institutionally legible" is an ambiguous process. Men construct performances to fit into institutionally prescribed categories of how an idealized reformed man should act. However, these performances cannot be neatly categorized as authentic reflections of men's internal selves or as superficial pantomimes designed to game the system. Indeed, as Sweet points out, "Authenticity and strategy are entangled" during institutional performances.[38]

Men were constantly negotiating this tension between authenticity and strategy in their performances of rehabilitation. For men who grounded their reformed identities in the rhetoric of twelve-step programs, the language of choice and personal responsibility resonated with their experiences of recovery. Taking accountability for their past wrongs was something they had done repeatedly in twelve-step meeting rooms. It wasn't a stretch for them to do the same in front of employers. At the same time, these men nonetheless recognized the strategic aspects of systems navigation and tailored their performances to fit the needs of the situation at hand.

For example, Eric had a long history of addiction and drug dealing. He expressed an abiding commitment to leading a lifestyle of recovery and committed himself to shepherding other men through the trials of reentry. But he also recognized the dramaturgical nature of performing rehabilitation for middle-class employers. Although Eric found meaning and identity in the rhetoric of recovery, he also learned how to leverage this language to make himself "legible" to institutional authorities as a reformed man deserving of inclusion. Indeed, part of Eric's journey of recovery was teaching other men how to use the language of remorse and personal responsibility to strategically navigate interactions with institutional gatekeepers. Similarly, Walter taught program participants how to play the "language game" to strategically present themselves in the least threatening way possible. At the same time, he emphasized how men's performances needed to be authentic expressions of remorse. According to Walter, if men's performances weren't coming from a sincere place of internalized reform, employers would see right through them.

The process of becoming professionally poor illustrates that the runaround is not only punitive and exclusionary; it is also a productive technique of social control. The runaround "molds, trains, builds up, and creates subjects."[39] Navigating the institutional circuit trains men to align their actions and identities with the state's categories of deservingness. In order to access public aid and avoid reincarceration, formerly incarcerated men must show that they are able to follow rules, control their emotions, remain sober, and accept the most immediate and available work. The routine hassles and indignities of the runaround train men to conform to these expectations of deservingness. Being constantly made to wait teaches men how to be patient; managing overstuffed appointment schedules teaches them time management skills; feeling constantly degraded by frontline actors trains men to distance themselves from negative stereotypes associated with the undeserving poor; living off meager welfare benefits teaches men budgeting and deferred gratification; and constantly interacting with overworked, street-level bureaucrats teaches them emotional control and conflict resolution.

Men who learn to navigate the institutional circuit are held up as reentry "success" stories who prove that with enough grit and the right attitude, it is possible to overcome the bureaucratic barriers to reentry. Their relative success reinforces dominant cultural understandings "of who is fit to belong as a permanent and full member of society and who is not."[40] By making themselves institutionally legible, men construct downward-facing symbolic boundaries between themselves and the undeserving poor.[41] This boundary work reinforces men's reformed identities and facilitates interactions with institutional gatekeepers. But in doing so, men unintentionally reify the state's categories of deservingness and "solidify a stratified system in their own communities."[42]

Their success reaffirms the notion that formerly incarcerated men are not entitled to social inclusion after their release. Instead, they must engage in bureaucratic labor to *earn* their place back in the social order.[43] Only men who undertake the impossible task of navigating the institutional circuit— who learn to tolerate the hassles and indignities of the runaround, who devote themselves fully to complying with a dysfunctional and disciplinary network of bureaucracies, and who learn to contort their biographies to align with dominant institutional understandings of worthy citizenship— deserve the fruits of social inclusion. Those who fail to live up to this task, who succumb to the stress and hardship of severe deprivation or who refuse to tolerate the frustrations of bureaucratic disempowerment, deserve to be punished and excluded until they can live up to these ideals.

And yet, even when men transformed themselves into reentry "success" stories, they remained trapped at the margins of mainstream social life. Although becoming professionally poor facilitates access to basic material necessities that kept formerly incarcerated men housed and fed, these resources were meager and temporary. They were only ever enough to patch men up from one crisis to the next, not enough to lift them out of poverty.[44] What is more, the bureaucratic labor required to access these meager benefits was so time consuming that it left little time to pursue economic independence, keeping men stuck in cycles of poverty and bureaucratic processing. Men could earn stacks of rehabilitation certificates and learn how to present themselves as "good" ex-prisoners and yet continue to accrue child support debt and face recurrent episodes of unemployment and housing insecurity.

Indeed, research suggests that the practices of becoming professionally poor actually have little material value. Sociologist Reuben Miller finds that certificates of program completion did very little to help the formerly incarcerated men in his Chicago study find work. As one program administrator observed, "My guys got 14 certificates and no job."[45] Similarly, sociologist Lynne Haney finds that child support judges give little regard to men's self-presentation in court or their certificates of completion for responsible fatherhood programs.[46] Instead, judges' sole concern is whether or not men pay. Other than paying child support, there is nothing men can do to prove that they are good fathers.

Over and over again, formerly incarcerated men are promised that by internalizing cultural narratives of individualism and personal responsibility, they will be rewarded with the fruits of social inclusion. But more often than not, men remain excluded from mainstream social life. As sociologists Timothy Black and Sky Keyes argue, these cultural narratives set men up for failure and disappointment.[47]

And yet despite these disappointments, men nonetheless hold onto these narratives of individualism. By casting themselves as masters of their own destiny, men were able to cling to a sense of dignity and autonomy amid the degradation and disempowerment of the runaround. These narratives also resonated with their personal biographies. As former drug entrepreneurs, men formed masculine identities during their young adulthood around narratives of self-reliance and competition. Men continued to draw upon this "hustler mentality" to help them remain resilient amid the constant hardships of reentry. Narratives of individualism also aligned with men's profound distrust of the state. Men had long histories of harassment and abuse at the hands of state actors; they had little faith that the institutional circuit would be any different. Instead of relying on the state for help, they took it upon themselves to achieve reentry success on their own terms, despite the steep odds. In the next chapter we explore how men coped with the incongruity between their desire to achieve reentry success on their own terms and the ongoing material hardships they experienced long after they had desisted from crime and become "good" ex-prisoners.

SIX

Backsliding

PETER WORRIES where his next meal will come from. "I'm not used to living like this. Being broke all the time," he tells me as we walk down the block after our interview. Peter was a 34-year-old Black man. I got to know him over several months in 2014 while he participated in the Responsible Fatherhood Program at Uplift. Peter had spent his teens and twenties embroiled in the underground economy, earning fast money selling drugs and committing robberies. At 19 he was convicted of manslaughter and served an 11-year sentence in state prison. When I interviewed him in April 2014, he had been out of prison for four years. Two months prior to our interview he had lost his apartment and moved into a homeless shelter. He was receiving public assistance and was in the process of applying for a scatter-site housing program, which required him to manage a schedule of HRA verification meetings, a mandated BTW program, a psychiatric evaluation for his housing application, and his fatherhood class at Uplift.

In addition to facing food insecurity, Peter struggled with various health conditions. A week prior to our interview, he had gone to the ER for severe back pain, where they gave him Motrin and a prescription for pain medication. Even though he has Medicaid insurance, he couldn't afford the $4 copay for the prescription. He seemed ashamed about his inability to pay for his prescriptions. He told his classmates at Uplift, "I got a prescription I can't even fill. I ain't got $4. I'm that broke. Being broke is like a disease." Peter worried that he wouldn't be able to afford his asthma inhaler the next time it runs out. "I could be running around without an asthma pump because I ain't got $4," he told the class.

Although Peter was enrolled in various employment programs, he struggled to find work as someone with a violent criminal past. He discussed how he wished that there was a time limit on how long employers could ask about his criminal history. "[E]verybody always says, move on, move on. But it's always over your head." He continued, "You wanna make sure that there's no liability to your company. I can understand that. But . . . again, I was 19 when that happened. Here I am, I'm 34, and I'm still facin' consequences. I thought the purpose of incarceration was to be my punishment. So, when I'm out now, my punishment is supposed to be over. Why is it I'm still bein' punished permanently?"

Given the myriad obstacles he faced in achieving economic security, Peter discussed how he was struggling to avoid falling back into his old lifestyle. He told me, "I have to admit, right now I'm still hangin' on to like the last string. I'm still ready to just say, you know what? Forget doin' this the right way. Go find a couple of my old friends and [say], 'Like, listen, let's set up shop again.' I don't wanna do that."

• • •

Our most common measure of reentry success is the absence of recidivism. People "succeed" in reentering society when they no longer have contact with the criminal legal system. By this metric, Peter is a reentry "success" story. He had avoided criminal legal contact for four years.[1] But as Peter's case illustrates, simply avoiding contact with the criminal legal system does not equate with societal reintegration. Peter struggled to attain basic aspects of social inclusion. He struggled with housing instability, food scarcity, unemployment, and chronic health conditions. In his efforts to access basic material necessities, he became enmeshed in the institutional circuit of transitional housing facilities, public assistance programs, and community-based service providers. Although he had avoided criminal legal contact, he remained trapped at the margins of mainstream social life.

Like Peter, almost half the men I interviewed had avoided reincarceration for at least three years but continued to find themselves in dire economic straits. Many of these men had internalized cultural narratives of individualism and were actively compliant with state authorities. Some had obtained stable employment and housing, sometimes for several years before our interview. But despite attaining nominal reentry "success," these men constantly lived their lives on a razor's edge of poverty. In many cases, a job loss, a relapse, or an eviction had derailed relative economic stability and pushed them back into poverty. Even formerly incarcerated staff members at Second

Chances and Uplift lived at the precipice of poverty. They continued to live in disadvantaged neighborhoods, struggled with debt, and suffered from chronic health conditions.

This chapter explores how the "afterlife of incarceration" lingers in the lives of formerly incarcerated men for years after surviving the initial shock of reentry.[2] The shadow of their criminal records continues to circumscribe their life chances, limiting their employment and housing options and straining their family relationships. It also lives on in their minds and bodies, in the form of chronic physical and mental health conditions that are compounded by severe deprivation. This chapter illustrates how dominant metrics of reentry success miss the ongoing material struggles returning citizens face long after they leave behind criminal careers. And it illustrates how the institutional circuit functions to keep returning citizens trapped in cycles of poverty and bureaucratic processing rather than serving as conduits for social inclusion.[3]

LIFE AFTER REENTRY

Most longitudinal studies of prisoner reentry focus on measuring broad patterns of recidivism over time. Perhaps the most comprehensive statistical analyses come from the Bureau of Justice Statistics. Using administrative records from 30 states, BJS researchers found that 83 percent of people released from prison in 2005 had been arrested at least once over a nine-year period, with the vast majority of arrests occurring within the first three years of release.[4]

These numbers suggest that avoiding criminal legal contact is difficult to achieve for the majority of returning citizens. However, these studies tend to flatten the reentry process and paint a superficial picture of life after release. They reduce returning citizens' complex biographies and lived experiences to a binary outcome that tells us little about the context of returning citizens' daily lives and the factors that precipitate criminal legal contact. In recent years, a growing body of qualitative research has worked to add nuance and context to our understanding of the period following release. However, most of this work focuses on the initial shock of transitioning from incarceration to community, the period when the risk for recidivism is at its highest. The most comprehensive qualitative study to date followed a cohort of returning citizens for three years.[5] But what happens to returning citizens after the initial period of release? This chapter sheds light on the ongoing material struggles that formerly incarcerated men continue to face in the long "afterlife" of incarceration.[6]

Of the forty-five men I interviewed, eighteen reported no criminal legal contact, including arrest or reincarceration, for at least three years prior to our interview. Nine had avoided contact for three to five years and nine had maintained no contact for six years or more.[7] Despite complying with state authorities and avoiding reincarceration, these men continually struggled to attain a basic level of living commensurate with full community membership. They lived in a constant state of material insecurity. Almost all lacked independent housing. Only three men reported living in their own apartments. Everyone else I interviewed relied on family members, romantic partners, and transitional housing facilities for shelter (see table 1 in the introduction). As men of color with criminal records, limited education, and spotty work histories, they also struggled to maintain stable jobs. They experienced recurrent episodes of unemployment and had to turn repeatedly to family members and safety-net bureaucracies to meet their basic material needs. And many suffered from chronic physical and mental health conditions that resulted from years of trauma, substance misuse, and incarceration. For some men, their daily lives were marked by constant cycles of poverty and bureaucratic processing.

Severe Deprivation and the Institutional Circuit

Travis had been living in the shelter system for three and a half years when I interviewed him in 2014. At the time of our interview, Travis was 33 years old and was the sole caregiver for his 5-year-old autistic son.[8] Travis was born in Puerto Rico but moved to the mainland United States when he was 6 years old. He first began using drugs at 12 years old and began injecting heroin at 15. He used heroin and crack heavily for the next 13 years, racking up 29 arrests and five felony convictions for drug-related charges. He also contracted hepatitis C. "I went through a lot," Travis told me. "I had about three overdoses that I didn't think I was gonna come back from. . . . You know, I used to live in an old house, I used to eat out of trash cans, I used to smoke cigarette butts from the floor. I ain't had no problem sleeping next to a rat at night."

In 2008 Travis was released from prison and got sober. He said he hadn't had any contact with the criminal legal system since then. Travis was mandated to a residential treatment facility upon his release. He met a woman from the program, and they began a romantic relationship. She gave birth to a son in 2009 but claimed that another man was the father. Travis obtained a paternity test and proved that he was the child's biological father. He took sole custody of the boy when the child was two months old and has been the child's primary caregiver ever since.[9]

Travis was living in Philadelphia at the time, but after he split with his son's mother, he moved to New York City to live with his sister and her boyfriend. "I had nowhere to go," Travis explained. But his sister's studio apartment was too small for four people. "It was kinda crowded," Travis said. Travis's sister suggested that he move into the shelter system. "She told me to go to the shelter system and try to get a job and work your way out from there. And I've been there ever since [2011]."

Travis's son suffers from seizures and was diagnosed with autism at 18 months old. As the sole caregiver for a disabled child, Travis had little time to search for work. He last worked in 2012, waving a sign on a street corner for a tax preparation business. Since then, he has survived on food stamps and his son's SSI. "Right now, I'm only receiving $63 in food stamps a month for me and my son because they're saying he receives Social Security, but Social Security is not enough," he explained. Later in the interview he told me, "I budget and try to stretch it, but they want me to save some of it. I have no job, plus his diet, he has a special diet, and transportation's not cheap and his clothes and his . . . it's all so stressful. I'm doing it by myself."

In his spare time, Travis has been participating in various programs to "get on paper" to improve his résumé. "I just go to programs and try to get certificates or something so when I get a chance, I can have a better resume," he explained. Although his son attends school now, Travis has to take his son to neurology appointments and physical therapy sessions. Travis also has to manage his own health issues related to his hepatitis C. On top of managing his and his son's health-care appointments, Travis spends significant time managing the runaround of HRA. He is constantly running back and forth to verification appointments and scrambling to fix clerical errors that block his access to benefits (see chapter 2). "It's like they're always closing out my case and telling me to go all the way there, to have me go back and forth," Travis told me.

Travis embodies many of the characteristics of reentry success. He discussed having left behind his previous lifestyle as a drug user to embrace an identity as a reformed man who takes personal responsibility for his life:

TRAVIS: I went from having cars and stuff to now I'm comfortable walking everywhere, I just got so used to it. And you know, living off welfare, every two weeks depending on a hundred something dollars and going to programs trying to better yourself. . . . [I]t just forces yourself to be humble. Because what can you do about it? Be mad at nothing but yourself.

He has maintained sobriety and avoided criminal justice contact for six years. And he is an involved father who cares for a disabled son. Yet Travis lives life on the margins of mainstream society. He has been unemployed for four years and has spent three and a half years in the shelter system with his son. In addition to being a full-time caregiver for his son, he spends significant time circulating through employment programs and managing a litany of health-care and HRA appointments. Travis's case illustrates how the hassles and degradations of the runaround persist long after formerly incarcerated men attain reentry "success." Despite his struggles, Travis expressed gratitude that he had survived the trials of addiction and incarceration. Toward the end of our interview, he told me, "And you know for me to still have all my teeth, and, um, I don't have HIV or nothing like that, I never caught an STD. You know, I'm not dead. And I'm sane. I have sanity, I'm still intelligent, kinda handsome, I still could attract ladies, and you know, I'm grateful now."

Stability and Backsliding

Even men who were able to find steady employment and independent housing were constantly on the brink of backsliding into severe deprivation. A job loss or an eviction could trigger a major crisis in their lives, erasing years of progress and requiring men to turn to family members or the institutional circuit for material support. Leon, whom we met in chapters 3 and 4, is a prime example. At first glance, Leon appears to be a reentry success story. Leon had spent most of his adult life embroiled in the drug economy and cycling in and out of prison. After being released from jail on gun charges in 2007, he made the decision to go straight for good. When I interviewed him in 2015, he had not had any criminal legal contact for eight years.

After his release, Leon found a steady job working for a bread factory. However, around 2010 Leon and his wife were both laid off from their jobs, and their landlord increased their rent by $400. They decided to move to Pennsylvania with their daughter, where the cost of living was significantly cheaper. After working at Walmart for a few months, Leon was able to land a steady job working for the local water district, while his wife got a job at a hospital. They were able to rent a five-bedroom, two-bathroom house with a yard for $750 a month, about half of what they were paying for their small apartment in New York City. Leon had all of the trappings of reentry success. He had avoided crime and reincarceration for eight years. He had a steady job, independent housing, and strong family bonds. But Leon was just a job loss away from backsliding into poverty.

In 2015 Leon and his wife were both laid off from their jobs, and they were forced to move back to New York City to live with family members. "It was just like a domino effect. Because we didn't even want to come back," Leon told me. They arrived in New York City in late March 2015, about five months before our interview. The move forced Leon to live apart from his family. Leon's mother-in-law offered to take in Leon's wife and daughter, but there wasn't enough space for Leon, so Leon was forced to move in with his aunt in another borough. Although this arrangement was allowing Leon and his wife to save money so they could afford their own place, living apart put a strain on the family:

LEON: Honestly, I'm only there [at my aunt's house] because I'm trying to save money, so me and my wife can put up and get our own place. Because New York is very expensive. You know, she's going through it over there with her parents because she doesn't wanna be there. I'm at my aunt's house, I don't wanna be there. We see each other twice a week and on the weekends and this has been frustrating, very frustrating.

Leon worked tirelessly to save up money for a new apartment for his family. Within a month of moving back to New York City, he was working seven days a week at two jobs. "I was working from 8:00 in the morning to 12:00 at night. Every day, Monday to Friday, and then, the weekends, I would open up my second job and stay 'til closing. So, I was pulling 32 hours just on the weekends. Like, I was getting some money," he told me.

However, in July, about a month before our interview, he was laid off from both his jobs. He enrolled in the Workforce Development and Parents in Transition programs at Second Chances and was placed in a part-time paid internship, earning $8 an hour for 21 hours per week. Although Leon appreciated the internship opportunity, the money he earned "doesn't cut it" compared to what he was earning when he was working two jobs.

As we learned in chapter 4, Leon owed $17,000 in child support arrears to the DSS. Now that he had returned to New York, his debt had caught up with him. His license was still suspended for nonpayment, which blocked him from several job opportunities. Staff at Second Chances had recently set him up for a job interview for a maintenance position. The interview went well, and staff members told Leon that he was a shoo-in for the job, but Leon was still waiting for the final confirmation. "I need to actually hear it from them, you know, and be called in to actually start, to see that employment before I can feel good about it. Because, now, this just has me antsy," he told me.

Leon was struggling with anxiety, and the uncertainty of waiting to hear back about the job was compounding the psychological stress he was under. Indeed, the last year had been incredibly stressful for Leon. Leon was seeing a counselor at Second Chances to help him manage his anxiety, but he discussed the devastating toll this stress had taken on his mental and physical health. He said that he had lost 37 pounds over the last three months due to stress. He explained:

> LEON: [S]tress played a big factor [in the weight loss]. For one point, like, I only eat one meal a day because I'd be depressed. I . . . I . . . I just can't find the urge to eat. I don't sleep well; I've been up for two days now. I took two Ambiens the other night and I can't sleep because I'm constantly worried about employment, job, how I'm gonna put my family back under one roof.
>
> Like, hearing my daughter cry every day, she had this big beautiful bedroom in Pennsylvania. And, now, she's confined to sleeping with her mother in a twin-sized bed at her grandmother's house because my wife's siblings live there with their children. It's . . . it's, kind of, crowded in the house, you know, so, we're, like, trying to put each other back under the same roof, but it's not at our pace. It's at your financial pace, you know. But, listening to my daughter cry, it hurts, like, "Dad, am I gonna see you today?" And, it hurts because she used to see me every day, you know. We lived together. So, it bothers me, you know, but I can't rush. So, you know, I'm faced with that every day. Keeps me up.

Leon's case illustrates how formerly incarcerated men are constantly teetering on the precipice of crisis. Leon enjoyed relative financial stability for several years, but a series of economic downturns left him unemployed and homeless, forcing him to split up his family and move in with relatives. Leon worked tirelessly to save money so he could rent a new apartment but kept encountering setbacks. These financial strains had a corrosive effect on Leon's psychological and physical well-being. He constantly worried about his ability to save enough money to reunite his family under one roof. He stopped eating, lost weight, and couldn't sleep. Despite these strains, Leon nonetheless tried to remain hopeful. Toward the end of our interview he told me, "God has been kind. I'm free, I'm alive, I can walk, I can talk. I can be with my children and my grandchildren. Things will get better. Patience. Rome wasn't built in a day."

Like Leon, Eddie had also established economic stability for several years before being derailed by a layoff. As we learned in chapter 2, Eddie had a steady office job at an insurance company for seven years. He was laid off in 2009 and was still unemployed and receiving public assistance when I interviewed him in 2014. Over a four-year period, Eddie had cycled through multiple BTW programs but had found little help in landing a job. He has dutifully complied with program mandates to apply widely for jobs and accept any available work. "I kept applying, and everywhere I would go, they would . . . I would never get any calls," he told me. He continued, "I put my résumés out, I do all the things they tell me to do, and it's like, 'Nah, nah.' Either I got too much experience, or I don't have enough."

Eddie had extensive experience doing office administration and customer service work, but his BTW program kept sending him for job interviews doing building maintenance or security, jobs for which he had no prior experience. He described the awkward job interviews he went on:

EDDIE: So, I would go to these interviews, but of course my resume says nothing about maintenance. They actually, one time, one of the Back to Work . . . locations, actually took my resume, changed it, and put a job stating that I had maintenance experience. And that was . . . supposedly the last job I had. Then they put the other jobs [doing office administration and customer service below that]. So, the people were like, "I see here your last job was [building maintenance]. Um, prior to that . . . why did you change your, y'know, the field of work?" [I'm] sorta like a deer in headlights, like . . . um, I had to come up with some [story], "Oh, you know, right now, there's hard . . . so, um, I'm pretty much good with my hands and I'm really in need for a job so I would pretty much take anything that I can get, but I am good with my hands, and I know I have experience working with, um, in the field, so . . . ." But they never called me, of course.

Eddie, like many of the men I met at Second Chances and Uplift, found mandated BTW programs entirely unhelpful. Men routinely complained that these programs were not equipped to address the needs of people with criminal records. They reported cycling through BTW and other employment programs for months or even years with little success.

Russell also described his BTW program as more hassle than help. Russell was a 28-year-old Black man who lived with his 5-year-old son, his 1-year old daughter, and their mother. Russell had avoided reincarceration for almost seven years prior to our interview. He was incarcerated on drug distribution charges at 16. He served four years, two in a juvenile facility and two in an adult facility, and has not had criminal legal contact since his release.

Russell was unemployed at the time of our interview and was participating in the Responsible Fatherhood Program at Uplift. Prior to seeking employment help at Uplift, he had worked a series of jobs as a construction laborer and stockroom worker. He had recently participated in a vocational training program in which he earned a half dozen certificates in "green" construction and building maintenance. But like Eddie and Leon, Russell struggled to navigate the labor market with his criminal record. Russell's girlfriend works as a nurse, but her income is not enough to cover household expenses. They recently applied for SNAP benefits, and Russell is required to attend BTW programs.

Since his girlfriend works full time, Russell has taken on the role of primary caregiver for their two sons. He is desperate to find work so he can also contribute financially to his household, but he complains that his BTW program is actually preventing him from finding a job. He says that he is required to show up at his BTW program and sit in front of a computer all day searching for jobs on the internet and sending out his résumé. He sees this as a huge waste of time. He wants to be out conducting face-to-face job interviews at construction sites, not sitting in a computer lab all day. He told me:

RUSSELL: You're taking up my time when I could be going somewhere, going out to interviews and all of this. Don't have me sitting here wasting my time on somebody computer and all of this when I could be going trying to do a face-to-face [interview] . . . Them guys [at BTW] is really not a source for me.

The experiences of men like Leon, Eddie, and Russell illustrate how even formerly incarcerated men who establish a degree of economic security are vulnerable to backsliding into poverty. A sudden layoff had thrust these men back into an unforgiving labor market, where their criminal records were liabilities. Unable to regain their foothold in the labor market, they were forced to rely on family members and safety-net programs to meet their basic material needs. But their experiences illustrate how poor families and public assistance programs can do little to lift formerly incarcerated men out of poverty. They can help men survive conditions of severe deprivation by providing food and shelter, but they are not sustainable conduits to social mobility.

Leon's wife and daughter were forced to move into a crowded apartment where resources were stretched thin. Eddie was reliant on public assistance, but as we learned in chapter 2, he has dealt with repeated clerical errors that resulted in sanctions and lost benefits, requiring him to repeatedly attend fair hearings to restore his benefits. The BTW programs designed to foster economic independence offer little support to people with criminal records. According to Russell, these programs are hollow bureaucratic routines rather than meaningful conduits to employment and social mobility.

For many men, Second Chances and Uplift represented meaningful alternatives to unresponsive BTW programs. Indeed, many of the men I met at Second Chances and Uplift sought out these organizations after having had negative experiences with BTW programs. Peter discussed finally finding the support he needed at Uplift: "[I]t took me four years to finally find some help." Like Peter, other men routinely expressed their gratitude for the support they received at Second Chances and Uplift after feeling excluded and abandoned by other programs for years. But behind the scenes, the formerly incarcerated "success stories" who staffed these programs were experiencing their own struggles.

Staff Struggles

Eric, one of the job readiness facilitators at Second Chances, is a prime example. Eric had a long history of addiction and incarceration. He grew up in the Lower East Side of Manhattan during the 1970s and 1980s, a period when open air drug markets and violent crime were pervasive in the neighborhood. Eric said he was raised by "two heroin parents" and grew up around an extended family of uncles and cousins embroiled in the drug trade. Eric witnessed his first murder at age 12. His cousin was shot and killed while Eric was walking beside him down the street. That same year, Eric experienced his first arrest and incarceration. He would spend the next two decades entangled in the criminal legal system. Over that time, Eric amassed 72 arrests, 30 misdemeanor convictions, and 8 felony convictions, and he served 5 state prison sentences.

Over the years, Eric had made several attempts at going straight. He got his first job as a job readiness facilitator in 1995. He discussed how this early success went to his head. He said he became overconfident and thought he could still sell dope and use drugs on the side while holding down a legitimate job. Eric was eventually arrested on drug charges and went back to prison. Upon his release, Eric got back on his feet, moved to Maryland, and remained out of prison for several years. He got another job, teaching GED prep classes and facilitating job readiness workshops. "I fucked that up too," he told the class. "I was stuck in between two worlds. I wanted to stop going to jail, but I didn't know how to act." Eric's last conviction was in 2007. He was offered the opportunity to participate in an alternative to incarceration program in lieu of incarceration. Since completing the program, he has committed himself to leaving behind his lifestyle of "getting high and hustling."

By the time I met Eric in 2012, he embodied the characteristics of a reentry "success story." He had been out of prison for five years without criminal legal contact. He was maintaining sobriety after three decades of addiction and expressed an abiding commitment to leading a law-abiding lifestyle. He had completed his last stint of probation and was no longer under criminal legal supervision. He had earned an associate's degree and was working toward his bachelor's degree in public policy. And he was economically independent. He rented his own apartment and was on an upward trajectory in his career as a social service facilitator, earning around $40,000–$50,000 a year plus benefits.

The men at Second Chances looked up to Eric as a role model. Most were struggling with conditions of severe deprivation. Their daily lives were marked by the constant stress of hunger and housing insecurity, compounded by the hassles and degradations of the runaround. They aspired to attain the type of material stability that Eric had achieved: a steady career, an apartment of their own, and freedom from the institutional circuit. But despite Eric's outward success, he continued to struggle with material hardship.

On the last day of the workshop, Eric would go around the classroom and ask participants for feedback about their experiences. Participants would often take this opportunity to thank Eric and Walter for their mentorship during the two-week class. One man thanked Eric and told him that Eric should splurge and buy himself a new car as a reward for all the hard work he did in the workshop. Eric replied that he wasn't in a financial situation to afford a car. He told the class, "You have to start stackin or saving money. If I lost my job today it would be really hard for me. I don't have enough money saved to cover my bills for 3 months. You should all have enough money saved up to cover your bills for 3 months." On another occasion, Eric explained to the class, "A lot of people in this workshop get mistaken that Walter and I are riding high and it's not the case. I'm one step ahead of y'all. I just got here first."

Indeed, Eric struggled to keep his head above water financially. He had accumulated tens of thousands of dollars in legal debt over the course of 20 years entangled in the criminal legal system.[10] Upon his release in 2007, Eric owed $22,000 to the Department of Motor Vehicles (DMV). He owed $7,000 of this in fines for multiple counts of driving without a license and other moving violations. The remaining $15,000 was for interest, surcharges, and court fees that had accumulated while he was incarcerated and unable to pay. Eric also owed $15,000 in fines for selling drugs in a school zone, another $2,000 in probation fees, and another $5,000 in other court-related fees and restitution. Eric also had significant medical debt. A few years after his release, Eric was between jobs and was hospitalized for four days because of a gastrointestinal issue. He was uninsured at the time and left the hospital with a $10,000 bill. Eric also took out a student loan to attend community college. While attending, he was reincarcerated and his loan accumulated interest while he was unable to pay.

By the time I met Eric in 2012 he had enlisted the help of pro bono attorneys, who helped him file for bankruptcy and consolidate and reduce some of his $50,000 of debt. Despite negotiating lower payments and working out payment plans, Eric still owed $10,000 to collection agencies related to DMV surcharges and an additional $7,000 in outstanding court fees, probation fees, and other fines. Despite excelling in his career, Eric still had to rely on family and friends for financial support.

Eric's financial struggles were a constant source of stress. At times he flirted with the idea of earning fast money in the underground economy. One Monday in 2013, Eric discussed how he had felt depressed all weekend. He had paid all of his monthly bills that week and was broke until his next paycheck. Unable to go out and spend money, he spent the weekend alone in his apartment. He told the class, "Don't think because you're out of the lifestyle that opportunities aren't there." Over the weekend, a friend approached Eric asking him to vouch for him to another drug dealer. His friend would pay Eric a fee if Eric would assure the dealer that Eric's friend could reliably sell "50 bricks." Despite being desperate for cash, Eric refused to get involved. "These are not options for me anymore," he told the class.

Throughout the course of my fieldwork, Eric was also suffering from a chronic stomach condition. He complained of constant stomach pain and other intestinal issues. He had to repeatedly miss work due to illness or doctor's appointments for diagnostic tests and outpatient procedures. In addition to his stomach issues, he experienced constant colds during the winter. "My immune system is shot," Eric told me. He said that he had seriously considered resigning because he had missed so much work due to his illnesses.

During this time, Eric never got a clear diagnosis for his stomach condition. He suspected that his symptoms might be psychosomatic. Eric often discussed how he suffered from post-traumatic stress disorder (PTSD). During his two-decade career as a drug dealer, he was "shot at, stabbed, robbed, almost murdered." His joints hurt during the winter because he had "broken bones" and had been "beaten up by the police." The constant threat of violence that came with Eric's previous lifestyle took a toll on Eric's mental health. For two decades he lived in a constant state of vigilance against the threat of violence from rival drug dealers, fellow inmates, police, and corrections officers. Although Eric had left this lifestyle behind, he continued to experience intense anxiety. "I got real bad nerves," he told me. Eric was particularly worried about encounters with law enforcement.

Over lunch in spring 2013, Eric told me that he thought his stomach pain was related to his PTSD. He told me how a recent encounter with law enforcement had triggered intense anxiety. Eric had been ticketed for smoking a cigarette on an outdoor train platform. Since the incident, his stomach pain had gotten worse and he had been experiencing intense anxiety every time he saw a police officer. He was afraid that there was an open warrant that he didn't know about, and that at any point he could be rearrested and sent back to jail, ruining everything he had accomplished.[11]

He told me that over the weekend he was standing outside of his brother's house smoking a cigarette and talking to a friend when a cop car slowly drove down the block. He said that even though he wasn't doing anything illegal, he started sweating, his heart started racing, and his hand started shaking. Eric told me that every encounter he had ever had with law enforcement had been negative. "I've had my teeth kicked in. They tried charging me with murder," he told me.

Eric's neighborhood context also took a toll on his mental health. He routinely discussed how he lived in a neighborhood with high rates of violent crime. He discussed living with a pervasive sense of fear that he would be victimized. Seeing teenagers on the corner would trigger his anxiety because it reminded him of the violence he experienced in his youth. I once suggested that Eric deal with stress by exercising. He replied half-jokingly, "You can't jog in my neighborhood. It becomes a sprint. You got kids throwing bottles at you."

Even though Eric was able to avoid victimization, being constantly surrounded by violence took a toll on his mental health. Over coffee one morning, Eric told me that on his 15-minute bus ride to the train station, he passed three murder scenes. At one scene, he saw a woman crying over a dead body. He told me, "It's depressing, John. I'm telling you, I gotta get out of my neighborhood."

Indeed, Eric desperately wanted to move. During a class discussion about managing stress, Eric discussed how he was afraid of the violent crime in his neighborhood. However, his old ways of managing fear were unhealthy, and he needed to learn new ways of dealing with stress. "Is it healthy for me to buy a gun?" he asked the class rhetorically. "No. I need to save money to move out of my neighborhood." On another occasion Eric discussed creating options for himself to avoid resorting to old habits. He told the class, "My neighborhood is not conducive to my recovery. There has to be another option. I've worked hard to make options for myself. When I first got out, I didn't have any options. I had to live in the ghetto. I have options now. I'm not gonna buy a handgun; I'm gonna move out to another neighborhood with a lower crime rate."

But with bad credit and a criminal record, moving to a safe and affordable neighborhood was difficult for Eric. One day in May 2013 while we ate lunch, Eric showed me pictures of a brand-new apartment complex he was hoping to move into. The complex had a pool, a community area, private yards, and scenic views. What's more, a certain proportion of the housing units were set aside for low-income residents. I was excited for Eric. "Nice, dude, get in there!" I told him. Eric was quick to deflate my excitement. "You know what gets me shut down," he replied, referring to his criminal record. Eric later told me that he had been discriminated against five times by real estate agents because of his criminal record. "Yea, I hear ya," I sighed. "I'm trying to find someone to cosign with me," he told me.

Eric did eventually find a cosigner. A year later, in May 2014, Eric moved into a new apartment in a safe neighborhood with the help of his longtime girlfriend, who had good credit and no criminal record. On a Friday morning, Eric was ecstatic to tell me that he was getting the keys to his new apartment that day. He proudly showed me pictures comparing his old apartment to his new apartment. "I'm going from this . . . ," he scrolled through a series of pictures on his phone of his old apartment building: trash and uncollected garbage on the streets, metal bars on all the doors and windows, and uncut grass that is nearly three feet tall. "Fuckin dude never comes by to cut the grass," Eric commented. "To this . . . ," he scrolled through pictures of his new apartment building. It's brand-new construction in what looks like a suburban area. The complex has well-manicured lawns and a tree-lined courtyard. The interior sports brand-new granite countertops and appliances. Eric was elated. "No more fuckin gun shots," he told me triumphantly.

Eric was beaming for the rest of the day. He proudly announced his move during our staff meeting later that day, to a round of applause from his co-workers. As I was leaving the office that day, I overheard Eric talking to two program participants about the importance of making changes in their lives. Using his recent move as an example, he told the men, "I'm trying to live and everything around me is dying. What are you gonna do in a situation like that? Are you gonna die with everything around you or are you gonna get out and live?"

However, despite moving to a safer neighborhood, Eric continued to have ongoing mental health struggles. In August 2014, a few months after his move, Eric confided in me that he was struggling with burnout at work. "I'm tired. I'm this close to losing my mind," he told me, pinching his thumb and index finger together.

Eric had been running back-to-back workshops with no break for the last several months. Usually he would have a weeklong break between workshops to allow him to catch up on other work and prepare for the next cohort of participants. But in recent months Second Chances had taken on new funding contracts, which had increased pressure on the program to move more participants through the workshop. The relentless pace of running back-to-back workshops had taken a toll on Eric's emotional health. "I'm in here, in this workshop trying to help other people, but I'm still going through my own reentry process," Eric told me. He continued, "It's like they tell you, 'Just get a job and you'll be fine.' No mother fucker, I got crazy shit going on in my head."

. . .

I observed similar struggles among staff members at Uplift. Ray was a 59-year-old Black man and the class facilitator for the Responsible Fatherhood

Program at Uplift. Ray had a long history of addiction and incarceration but had been sober and crime free for about a decade when I met him in 2014. Ray parlayed his experience of recovery into a successful career as a group facilitator. Despite these successes, however, Ray struggled with housing insecurity.

I first learned about Ray's housing struggles in late May 2014. Ray facilitated the evening fatherhood class, which ran from 4:00 p.m. to 8:00 p.m. and included a dinner provided by the program, usually pizza. When I arrived at Uplift Ray was in the kitchen getting ready to serve dinner to that evening's Responsible Fatherhood class. As he was setting up pizza boxes and paper plates, I asked Ray how his weekend went. He sighed and began explaining that he had had to move out of his apartment over the weekend. Ray told me that his roommate had been smoking crack and not paying his share of the rent. His roommate owed $5,000 in rental arrears.

Ray had a history of addiction and decided it was best to remove himself from an unhealthy situation. Ray said that he had tried multiple times to get his roommate help. He had lectured his roommate over and over again about how he needed to get sober. Ray told me, "I'm tired of leading a horse to water. He's sick, he's on disability, and he's smoking that stuff. It's not good!" Although Ray was able to remove himself from a bad situation, he had nowhere to go.

Our conversation was interrupted as program participants arrived and began making themselves plates of food. A few minutes later we continued our conversation. "So, this all went down this weekend?" I asked him. Ray took a seat. He stared off into the distance and began grinding his teeth. He sighed and said, "Yeah . . . I don't even have anywhere to go tonight. . . . I might have to go to one of them drop in places [shelters]." He sighed again and shook his head, "I don't know. It is what it is."

Our conversation trailed off as more participants arrived and Ray had to prepare for class. After class, I checked back in with Ray as he was tidying up the classroom. It was around 8:30 p.m. Ray told me that he didn't have anywhere to sleep that night. He told me that the night before he had slept in a 24-hour laundromat. "I wouldn't say I slept, really," he said. His plan for that night was to stay at the office as late as he could and then figure out somewhere to "bed down."

Ray's long-term plan was to rent his own apartment, but he didn't have enough money to afford the upfront costs of an apartment, which in New York City is typically three times the monthly rent (first month, last month, and security deposit). He said that he was going to have to ask payroll for an advance on his paycheck to cover at least his security deposit. Ray hoped to rent an apartment for $800 a month, which was at the upper end of his monthly budget.[12] He would have to tap into his savings to afford the monthly rent, but "at least I'll have my own," Ray said with a shrug. Our conversation trailed off and I started making my way home. I shook Ray's hand and wished him the best of luck, telling him that I'd keep him in my prayers. "I'll be alright," Ray assured me. "This too shall pass."

The following Monday I was back at Uplift to observe a Responsible Fatherhood class, but no one showed up, so Ray canceled the class. I sat with Ray in the computer lab while he searched for apartments on Craigslist. Ray mentioned that he had family members who would probably take him in if he asked them, but Ray would rather keep his distance from his family. Over the years Ray had had multiple disputes with family members over money and felt that staying with a family member would cause more problems than it would solve. Ray continued to search through apartment ads. He had lowered his budget to $600 a month, but most of the places he found looked run down. Even with his modest budget, Ray continued to worry about affording the $1,800 in upfront costs to rent an apartment.

I saw Ray again the following week. His housing search was still ongoing, and he had begun to explore options for moving into a scatter site housing program. Over dinner he traded stories with one of the program participants about the difficulties of completing the onerous application packet. Ray worried aloud that his ongoing housing crisis was putting him at risk of reverting to criminal behavior. He told me, "I'm homeless right now, but I have a job and that's the only thing keeping me from going back. If I wasn't getting an income, I would revert to the things I know how to do. I don't know if I would be a drug dealer. I tried that and I wasn't very good at it. I got three to four years."

Around this time, I began to see Ray less often. Ray kept having to cancel evening classes due to low attendance, so I decided to change my schedule to observe daytime classes, when attendance was more consistent. I saw Ray one more time at the end of July but didn't get an update on his housing situation. I took a hiatus from fieldwork during the month of August. When I returned to Uplift in early September, I stopped by Ray's desk to see how he was doing. Ray's things were gone, and his desk was being used to store old files. I thought that maybe Ray was on a temporary hiatus and would return once attendance for evening classes was more consistent. I asked a staff member if that was the case and they explained, "No, Ray is no longer with us unfortunately." No one mentioned why Ray had been let go, and I didn't feel it was my place to ask Ray's supervisor about what had happened.

Two months later I was chatting with Brandon, a Black formerly incarcerated staff member in his late thirties. Brandon had been an intern at Uplift and was getting ready to take over the evening fatherhood classes. I brought up how Ray used to facilitate the evening class when I started doing my fieldwork. I ask Brandon if he knew what happened to Ray. "Between you and me, he was fired. He was doing some shady stuff," he told me. I told Brandon that I knew Ray was "struggling with some major housing issues," but I didn't know that he had been doing anything "shady." Brandon replied, "Yea and the thing is, this is the type of place where if you need anything all you have to do is ask." I never found out exactly why Ray was fired. Regardless of the exact details, Ray's experience illustrates how formerly incarcerated men are constantly at risk of backsliding into severe poverty. Despite attaining relative economic stability, losing his apartment sent Ray into a downward spiral that left him homeless and unemployed.

* * *

Eric's and Ray's experiences illustrate that reentry "success" is a precarious status. They demonstrate how even formerly incarcerated men who attain career success and economic stability are constantly teetering on the edge of various crises. They show that reentry is not a linear process of transitioning from prison to community, but occurs in fits and starts, with periods of progress and stability interspersed with setbacks and crises.[13]

Eric's housing saga is illustrative of the ups and downs of reentry. Eric lived in a high crime neighborhood where violence and criminal opportunities abounded. Despite his poor credit and criminal history, Eric was able to move into a new apartment in a safe neighborhood with the help of his girlfriend. This was an important step in the right direction, but his ongoing financial and health struggles were constant liabilities that loomed in the background, threatening to derail all of the progress he had made. Eric acknowledged that many of his struggles were, at least in part, self-inflicted. He was realistic that it could take him years to fully achieve reintegration. "It takes 10 years for someone with my background to fully catch up to where I should be as an adult," he told the class.

Ray's case also illustrates how formerly incarcerated men constantly live on the edge of poverty. Ray had remained out of prison and was holding down a steady career in the social service field. But Ray was just one crisis away from backsliding into poverty. When he was forced out of his apartment due to a drug-addicted roommate, Ray found himself homeless. Ray had meager savings and was living paycheck to paycheck. He couldn't afford the upfront cost of an apartment and was experiencing homelessness at the same time that he was trying to serve as a mentor and role model to formerly incarcerated fathers.

CONCLUSION

According to research from the BJS, returning citizens remain at risk for rearrest for up to nine years after release. Indeed, less than 20 percent of people released in 2005 were never arrested again after nine years.[14] However, these numbers tell us little about the context of returning citizens' daily lives that creates the conditions for recidivism. When we look beyond the numbers, we can see how the stress of material insecurity and bureaucratic processing constantly threaten to derail men's progress toward reintegration.

Men like Travis, who subsist on meager public assistance benefits and juggle chronic health conditions and child-care responsibilities, become ensnared by the institutional circuit. They constantly labor to free themselves from cycles of poverty and bureaucratic processing but are beset by bureaucratic barriers that undermine their independence. The institutions ostensibly designed to lift them out of poverty offer minimal support, enough to patch them up from one crisis to the next, but not enough to lift them out of poverty.[15] Accessing these meager public benefits requires so much time and energy that the men are left with few resources to pursue economic independence.

Men like Leon, Eddie, and Russell, who were able to establish stable employment, were derailed by a sudden job loss. They struggled to navigate the labor market under the weight of their criminal records and were forced to rely on family members, public assistance programs, and community-based service providers to meet their basic material needs. And men like Eric and Ray, who had established successful careers and were independently housed, were constantly teetering on the edge of various crises. In all of these cases, men had avoided criminal legal contact for at least three years and expressed a commitment to leading a reformed lifestyle. But their daily lives were marked by constant material insecurity.

These findings illustrate how metrics of reentry "success" that equate successful reentry with the avoidance of criminal legal contact ignore the material realities that shape returning citizens' daily lives. Men's ability to avoid rearrest tells us little about their income, employment, and housing. It offers little insight into their physical and mental health or their relationships with family. In sum, it tells us very little about whether they have attained the most basic elements of social inclusion.

Moreover, metrics of success that focus on arrest or incarceration imply that recidivism results from individual, rather than institutional, failure. It suggests that people who are rearrested continue to make criminal choices and are thus in need of ongoing state surveillance and punishment until they can make better choices. Such an approach ignores the litany of institutional failures that leave returning citizens vulnerable to conditions of severe deprivation.[16] It also ignores the ways in which the recurrent experience of procedural injustice exacerbates the stress of severe deprivation and undermines trust in state authority, creating conditions that increase the risk of recidivism. Our metrics of reentry success must look beyond recidivism to include metrics of social inclusion like employment, housing, and health. They must also measure the behavior of institutions, not just individuals, to identify gaps in the safety net and use these data to hold the state accountable for failing to protect vulnerable citizens and foster their social inclusion.

Conclusion

CITIZENSHIP AND SOCIAL JUSTICE IN
THE AGE OF MASS PRISONER REENTRY

AVOIDING REINCARCERATION and accessing public aid requires formerly incarcerated men to navigate a fragmented and punitive institutional circuit of parole, public assistance agencies, transitional housing facilities, community-based service providers, and family welfare bureaucracies. But rather than serving as a conduit for social inclusion, the institutional circuit perversely undermines reintegration. Men experience a litany of hassles, costs, and degradations as they navigate the institutional circuit, an experience I call "getting the runaround." More than just a series of inconveniences, the runaround functions as a bureaucratic barrier to reentry that extends the state's power to punish. The runaround exacerbates the stress of severe deprivation, reinforces distrust of state authorities, and ultimately undermines successful reintegration. As men grew older and embraced identities as reformed men, they learned to cope with the stress of the runaround by treating systems navigation as a full-time job. But even when men embraced ideologies of personal responsibility and complied with state authorities, they experienced persistent material hardship for years after attaining nominal reentry "success."

What can these men's experiences of "getting the runaround" teach us about punishment, welfare, and citizenship in the era of mass prisoner reentry? What can they tell us about the role of the state in shaping life course transitions and masculine identities? How can their experiences inform how we measure and assess reentry success? And how can their experiences help us to imagine alternative systems of prisoner reintegration organized around principles of social justice and inclusion?

Men's experiences of the runaround provide insights into the ways in which citizenship is diminished in the era of mass prisoner reentry. Claiming status as a member of a political community is a dynamic and often inconsistent process. Sociologist Evelyn Nakano Glenn argues, "Citizenship is not just a matter of formal legal status; it is a matter of belonging, including recognition by other members of the community. Formal law and legal rulings create a structure that legitimates the granting or denial of recognition. However, the maintenance of boundaries relies on 'enforcement' not only by designated officials but also by so-called members of the public."[1] Glenn differentiates between formal citizenship and substantive citizenship. Formal citizenship refers to "law on the books" or the formal written statutes, policies, and court cases that confer citizenship rights. Substantive citizenship, on the other hand, refers to "law in action" or "the actual ability to exercise rights of citizenship."[2]

There are thousands of "laws on the books" that formally block returning citizens from accessing basic aspects of citizenship. But the runaround draws our attention to the "law in action," highlighting the informal institutional processes that undermine the ability of returning citizens to exercise the substantive rights of citizenship. In these ways, the runaround contributes to what sociologist Susan Sered calls "diminished citizenship."[3] The concept of diminished citizenship highlights the dynamic and inconsistent "*processes* by which various populations, at various times, can experience some but not all of the rights of citizenship."[4] Although study participants enjoyed some aspects of formal citizenship and were free from the most coercive aspects of carceral control, their inclusion as full community members was routinely diminished by the runaround.

First, the runaround weakened returning citizens' social rights. The financial and opportunity costs of the runaround routinely undermined study participants' ability to attain a basic standard of living commensurate with full community membership. Long waits, overlapping appointments, complicated paperwork, rigid rules, and frequent clerical errors cumulatively functioned as bureaucratic barriers that blocked men's access to social welfare benefits, such as food stamps, general assistance, and supportive housing. Without access to these stabilizing resources, men faced a constant grind of poverty survival, with the strains of hunger and housing insecurity eroding their physical and psychological well-being. For men unable to rely on family members or romantic partners for material support, they had to turn to shelters and three-quarter houses, which exposed them to violence, drug use, crowded conditions, and exploitation by landlords that further weakened their social right to adequate living standards.

The runaround also undermined men's right to participate in the economic sphere as workers and consumers.[5] Men spent so much time keeping up with the litany of overlapping bureaucratic mandates necessary to avoid reincarceration and access public aid that they felt unable to pursue economic independence. These opportunity costs undermined men's ability to conduct job searches or participate in educational or vocational training programs, activities that would allow them to attain not only a better standard of living but also the dignity associated with paid work and the ability to "freely purchase goods and services" in the consumer economy.[6]

Additionally, the runaround diluted men's civil rights. Men had to constantly relinquish their rights to privacy, personal liberty, and free movement to comply with the mandates of the institutional circuit. To avoid reincarceration, men on parole had to acquiesce in constant surveillance, including frequent appointments, home visits, and drug tests. They also had to abide by curfews, comply with restrictions on where they could travel or reside, and participate in mandatory rehabilitative programs. Accessing public assistance similarly required men to submit to surveillance and comply with various work-related mandates or risk losing access to basic material necessities.[7] Residing in transitional housing facilities also entailed deprivation of personal liberty. Men residing in shelters had to abide by a curfew and comply with mandatory programming to maintain access to their beds. Those living in three-quarter houses had to attend mandatory treatment sessions or risked eviction. Residential treatment facilities entailed the most significant deprivations of liberty.[8] Residents were under constant surveillance, from both staff and other residents. They had to attend mandatory treatment sessions, submit to drug tests, and complete house chores. They were also not allowed to control their finances and had to earn the privilege to use a phone, receive visitors, or leave the facility. Breaking the rules meant further losses of personal liberty and potential eviction. These forms of surveillance and punishment are linked across these various systems. For example, a sanction from HRA could cascade into a sanction from a transitional housing facility, which in turn could trigger a sanction from parole.

Men's experience of diminished citizenship reflects how the runaround is rooted in profound power asymmetries between returning citizens and the state. Returning citizens are subject to the decisions of institutional gatekeepers, who wield power over men's ability to access public benefits or exercise personal liberty.[9] Men experience these unequal power relations as extensions of the state's power to punish. The runaround functioned as a kind of procedural punishment that communicated stigma and diminished returning citizens' rights through mundane, often hidden bureaucratic processes that operated outside the bounds of formal criminal sentencing. However, the runaround was not only repressive and exclusionary. It also has productive effects, working to mold and train returning citizens into governable subjects.[10]

On the one hand, the stress and hassle of the runaround push men to be the types of defiant and unruly men the system is designed to govern. The runaround exacerbates the strains of severe deprivation and reinforces men's distrust of state authorities. Under these conditions, men become vulnerable to interpreting what may have been minor inconveniences as forms of intentional abuse or disrespect. Men respond to this sense of disempowerment with resistance. They get into arguments with frontline staff, disobey institutional rules, and engage in "system avoidance."[11] These "compensatory manhood acts" allow men to regain a sense of autonomy amid the degradation of the runaround, but they result in losing access to material resources and increasing the likelihood of reincarceration.[12] What's more, their resistance confirms cultural expectations that criminalized men of color are aggressive and oppositional to authority—the kinds of men in need of ongoing state surveillance and punishment.

On the other hand, the routine hassles and indignities of the runaround train men to align their identities with the state's categories of deservingness. Despite their ongoing experiences of diminished citizenship, men labored to gain recognition as deserving citizens. As they aged out of crime and embraced identities as fathers, they yearned for the trappings of a respectable middle-class lifestyle. They viewed complying with the demands of the institutional circuit as a means of achieving their goals of economic independence and involved fatherhood. To that end, they developed a variety of psychological tools to cope with the stress of the runaround. They constructed reformed masculine identities, casting themselves as men capable of rising above the stress and degradation of procedural injustice through grit and self-reliance. The institutional circuit played a significant role in shaping these practices of identity work. Cultural narratives of individualism and resilience were institutionalized in the curriculum of rehabilitative programs inside prisons and throughout the institutional circuit. Over time, men internalized these narratives and drew on them to craft reformed identities.

Gaining recognition as worthy citizens also required a significant amount of bureaucratic labor, so much so that men had to treat it as a full-time job, what Andre called being "professionally poor." Men labored to make themselves "legible" as deserving citizens by "getting on paper" and "performing rehabilitation."[13] This "rehabilitative labor" trained men to become the kind of idealized worker-citizens the state seeks to produce: men who are disciplined, personally responsible, and willing to fulfill their roles as wage workers and family breadwinners.[14] However, by aligning their identities with the state's narrow categories of deservingness, men reified boundaries of deservingness and reinforced patterns of diminished citizenship.

Indeed, the fact that formerly incarcerated men had to treat rehabilitative labor as a full-time job in order to access basic social and civil rights illustrates the degree to which they occupy an "alternate legal reality" wherein they "are subject to laws that conventional citizens are not, and have responsibilities that conventional citizens do not have."[15] It illustrates how formerly incarcerated men are expected to pay an ongoing "symbolic debt" to society in exchange for recognition as citizens. Only men who can pay this debt—those who are capable of tenaciously enduring the hardships and indignities of the runaround, who are willing to internalize the state's messages of personal responsibility, and who are able to engage in the rehabilitative labor of system navigation—are deserving of recognition as full community members. Those who are unable to pay this debt—those who become overwhelmed by the stress and exhaustion of severe deprivation or who refuse to tolerate the frustrations of bureaucratic disempowerment—do not deserve recognition as full citizens.

Thus, in addition to having their social and civil rights routinely diminished by the runaround, formerly incarcerated men are also expected to engage in additional obligations of citizenship that are not required of conventional citizens. As sociologists Reuben Miller and Forrest Stuart observe, formerly incarcerated people are obligated to "offer some social or material benefit to their home communities. No other group is expected to 'give back' in this way, raising questions about what to expect from the most marginalized members of the polity."[16]

What's more, even when men internalize the state's messages of personal responsibility and learn the skills to be professionally poor, they remain trapped at the margins of mainstream social life. Despite attaining nominal reentry "success" by avoiding criminal legal contact, they live their lives on the razor's edge of poverty, just a job loss or an eviction away from backsliding into severe poverty. When men inevitably fall on hard times, the safety-net programs designed to catch them do little to extend their life chances beyond basic survival and low-wage work, providing enough resources to patch them up from one crisis to the next but not enough to lift them out of poverty.[17] Thus, even when men live up to the cultural ideals of deserving citizenship, they continually struggle to attain a level of economic security commensurate with social citizenship.

TOWARD A SOCIAL JUSTICE MODEL
OF PRISONER REENTRY

In this section I present a set of orienting principles for developing a social justice approach to reentry and public safety. I begin by addressing dominant approaches to reducing administrative burden that focus on technological innovation and service coordination. Next I discuss the need to redesign metrics of reentry success so that they focus on addressing the needs of returning citizens. In the final two sections I focus on broader reforms, particularly the need to shrink the carceral state and invest in a more expansive social safety-net.

The Promises and Pitfalls of Reducing the Runaround

Throughout the preceding chapters we have seen how the runaround undermines reintegration. It obstructs access to material resources, exacerbates the stress of severe deprivation, and undermines trust in state authority. How can we reduce the burdens of the runaround? Current approaches to reducing administrative burden either focus on implementing small-scale technological fixes to service provision or involve improving coordination between service providers. Both approaches are promising for reducing various administrative burdens, but they are also limited in their ability to address the root causes of the runaround.

In recent years a variety of technology-based nonprofits have emerged offering digital platforms "to create a more user-friendly safety net."[18] For example, Single Stop provides a digital platform to screen low-income individuals for eligibility for government benefits across a range of programs. Second Chances utilized this technology to provide men with a centralized location to obtain information about benefits eligibility as well as legal debt. For example, Eric utilized Single Stop to find out how much money he owed to the DMV, which helped him coordinate with pro bono lawyers to reduce his debt. Code for America is another technology-based nonprofit that utilizes digital technology to create a "human-centered safety net." In California the organization collaborated with state and local agencies to develop GetCalFresh, an online portal designed to streamline the application process for food stamp benefits. Using their mobile phones or computers, people can apply for food stamp benefits in as little as 10 minutes. All 58 counties in California now use GetCalFresh, leading to a significant reduction in the participation gap between those eligible for benefits and those who have access.[19] Similarly, tech start-up Propel provides a free mobile phone app to five million households that helps them manage their food stamp benefits.[20] The app allows users to check their account balances and track their spending.[21] By functioning more like a banking app, Propel is designed to make users feel more in control of their finances and reduce the stigma associated with receiving public assistance.

Digital technologies offer concrete solutions for reducing administrative burdens and expanding access to social services. However, creating a socially just approach to prisoner reentry cannot rely on small-scale technical fixes alone. Organizations like Single Stop, Code for America, and Propel represent innovative approaches for reducing the burdens of the runaround and reforming our fragmented and stigmatizing safety net. But their existence speaks to the deeper dysfunctions of our contemporary system of poverty governance. The fact that a market exists for tech organizations to "hack" our safety net to make accessing social rights of citizenship more "user friendly" illustrates the failures of the state to protect vulnerable populations from market forces and environmental risks.[22]

Efforts to improve service coordination offer similar promises and limitations. The "one-stop" service model has emerged in recent years as a promising solution for delivering the kind of wraparound services necessary to address the complex needs of people leaving prison. By housing multiple social service agencies under one roof, reentry one-stop centers can improve cross-agency collaboration and continuity of care while reducing redundant paperwork and conflicting appointments. Second Chances was an early adopter of this model, offering a menu of services under one roof, including employment services, substance use and mental health treatment, anger management classes, parenting and relationship counseling, legal aid, benefits application assistance, and GED prep classes.

The one-stop model has been cited as best practice for addressing the diverse needs of people leaving prison.[23] However, the one-stop model has the potential to "widen the net" of carceral control, especially if these programs are administered by sheriff's departments or community corrections agencies rather than private nonprofits like Second Chances. Indeed, Second Chances was uniquely positioned to resist direct collaboration with law enforcement agencies. Its location in a large, well-resourced city meant that it was able to collaborate with an existing social service infrastructure and tap into a variety of funding streams that were not directly tied to the criminal legal system. By contrast, service agencies operating in many small cities, suburbs, and rural areas are forced to rely heavily on collaboration with "police, community corrections, and jails to provide continuum of care so often cited as a necessity for people with complex needs after incarceration."[24] In these remote and resource-scarce places, "police, courts and jails are at the center of the existing social service infrastructure," forcing service providers to rely on the carceral state for funding and service delivery.[25] This blending of law enforcement supervision and social service provision raises questions about whether one-stop centers function as progressive alternatives to social service fragmentation or represent an intensification of the state's capacity to surveil and punish the poor.

For one-stop centers to advance the goals of social justice, they must focus on increasing service coordination without increasing surveillance and punishment. However, much of the political support for one-stop reentry centers is framed around the discourse of recidivism reduction, and funding is often contingent on direct collaboration with law enforcement agencies. As a result, one-stop centers tend to focus myopically on the law enforcement goals of risk management rather than on social justice goals of alleviating poverty and addressing the structural inequalities that underlie mass incarceration. Shifting the dominant paradigm of reentry away from law enforcement and toward social justice means that reforms must go beyond short-term solutions that focus on technological innovation and service coordination. Instead, we must focus on addressing the deeper structural inequalities and institutional failures at the root of mass incarceration in the United States. This will involve long-term investments in universally accessible public infrastructure to reduce our reliance on the carceral state to manage social problems. This work begins by fundamentally reorienting how we conceptualize and measure reentry "success."

Redefine Reentry Success

Over the last decade, policymakers have identified recidivism reduction as a key strategy to reduce the economic and social costs of mass incarceration. Indeed, much of the discourse surrounding prisoner reentry is filtered through the lens of public safety and austerity. Policymakers are only willing to justify reentry services insofar as they can lower recidivism rates and reduce taxpayer spending without jeopardizing public safety.

Under this model, reentry policy making begins and ends with the question of recidivism reduction. Little attention is paid to whether these interventions improve the quality of life of returning citizens. Indeed, as criminologist Marina Bell argues, by making recidivism reduction the standard metric of reentry success, policymakers set "markedly low expectations for what a successful, fulfilling life is supposed to be for populations who are put through reentry programs."[26] She continues, "When these individuals manage to struggle by at minimum baseline standards under oppressive social conditions that led many to crime in the first place, the intervention is considered a success as long as they are tolerating those conditions without acting out in a 'criminal manner.'"[27]

As we saw in chapter 6, formerly incarcerated men toil at the margins of mainstream life for years after successfully avoiding criminal legal contact. But current reentry metrics overlook the experiences of these men. By myopically focusing on men's ability to avoid reengagement with the criminal legal system, current standards of reentry success ignore the material insecurities that formerly incarcerated men continue to face after desisting from crime. These metrics create policy feedback loops that undermine efforts to address the needs of returning citizens. When recidivism reduction becomes the standard metric of rehabilitation, and when that metric becomes tied to funding, it incentivizes service providers to design programs focused on achieving only that metric. As a result, it crowds out other metrics of reintegration and reinforces the idea that reentry success can only be defined in negative terms (i.e., the absence of criminal legal contact) instead of positive terms (i.e., the presence of employment, housing, and other markers of well-being).

Making recidivism the standard metric of rehabilitation also allows policymakers to claim policy success while ignoring the social suffering that returning citizens continue to face.[28] By equating reentry policy "success" with lowered recidivism rates, policymakers are able to claim that money is being saved, prisons are downsizing, and the public remains safe. But such claims obfuscate the fact that "successful" returning citizens (i.e., those who avoid reincarceration) nonetheless remain trapped in cycles of unemployment, housing instability, and institutional processing for years after attaining so-called reentry success. By only measuring reentry success in relation to recidivism, policymakers effectively "disappear" the social suffering that returning citizens experience.[29]

Because the suffering of returning citizens slips through official measures, it becomes easy to ignore, and it allows us to become complacent with the status quo. If we are serious about ending mass incarceration and improving the well-being of returning citizens, we must begin by redefining how we measure reentry success.

Political scientists Elsa Chen and Sophie Meyer illustrate the need for scholars, practitioners, and policymakers to move "beyond recidivism."[30] They argue that even the best measures of recidivism are inadequate for understanding the factors that explain why people recidivate in the first place. Binary metrics that focus on success or failure in avoiding criminal legal contact offer little insight into the material insecurities and institutional failures that create the conditions for recidivism. Moreover, a myopic focus on recidivism overlooks other indicators of progress and vulnerability. As we saw in chapter 6, reentry is a nonlinear process that occurs in fits and starts, with periods of progress and stability interspersed with setbacks and crises.[31] A person's rearrest could indicate reentry failure, but it ignores incremental progress in other areas of reintegration, such as employment, housing, family, or health. Conversely, just because a person is free from criminal legal contact does not mean that they are free from material insecurity or other vulnerabilities that jeopardize their ability to achieve a quality of life commensurate with full community membership.

Chen and Meyer argue for the need to move beyond a threat-based model of reentry that focuses only on measuring returning citizens' risk of recidivism and instead shift toward a reintegration model that focuses on measuring indicators of social inclusion.[32] Indeed, our current metrics of reentry success lack "any standard for a person's quality of life following release."[33] Moving "beyond recidivism" would involve expanding measures of reentry success to encompass indicators of individual well-being and economic security, such as income, employment, housing, and health. Such data would provide indicators of incremental progress and highlight the material insecurities that shape returning citizens' daily lives. This would also mean "collecting information on the availability of programming and resources."[34] Do returning citizens have access to income support, education, vocational training, housing, substance abuse treatment, or health care? If not, such data could identify holes in the safety net and direct resources to address these policy deficits. Moreover, rather than reinforcing a paradigm of reentry that focuses on individual failure, such data could highlight the institutional failures that lead to social suffering and recidivism.

This holistic approach to measuring reentry success would entail a significant project of data integration. It would involve data sharing "between different levels of government and policy domains, between custody and community, and across the public and nonprofit sectors."[35] It would also involve incorporating the voices of returning citizens by combining qualitative interview and ethnographic data with official administrative data sets.[36] As with one-stop reentry centers, projects of data integration must prioritize improvements in service coordination without increasing the capacity of the state to criminalize marginalized populations. Firewalls must be in place to not only protect confidential information, such as health records, but also ensure that law enforcement agencies cannot use integrated data systems as surveillance tools to expand the reach of the carceral state.

With such safeguards in place, data integration will not only provide a more empirically nuanced and accurate picture of the reentry process, but it also can help to fundamentally shift the paradigm of reentry from one "based on risks and failures to a more productive emphasis on needs, resources, and incremental measures of rehabilitative success."[37] Such data can be utilized to identify gaps in services and foster "systems of accountability within the local government that can be rapidly addressed, creating new policy feedback loops that reinforce a re-integrative approach to reentry."[38]

Shrink the Carceral State

A social justice approach to reentry must begin from the premise that there should be fewer people locked in cages in our country. If we lock up fewer people, fewer people will face the challenges of reentry in the first place. However, reducing the penal population is no easy task. It involves not only diverting the "low hanging fruit" of nonviolent, nonsexual, nonserious offenders into community-based alternatives, but also seriously reconsidering how we treat people who are convicted of violent crimes. Indeed, the majority of people incarcerated in the United States are serving time in state prisons for violent offenses.[39] Any serious conversation about reducing the penal population must grapple with the problem of violent crime.

Although ending the war on drugs is an incredibly important step in shrinking the carceral state, drug offenders represent only a fraction of the penal population. People serving time for nonviolent drug offenses account for about 20 percent of all prisoners nationwide. As civil rights attorney James Forman Jr. puts it, "Even if we decided today to unlock the prison door of every single American behind bars on a drug offense, tomorrow morning we'd wake up to a country that still had the world's largest prison population."[40] To truly shrink the carceral state, we must fundamentally reconsider how we punish people who commit violent crimes. Such a shift in penal sensibilities will require us to seek accountability for violence without resorting to incarceration.

First, we must acknowledge that violence is pervasive in the lives of formerly incarcerated people.[41] Most of the men featured in this book grew up in violent contexts and had histories of trauma dating back to their early childhoods. For some, violence was embedded in their households. Travis witnessed his mother's abuse at the hands of a series of violent boyfriends for most of his childhood, with one man even showing up at his mother's workplace, threatening to kill her with a box cutter. Outside their homes, violence was a pervasive aspect of their neighborhood contexts. Growing up in New York City's poorest and most racially segregated neighborhoods during the 1980s and 1990s, most of the men experienced historically unprecedented levels of violent crime unfolding outside their front doors. Eric witnessed his cousin's murder at age 11, seeing him gunned down as they walked down the street together.

Levels of violence continued to escalate in men's lives as they grew into adolescence and young adulthood. Seeking money and respect in the drug economy, they were drawn into a world of predation and violence. Men lived their lives in constant fear of being victimized and had to be willing to engage in violent acts to defend themselves. Indeed, the boundary between "victim" and "offender" is often blurred in these contexts.[42] Men who perpetrate violent acts are also victims of violence themselves. Leon spent over a decade cycling in and out of prison for a series of violent felonies stemming from his involvement in the drug economy. But Leon was also a victim of this cycle of retaliatory violence. He had been shot, stabbed, and slashed multiple times, leading to a variety of physical ailments later in life. Similarly, Eric had been shot at, stabbed, and beaten multiple times throughout his career as a drug dealer and struggles with PTSD as a result.

Sociologist Bruce Western argues that our practices of criminal sentencing must recognize the complexity of violence in the lives of criminalized populations. "The great moral challenge is not to find the innocent among the guilty," he argues, "but to treat with decency and compassion even those who engage in violence."[43] Western advocates for the use of "social adversity mitigation" in criminal sentencing. This approach to sentencing argues that our assessments of moral culpability should not only focus on questions of choice and personal responsibility but also take into account a defendant's wider biography. Such an approach acknowledges how poverty, trauma, housing insecurity, and discrimination circumscribe people's choices and create the conditions for crime to occur. "Social adversity mitigation admits the moral complexity of the social world and acknowledges that a defendant too has suffered harm."[44]

Community-based restorative justice programs are also important avenues for reducing our reliance on incarceration to address the problem of violence. People who have survived violence do not unequivocally equate incarceration with justice. When given multiple options, most survivors say they want accountability from the person who harmed them, not vengeance. In a 2016 study by the Alliance for Safety and Justice, most survivors said that they wanted the person who harmed them to "understand the pain they caused, to acknowledge their accountability in person, and to make a commitment to transform their behavior."[45] Restorative justice programs have a proven track record of delivering this kind of accountability while also maintaining public safety.[46] Expanding these types of pretrial diversion programs, along with eliminating mandatory minimum sentences for all crimes, providing adequate funding for public defenders, and restoring judicial discretion in sentencing, are all crucial steps in shrinking the footprint of the carceral state.[47]

Shrinking the carceral state and addressing violence also means making investments in communities to promote what Western calls "thick public safety."[48] Western argues that "it is not police, courts, and the threat of punishment that create public safety, but rather the bonds of community produced by a raft of social institutions—family, schools, employers, churches, and neighborhood groups."[49] It is this "thick" web of social relationships and institutions that provides stability and predictability in daily life and creates mechanisms of informal social control and collective efficacy that prevent crime in the first place. People who attain economic stability after incarceration do so not because of heavy-handed parole surveillance or the threat of incarceration, but rather through access to the stabilizing institutions of family, education, work, and community. Thick public safety not only protects returning citizens from bodily harm but also provides them with a sense of material security that "lengthens [their] time horizons, allowing them to imagine a future in which it makes sense to invest in themselves and their children."[50]

However, our current approach to public safety continues to rely heavily on the "thin public safety" offered by authoritarian policing and mass incarceration. While these punitive approaches to crime control have been shown to decrease violence, they come at an incredibly high social cost.[51] "Thin public safety" can create order, but it inflicts violence on poor communities of color, erodes public trust in the legitimacy of the criminal legal system, destabilizes families and neighborhoods, and reinforces patterns of poverty and racial inequality.

Sociologist Patrick Sharkey argues that community-based institutions can play a vital role in reducing violence and strengthening community bonds without the social costs associated with militarized policing and mass imprisonment. For example, after-school activities and summer job programs dramatically reduce the chances that young people will become involved in violence. Violence interruption programs have been shown to be highly effective at de-escalating conflicts before they erupt into cycles of retaliatory violence. Reclaiming abandoned lots and turning them into green spaces reduces violence by activating mechanisms of informal social control and collective efficacy.[52] But as is the case with reentry nonprofits, we ask residents and local organizations to do far too much with far too little. If we are to ask local community groups to play a central role in creating safer neighborhoods, then we must commit the same financial resources to them as to law enforcement. Activating community groups should not entail a shrinking of the state, but rather a reorganization of state resources in the name of strengthening communities. We cannot achieve "thick public safety" on the cheap. Instead, it will require proactive investments of state resources to serve the needs of our most vulnerable citizens.

These "front end" reforms must be accompanied by "back end" reforms to the criminal legal system. As we have seen throughout the previous chapters, parole supervision creates a variety of obstacles in returning citizens' daily lives that undermine reintegration. Frequent appointments and long waits destabilize men's daily routines, undermine trust in state authority, and reinforce feelings of degradation, all of which increases the likelihood of noncompliance. Attending mandatory rehabilitative programs occupied significant amounts of men's time, and they were experienced as hollow bureaucratic performances or as punitive social control tactics rather than as meaningful therapeutic interventions. Residency restrictions and other parole conditions forced men into often dangerous, crowded, and exploitative transitional housing facilities.

Many of these hassles stemmed from the fact that parole in New York continues to be primarily oriented toward punishing failure rather than promoting success.[53] Frequent appointments, long waits, mandatory programs, and residency restrictions are all designed to closely monitor the daily lives of people on parole and catch them when they violate the rules. Such practices are grounded in a mission to "trail 'em, nail 'em, and jail 'em," rather than in a fundamental concern with facilitating the reintegration of returning citizens.[54] To the degree that parole focused on promoting reentry success, it largely involved providing referrals to third-party service providers. Thus, eliminating these burdens requires a fundamental paradigm shift in community corrections.

In 2017 the Executive Session on Community Corrections, a group of over two dozen criminal legal scholars, practitioners, and activists, convened at the Harvard Kennedy School of Government to create a blueprint for what such a paradigm shift might encompass. First and foremost, they argue that parole should focus on promoting success rather than punishing failure. Instead of myopically focusing on catching rule breakers, parole should focus on rewarding incremental progress through shorter periods of supervision and less restrictive conditions as people make progress toward their goals. People under supervision should be incentivized to reach reintegrative goals, such as obtaining education or maintaining sobriety, rather than being motivated to just "make it to the end" of their supervision period without being caught for a rule violation. "The supervision period should focus on positive outcomes rather than mere compliance," the group argues.[55]

Community supervision should be less expansive, focusing on a smaller number of high-risk individuals and not lasting for periods longer than two years. Since most reoffending occurs within the first two years of release, periods of supervision should generally not last beyond that. Longer periods of supervision yield diminishing public safety returns and perversely increase the likelihood of recidivism, especially for people at low risk for reoffending. The longer a person is under supervision, the more likely they are to be caught violating a rule. Focusing on catching low-risk rule violators does not enhance public safety and diverts resources away from those most in need of supervision and support.[56]

Community corrections agencies should also work to cut down on "back end" prison sentences for parole and probation violators. This is especially important for reducing the "net widening" effects of community corrections, as community supervision has become an increasingly popular alternative to incarceration.[57] Imposing fewer parole conditions, such as less frequent appointments, eliminating fines and fees, and reducing restrictions on movement and housing, could lead to fewer violations in the first place. Where sanctions are necessary, they should avoid incarceration as much as possible. So-called intermediate sanctions remove people from the community for short periods of time and provide them with supportive services to address the underlying issues that led to the violation. Such sanctions may involve a short jail sentence or a mandatory stay in a residential treatment facility.[58] As part of New York's broader effort to get "smart on crime," its parole officials have begun utilizing intermediate sanctions to punish parole violators. Some men in the study had avoided being sent back to prison through intermediate sanctions. For example, Dwight was required to spend a year in a residential treatment facility for relapsing on heroin instead of being sent back to prison. However, despite being less punitive, intermediate sanctions have been shown to disrupt residential stability and employment.[59] To prevent creating household ruptures, evictions, or unemployment, intermediate sanctions might involve spending weekends or nights in jail or attending mandatory outpatient treatment programs.[60]

Invest in Public Infrastructure

Although this book has been critical of the institutional circuit, particularly the burdens and hardships it creates in the lives of formerly incarcerated men, many institutions on the circuit do indeed provide formerly incarcerated people with vital material support. We should not overlook the fact that programs like Second Chances and Uplift provide real support to real people in real time.[61] They fill crucial holes in our frayed and fragmented social safety net and provide essential support to a vulnerable population that might not otherwise have access to social services. They are also important institutions of civic engagement, providing important venues for community fellowship and political organizing.[62] But we ask nonprofit service providers like Second Chances and Uplift to do far too much with far too little.

We look to community-based nonprofits to resolve large-scale social problems with deep structural root causes, but do not provide them with the resources or public infrastructure to tackle these issues. Instead, we force them into an endless competition over a small pot of public grant dollars, which they must subsidize with private charitable donations. If we were serious about supporting programs like these, we would provide them with more long-term and sustainable funding streams so that they could focus on providing quality services rather than on chasing performance metrics tied to grant dollars. And we would build a more robust public infrastructure around these programs. So many of the problems that frontline staff encountered were due to the fact that formerly incarcerated men had slipped through the cracks in the safety net. Histories of trauma, substance misuse, and institutional failure had left men in a state of "human frailty."[63] Administrative burdens had blocked their access to public benefits, lack of available public housing and lax regulations had forced them into burdensome and exploitative transitional housing facilities, and lack of protection from discrimination meant that they were chronically unemployed and desperate for help from community-based nonprofits. But there was often little frontline staff could do to address these deep structural inequalities beyond teaching returning citizens how to cope with the hardships of reentry. Although Second Chances and Uplift played a vital role in plugging these holes in the safety net, they should be supplements to rather than replacements for a functioning safety net for the poor that provides protection from market forces and discrimination.

Rather than relying on local nonprofits to resolve large-scale social problems, the state must take a more proactive role in fostering the social inclusion of the formerly incarcerated. For example, Second Chances and Uplift could do little to prevent employer discrimination or hold firms accountable for their discriminatory behavior. Protecting returning citizens from discrimination is the job of the state, and the state must play a more proactive role in reducing the collateral consequences of criminal convictions. Reformers have long advocated for lifting formal occupational bans for people with certain criminal histories, as well as "restoring access to social welfare benefits, education grants and loans, and public housing, and doing more to protect an individual's criminal record from public scrutiny or at least disallowing the use of a criminal record in hiring and renting conditions after some reasonable period of time has elapsed."[64]

Ban the box legislation has been a popular policy tool to protect people with criminal records from employment discrimination. New York City's Fair Chance Act prohibits employers from inquiring about an applicant's criminal record until a conditional offer of employment has been made. Moreover, an employer may only rescind an offer of employment based on an applicant's criminal history after they have provided the applicant with a written copy of the criminal background check and a written analysis of the applicant's criminal history in light of mitigating factors, and they must provide the applicant with three business days to provide a written response to the analysis.[65]

New York City's ban the box law is among the most extensive in the country and represents an important step in protecting the rights of the formerly incarcerated. However, discrimination in hiring continues to be widespread. Some evidence suggests that ban the box legislation actually *increases* the likelihood of racial discrimination for low-skilled Black men. When information is unavailable about individual job candidates, employers engage in statistical discrimination. Given Black men's overrepresentation in the prison population, employers assume that every low-skilled Black man they encounter has a criminal record and sort them out of the hiring pool based on this assumption.[66] Moreover, recent evidence suggests there is significant noncompliance with ban the box regulations. One study found that one in five firms was noncompliant with statewide ban the box legislation, with lack of enforcement being a significant driver of noncompliance.[67] These findings illustrate that the state needs to play a more proactive role in protecting vulnerable groups from employer discrimination. Most antidiscrimination enforcement is initiated through private litigation after discrimination has occurred.[68] For returning citizens struggling to survive conditions of severe deprivation, pursuing a high-profile antidiscrimination lawsuit is not a realistic option for protecting their civil rights. Regulators need to take a more proactive role in auditing firms for compliance with antidiscrimination regulations and meting out fines and other punishments for noncompliance.

Expanding opportunities for records expungement would also be an important step. People who obtain records expungements experience significant improvements in their wages and employment trajectories. One study in Michigan found that within one year of obtaining an expungement, average wages increased by 22 percent, driven by unemployed people finding work and underemployed people finding better or steadier jobs.[69] However, obtaining an expungement is difficult. It typically requires a waiting period of several years. It is also a complicated and costly process that entails a significant amount of bureaucratic labor. In New York, an expungement can entail "up to 40 hours from an attorney and court officials over several months," costing an average of $2,200.[70] As a result, there is a significant "uptake gap" between those eligible for expungement and those who obtain one. Just 6.5 percent of people legally eligible for expungement obtain one within five years of eligibility.[71]

Recent reforms have lowered the administrative burdens of obtaining records expungements. In New York, the state automatically expunges convictions for marijuana possession for up to two ounces without a court filing or the payment of fees.[72] These are important steps for expanding record clearance, but they do not help the vast majority of men exiting prison with serious felony records. In most cases, these men are not eligible for expungement.[73]

Even if expungement laws become more liberalized, many of the men had extensive criminal histories that would be difficult to expunge entirely. Moreover, publicly available criminal records databases are rife with errors and "subject to fewer regulations than are those maintaining publicly available credit scores."[74] Indeed, in the digital age criminal records have become a highly valued commodity for employers and landlords. In her study of "digital punishment," sociologist Sarah Lageson shows how the availability of criminal records has proliferated in recent years, driven by an unregulated online marketplace in which private data brokers buy, sell, and disseminate criminal records regardless of their accuracy.[75]

Where expungement is not available, certificates of relief for good conduct could provide "positive credentials" that can mitigate the stigma of a criminal record.[76] However, as we saw in chapter 5, obtaining a certificate of relief requires a significant amount of bureaucratic labor. Like expungement, there is likely an "uptake gap" between those who are eligible for such certificates and those who actually obtain them due to the litany of hassles and costs involved in obtaining one. Reducing these administrative burdens would be an important step in facilitating access to "positive credentials." An example would be utilizing digital platforms to simplify applications and integrating applications into other government databases to reduce paperwork burdens on former prisoners. Rather than requiring returning citizens to produce tax returns or proof that they receive government benefits, data integration would allow state authorities to have direct access to these records.

Beyond reducing criminal record barriers, the state must also play a more proactive role in improving the living standards of returning citizens by investing in universally accessible public infrastructure, such as adequate housing, basic income, public health, education, and employment. Setting stronger wage and benefit floors is one of the most important roles the state can play in improving the living standards of returning citizens.[77] Given their low levels of human capital, formerly incarcerated men tend to be relegated to jobs in the secondary labor market, where they receive low pay, scant benefits, and few opportunities for career advancement.[78] Since jobs in the secondary labor market tend to pay minimum wage, raising the minimum wage would significantly improve returning citizens' living standards and facilitate financial independence. Although the current minimum wage in New York City is $15 per hour, according to the MIT Living Wage Calculator, a single adult with no children living in the New York metro area would need to earn $20 an hour to cover living expenses.[79]

Raising the minimum wage would also have broader structural implications. Sociologist François Bonnet argues that the minimum wage sets the "upper limit" for the generosity of welfare and the humanity of punishment.[80] Bonnet's argument is based on his observation that the relationship between punishment and welfare in contemporary society is grounded in the Victorian concept of "less eligibility." According to the principle of less eligibility, welfare benefits must be less desirable than low-wage work. A person receiving public assistance cannot have a higher living standard than the lowest paid worker, otherwise the poor would abandon work for welfare. As a corollary, punishment must also be harsh enough so that welfare is more desirable than crime. A prison inmate should not have a higher living standard than a welfare recipient, otherwise the poor would turn to crime without fear of incarceration. According to Bonnet, this explains why countries with higher living standards for the lowest paid workers have more generous welfare benefits and more humane prisons than countries with low living standards for the lowest paid workers. He argues, "In Scandinavian countries, the minimum wage is so high that the upper limit for punishment and welfare allows for generous subsidies to the poor and lenient punishment; in the United States generalized low-wage work at the bottom of the labor market only allows for stingy welfare and harsh punishment. In Brazil, the poor survive through the informal economy and under the threat of death squads."[81] Thus, according to Bonnet, raising the minimum wage will not only improve the living standards of formerly incarcerated people, it can also help raise the "upper limit" of welfare generosity and the humanity of our criminal legal system.

Improving the living standards of returning citizens also requires the state to take a more proactive role in increasing housing capacity. This is especially important for returning citizens of color, whose lives have been circumscribed by histories of generational housing discrimination. As we have seen throughout the book, returning citizens struggle with housing insecurity not only in the period immediately following release, but also for years after sustained periods of desistance.

Housing insecurity is a particularly acute problem in New York City. New Yorkers have become increasingly rent burdened over the last two decades. Between 2005 and 2012, median rents in New York City increased by almost 40 percent, while median wages remained essentially stagnant.[82] Despite the high demand for affordable housing, such units are in short supply. For every two low-income households in need of an affordable unit, there is only one available. While housing insecurity is not a problem exclusive to the formerly incarcerated, their insecurities are exacerbated by the various formal and informal barriers that obstruct them from obtaining affordable housing, including bans on residing in public housing, parole restrictions, and discrimination by private landlords. As a result, formerly incarcerated men rely heavily on family members and romantic partners for housing, often straining already overcrowded households with overstretched family budgets. For men unable to rely on networks of support for housing, they must turn to the market for transitional housing facilities, where they are exposed to overcrowded conditions, violence, drug use, constant surveillance, and exploitation by landlords.

A variety of reforms could increase housing access for returning citizens. These include increasing access to housing by providing returning citizens with rental assistance vouchers during the period immediately following release and increasing the housing stock by building new affordable units or converting existing structures into affordable units.[83] However, both of these options rely heavily on private market actors and do not adequately protect returning citizens from market forces and discrimination.

An alternative to this market-driven approach is public investment in "social housing." Social housing policies are based on the principle that housing is a universal right of citizenship. Social housing seeks to decommodify housing and redefine it as a public good, "like schools, mass transit, and libraries."[84] Social housing includes traditional public housing, as well as resident-owned co-op buildings and mutual housing associations built and managed by nonprofits and community land trusts. By placing these units in the permanent stewardship of the public, such units can guarantee long-term affordability by shielding them from market forces that incentivize speculation.

· · · · ·

Returning citizens will continue to experience the runaround so long as the institutional infrastructure of prisoner reentry remains fragmented, underfunded, and animated by the disciplinary ideology of neoliberal paternalism. Creating a socially just approach to reentry cannot rely solely on small-scale technological fixes and improvements in service coordination. Although these reforms are necessary short-term steps for reducing the burdens of the runaround, they do not address the deeper dysfunctions of our contemporary system of poverty governance. Indeed, the runaround wouldn't exist in the first place if basic income, health care, and housing were universal rights of citizenship rather than means-tested programs associated with the undeserving poor. These observations illustrate the need for broad-based social movements to demand these state protections rather than relying on technological fixes.

Indeed, the need to raise the minimum wage and implement social housing programs illustrates that improving the lives of formerly incarcerated people cannot be limited to reforming the criminal legal system. Protecting returning citizens from discrimination, reforming parole, and reducing the hassles of the runaround are incredibly important goals, but they will fall short of truly improving the lives of returning citizens if they are not accompanied by proactive efforts to raise the living standards of formerly incarcerated people. Thus, the reentry movement must break free from its narrow focus on criminal legal reform and join broader grassroots racial justice and working-class movements aimed at improving the lives of the poor and demanding protection and accountability from the state.

NOTES

INTRODUCTION

1. All names are pseudonyms.

2. Andre had an unusual level of insight into the institutional circuit of reentry. Prior to his incarceration for real estate fraud, Andre had been the proprietor of a chain of "three-quarter" sober houses. As a former service provider in the reentry field, Andre had insider knowledge of how the system operated and why it was so dysfunctional. At the same time, Andre was also a service user and was experiencing this dysfunction firsthand. Because of this unique insider-outsider perspective, Andre was one of my most instrumental interlocutors for understanding men's experiences of the runaround. I got to know Andre over several weeks, and I formally interviewed him once. I draw on the insights I learned from these conversations throughout the book.

3. Hopper et al. (1997); Desmond (2015)

4. I use the term "reentry" throughout the manuscript to denote the experience of being released from incarceration and navigating the challenges of poverty, social exclusion, and criminalization. Reentry is the dominant term used in scholarly and policy literature to describe the process of leaving prison. However, it is an imperfect concept. It suggests a clean break between incarceration and community freedom and implies that people leaving custody were fully integrated community members prior to incarceration (Martin 2013; Wacquant 2010). This is not how I use the term. Instead, I use "reentry" to describe the liminal space between the total institution of the prison and the experience of full community freedom. As we will see throughout this book, people experiencing reentry are no longer incarcerated, but they are not totally free, either. They experience ongoing forms of state social control across a network of criminal legal and social welfare bureaucracies, and their lives continue to be circumscribed by criminal records and histories of social marginalization. In telling the stories of the men in this book, my goal is to push scholars and policymakers to adopt this more precise definition of reentry.

5. I use people-centered language as much as possible. When referring to people with incarceration histories, I use the terms "formerly incarcerated man," "woman," or "person." I also use the term "returning citizen" to highlight the fact that people released from prison have paid their debt to society and retain the rights, entitlements, and dignity of citizenship.

6. Middlemass (2017), Western (2018), Harding, Morenoff, and Wyse (2019), and Miller (2021) all provide ground-level accounts of how returning citizens navigate the hardships of reentry. They explore the challenges of desistance, the struggle to find stable employment and housing, and the complicated process of reuniting with family. However, these studies tend to address returning citizens' entanglements with the institutional circuit only in passing and do not provide a sustained analysis of the institutional mechanisms that undermine reintegration.

7. Haney (2018:4); S. Sered (2020)

8. See, for example, Rios (2011), Brayne (2014), Goffman (2014), Lerman and Weaver (2014), M. C. Bell (2017), and Cobbina (2019).

9. Throughout this book, I use the term "criminal legal system" to refer to the collection of state bureaucracies that administer criminal law and punishment, including police, courts, jails, prisons, probation, and parole. There is significant debate as to whether the criminal legal system delivers "justice" in the sense of applying the law equally, uncovering the truth, and delivering accountability for victims (Miller 2021). We see glaring racial disparities throughout the criminal legal process, calling into question whether the criminal law is applied equally to deliver fair and proportional punishments. Over 90 percent of criminal cases are adjudicated through plea bargains rather than trials. Such outcomes call into question the ability of the criminal legal system to uncover the truth when so many guilty pleas are entered by indigent defendants unable to afford adequate criminal defense. And there is growing evidence that survivors of violence do not equate incarceration with justice and do not obtain healing or accountability from the criminal legal process. Thus, rather than using the morally coded language of a "justice" system, I instead use the more descriptive language of a criminal legal system. This simply describes a set of institutions that administer criminal laws without implying the degree to which they may or may not deliver justice.

10. See Jones (2018) and Flores (2014, 2018) for exceptions.

11. Western's (2018) longitudinal study focuses on the first year after release, while Harding et al. (2019) document the first three years.

12. Western (2006)

13. Carson (2018); Visher and Travis (2003)

14. Shannon et al. (2017)

15. Shannon et al. (2017)

16. Western (2018:98); De Giorgi (2017)

17. Clear (2007)

18. Pager (2007); Western (2006, 2018); Harding et al. (2019)

19. Western (2006)

20. Western (2018)

21. Wang et al. (2013)

22. Testa and Jackson (2019)

23. Herbert, Morenoff, and Harding (2015)

24. Haney (2018:3); Geller, Garfinkel, and Western (2011:26); McKay et al. (2019)

25. Haney (2018:3)

26. Turetsky (2007)

27. Haney (2022:5–6)

28. See Hopper et al. (1997); Sered and Norton-Hawk (2014); Comfort et al. (2015)

29. Miller (2014).

30. Soss, Fording, and Schram (2011:1–2), cited in Halushka (2020:235)

31. Soss et al. (2011)

32. Stuart (2016:9–10); see Alexander (2010); Wacquant (2009)

33. McKernan (2017); Seim (2016); Miller and Stuart (2017)

34. Miller and Stuart (2017:536). They go on to argue that "the benefits of carceral citizenship are only made possible in the wake of the state's failure to ensure the social rights of citizenship to begin with, and to provide adequate protections against social and environmental risk. But however they accrue their citizenship status, citizenship includes benefits and political membership has privileges that must be accounted for if we are to understand the broad effects of crime control policy in the era of mass supervision" (543).

35. Comfort (2007)

36. Soss et al. (2011:3).

37. Glenn (2002)

38. Soss et al. (2011); Hays (2003)

39. Welsh and Rajah (2014)

40. Herd and Moynihan (2018)

41. Soss et al. (2011); Herd and Moynihan (2018); Headworth (2021)

42. Feeley (1979); Gonzalez Van Cleve (2016); Kohler-Haussman (2018); Eife and Kirk (2020); Cadigan and Kirk (2020); Clair (2020)

43. Miller and Stuart (2017:534); see also Mauer and Chesney-Lind (2002); Petersilia (2003); Travis (2005); Western (2006); Manza and Uggen (2006); Pager (2007); Clear (2007)

44. Western (2018)

45. According to sociologist Mustafa Emirbayer, relational sociology conceives of the social world as "a series of dynamic, unfolding relations" (1997: 281). This approach focuses on ongoing interactions *between* social actors as the central unit of analysis, rather than focusing on static structures or attributes of individuals. He writes, "What is distinct about the transactional approach is that it sees relations between terms or units as preeminently dynamic in nature, as unfolding, ongoing processes rather than as static ties among inert substances" (Emirbayer 1997:289; see also Desmond 2014; Clair 2020). A relational approach to studying the barriers to reentry conceptualizes them as a set of dynamic transactions *between* returning

citizens and institutional gatekeepers, not as simply a set of static public policies or individual attributes.

46. Herd and Moynahan (2018:26)

47. Miller and Stuart (2017:537)

48. Foucault (1977); Garland (1990); Eife and Kirk (2020)

49. S. Sered (2020)

50. Garland (1990:173), cited in Stuart (2016:16)

51. Ezzell (2012)

52. Haney (2018:4)

53. Haney (2018)

54. Halushka (2020)

55. Stuart (2016)

56. With over eight million residents, it is by far the most populated city in the country (US Census Bureau 2018). It is also a deeply unequal city. It has the fifth highest income inequality gap in the country (Bach 2020). It also ranks in the bottom third of the Urban Institute's overall inclusion rankings, a measure of the ability of low-income residents and residents of color "to contribute to and benefit from economic prosperity" in a city (Urban Institute 2020).

57. Small (2009)

58. See, for example, Mauer and Chesney-Lind (2002), Petersilia (2003), Travis (2005), Western (2006), Manza and Uggen (2006), Pager (2007), and Clear (2007).

59. I use the gender-neutral term "Latinx" to refer to groups of people of Latin American descent that include both men and women. When referring to specific people who identify as men, I use "Latino," and when referring to specific people who identify as women, I use "Latina."

60. The managerial staff in employment services—that is, staff who administered grants and oversaw curriculum—were mostly White and college educated, and I had little trouble fitting in with them. However, almost all frontline staff members—that is, the employees who carried out the day-to-day responsibilities of facilitating classes and addressing client needs—had backgrounds similar to the clients'. Almost all were Black and Latinx, had grown up in disadvantaged New York City neighborhoods, and had experienced incarceration.

61. I had no prior training or experience in résumé writing except for a one-hour seminar I took at my college career center as an undergraduate. Staff members simply assumed that because of my educational background I knew how to teach people how to make résumés. It took a few weeks of trial and error before I figured out how to best address the résumé needs of formerly incarcerated jobseekers.

62. See, for example, Western (2018) and Harding et al. (2019).

63. Western (2018)

64. Western (2018)

65. Halushka (2020)

66. Grant no. SES-1424309

67. Halushka (2020)

68. Jerolmack and Khan (2014)

69. Headworth (2019)

70. I follow the quoting conventions laid out by Emerson, Fretz, and Shaw: "Only those words actually taken down at the time are placed in quotes; a portion of the direct speech missed at the time is paraphrased outside the direct quotes" (2011:56; see also 63–69).

71. Herd and Moynihan (2018)

72. M. C. Bell (2017); Haney (2018)

73. Welsh and Rajah (2014); Gurusami (2017)

74. Sweet (2019, 2021); see also Miller and Stuart (2017)

75. S. Sered (2020)

I. THE INSTITUTIONAL CIRCUIT OF PRISONER REENTRY

1. NYC Department of Homeless Services (2021)
2. Kasdan and Youdelman (2008:16)
3. Wiseman (1979); Hopper et al. (1997); Sered and Norton-Hawk (2014, 2019)
4. Hopper et al. (1997)
5. Hopper et al. (1997:664)
6. Lara-Millán (2021); Seim (2020)
7. Lara-Millán (2021)
8. Haney (2018:4)
9. Paik (2021)
10. Haney (2018:40)
11. S. Sered and Norton-Hawk (2014)
12. Haney (2018:40); Paik (2021)
13. S. Sered and Norton-Hawk (2019:34)
14. Garland (2001)
15. See Phelps and Ruhland (2022); Petersilia (2003); Simon (1993)
16. Simon (1993); see also Garland (2001)
17. Simon (1993)
18. Simon (1993); Feeley and Simon (1992); Lynch (2000); Werth (2013)
19. Phelps and Ruhland (2022)
20. Lucken (1997); Petersilia (2003); DeMichele (2014)
21. Soss et al. (2011:6)
22. Haney (2010); Miller (2014)
23. Marwell (2004)
24. Allard (2008:31)
25. Allard (2008:27)
26. Garland (2001); Miller (2014); Haney (2010); Marwell (2004); Smith and Lipski (1994)
27. Miller (2014)
28. Aviram (2015); Gottschalk (2015)
29. Seeds (2017); DeMichele (2014)

30. DeMichele (2014); Lucken (1997)

31. Halushka (2017); Miller (2014)

32. Gottschalk (2015)

33. Goddard (2012); Miller (2014); Hannah-Moffat (2005)

34. Garland (2001:176)

35. McKim (2017:10)

36. Research suggests that POs more often utilize rehabilitation programs as techniques of risk management rather than as therapeutic interventions. For example, mandatory drug treatment acts as a means for POs to monitor returning citizens' daily activities and to determine their capacity for rule compliance. It also serves as a tool for punishing returning citizens for violating the terms of their parole. See Lynch (2000), Werth (2013), and Herbert et al. (2015). See also McKim (2017), who illustrates how the state systems of punishment and welfare have come to rely on addiction treatment as the dominant tool of managing marginalized populations.

37. Gottschalk (2015); Halushka (2016); Miller (2014)

38. Cuomo was governor throughout the period when research was conducted.

39. NYS Office of the Governor (2012 ,para 4)

40. Legal Action Center (2009)

41. In their study of parole in Michigan, sociologists Josh Seim and David Harding found that returning citizens under parole supervision were more likely to be employed than those not under supervision. However, they found that employment found through parole tended to be low wage and menial, and employment rates dropped off following completion of parole (Seim and Harding 2020:189).

42. Halushka (2017)

43. See, for example, Hays (2003). See also Halushka (2020); Western (2018); Harding et al. (2019)

44. Schott (2020); NYPWA (2009)

45. Polkey (2019)

46. These figures are rough approximations based on self-reports from interview respondents. Other sources provided some corroboration for these figures, but I was unable to directly verify the accuracy of these figures. See Prisoner Reentry Institute (2013) and NYPWA (2009).

47. Soss et al. (2011)

48. Kasdan and Youdelman (2008:1)

49. See Gustafson (2009); Soss et al. (2011); Headworth (2021)

50. Kasdan and Youdelman (2008)

51. Kasdan and Youdelman (2008:16)

52. Kasdan and Youdelman (2008:16)

53. See Haney (2018); Randles (2020a, 2020b)

54. Herbert et al. (2015); Lynch (2000); Werth (2013)

55. Stewart (2019); see also Hopper et al. (1997)

56. According to Roland, he was defending his wife from an attempted rape and beat the assailant to death.

57. NYC Department of Homeless Services (2021)

58. See Fairbanks (2009); Haney (2010); McKim (2017)

59. Prisoner Reentry Institute (2013); Barker (2015)

60. Prisoner Reentry Institute (2013); Barker (2015)

61. These experiences gave Andre an unusual level of insight into the institutional circuit compared to other interviewees.

62. Prisoner Reentry Institute (2013); Barker (2015)

63. Barker (2015:para. 7)

64. Barker (2015:para. 15)

65. Barker (2017)

66. See also Herbert et al. (2015)

67. Martin (2021)

68. Hopper et al. (1997); Soss et al. (2011); Sered and Norton-Hawk (2014); Comfort et al. (2015); Lara-Millán (2021)

2. JUMPING THROUGH HOOPS

1. I did not find out exactly what Calvin's sanction entailed. Typically, FTC sanctions suspend benefits for a period of time, usually 30–90 days.

2. Smoyer et al. (2021); Hamlin and Purser (2021)

3. Miller and Stuart (2017:537)

4. Herd and Moynihan (2018)

5. For a detailed discussion of how pressure to produce performance metrics shaped these organizational decisions, see Halushka (2017).

6. Kasdan and Youdelman (2008:7)

7. Kasdan and Youdelman (2008:7)

8. Returning citizens receiving public assistance must participate in mandatory BTW programs and WEPs as conditions of receiving aid. Failing to meet these requirements results in an FTC sanction, which leads to benefits being reduced, suspended, or terminated. Reasons for receiving an FTC include missed appointments, unexcused absences, inappropriate behavior, and not accepting a job offer (Kasdan and Youdelman 2008:16).

9. Haney (2018:26)

10. Haney (2018, 2022)

11. Haney (2018:4)

12. Sered and Norton-Hawk (2014)

13. Miller and Stuart (2017)

3. THEY SET YOU UP TO FAIL

1. The 1996 "welfare reform" law mandated that noncustodial parents reimburse the state for the cost of public assistance paid out to the custodial parent and their children. Under this policy regime, public assistance becomes, in effect,

a high-interest loan that custodial parents must repay. See Haney (2018, 2022) and Black and Keyes (2021).

2. At first, Leon didn't understand why his ex-partner was pursuing him for child support. He thought at the time, "Why would she do that? She knows where I'm at." Later, Leon found out that DSS was pursuing the case, not his ex-partner. According to Leon, his involvement in the case was triggered when his ex-partner was sanctioned for not reporting income.

3. Ezzell (2012)

4. Haney (2018)

5. Herd and Moynahan (2018:22)

6. Cf. Lubet (2017)

7. See Jerolmack and Khan (2014)

8. Headworth (2019)

9. Herd and Moynihan (2018:16–17)

10. Herd and Moynihan (2018:30)

11. Sociologist Matthew Desmond defines severe deprivation as economic hardship that is *acute*, characterized by "life below the poverty line" and a "scarcity of critical resources"; *compounded*, characterized by a "clustering of different kinds of disadvantage across multiple dimensions (psychological, social, material) and institutions (work, family, prison)"; and *persistent*, characterized by "enduring disadvantages" that begin with early life traumas, are experienced over long stretches of time, and are passed down generationally (Desmond 2015:3–4).

12. Clear (2007); Harding et al. (2019)

13. Western (2018:83); Pager (2007)

14. See Western (2018, Ch. 5)

15. Western et al. (2015:1513–14); see also Desmond (2015, 2016)

16. Pager (2007); see also Desmond (2016:379 n10)

17. Schrock and Schwalbe (2009)

18. Bourgois (1995); Anderson (1999)

19. Schrock and Schwalbe (2009:286); Ezzell (2012)

20. I also witnessed arguments between female program participants and staff members, but the vast majority of confrontations involved male participants.

21. Halushka (2017)

22. Miller (2021); Miller and Stuart (2017)

23. Miller (2021:318)

24. Miller and Stuart (2017)

25. Feeley (1979); Kohler-Haussman (2017); Gonzalez Van Cleve (2016); Eife and Kirk (2020); Cadigan and Kirk 2020); Clair (2020)

26. Foucault (1977); Garland (1990); Comfort (2008); Eife and Kirk (2020)

27. Kohler-Haussman (2017:215–16)

28. M.C. Bell (2017:2073)

29. In her research on the relationship between police and poor communities of color, sociologist Monica C. Bell has shown how these recurrent experiences of procedural injustice lead marginalized communities to become "estranged" from the

law. People who experience legal estrangement may view legal authority to be legitimate in the abstract, but their actual experiences with legal authorities teach them to expect arbitrary, unresponsive, and abusive treatment from state actors. Through these experiences, they learn that while they are subject to the law's coercive power, they exist outside of its protection. They develop an "intuition" that "the law operates to exclude them from society," rather than to provide inclusion, protection, and security (M.C. Bell 2017:2054).

30. Auyero (2011)

31. Kohler Haussman (2017); Eife and Kirk (2020)

32. Feeley (1979); Kohler-Haussman (2017); Gonzalez Van Cleve (2016); Eife and Kirk (2020); Cadigan and Kirk 2020); Clair (2020)

33. Goffman (1961); Foucault (1977)

34. Miller (2021)

35. Eighty-two percent of interviewees (n = 37) were either currently on supervised release or had been in the past.

36. I did not personally observe this. This vignette was reconstructed from Miguel's account.

37. Halushka (2020)

38. Stephan was one of only three White men I interviewed in the study. He was also one of only a few men with a college education, and the only man I interviewed who owned his apartment. However, his resentment of parole was typical of the men I interviewed. Indeed, the fact that Stephan was still resentful of his PO, despite not struggling under conditions of severe deprivation, speaks to the ways in which the degradation of parole provokes negative emotions.

39. In New York, POs have discretion to grant or deny driving privileges for people on parole (NYS Department of Corrections and Community Supervision 2020).

40. Halushka (2020:4)

41. Tony's case was unusual in that he had served his time in California state prison and was an out of state parole transfer. He was also convicted of manslaughter, which was the case for only a handful of interviewees. However, Tony's cynical views about state authority were quite common among the men who served time in New York state prisons and who were convicted of less serious crimes. Tony provides a distillation of the cynical worldview that circulated among the men I met at Second Chances and Uplift.

42. Legal Services for Prisoners with Children (2012)

43. Sociologist Sarah Brayne has shown that people who have had contact with the criminal legal system "are less likely to interact with surveilling institutions, including medical, financial, labor market, and educational institutions, than their counterparts who have not had criminal justice contact" (Brayne 2014:367; see also Sampson and Bartusch 1998; Tyler 2006). Similarly, political scientists Amy Lerman and Vesla Weaver (2014) show how contact with the criminal legal system has profound political consequences, leading to lower levels of trust in government and political participation.

44. It is important to note that this analysis is based solely on Tony's perspective. Had I been able to speak with Tony's PO, she would likely have had a different perspective on his actions. She might have pointed out that Tony has a violent criminal history and had just moved to the area. He needed to prove that he wasn't a public safety risk before he could be trusted with the full freedom of citizenship. Indeed, in the eyes of parole, Tony's actions proved that he wasn't ready for freedom. His noncompliance with parole rules was perhaps an early warning sign of a potential return to criminal behavior. From the perspective of Tony's PO, she needed to intervene early with tighter surveillance in order to prevent a more serious relapse into criminal behavior. Tony's PO might have argued that she wasn't trying to set Tony up for failure; she was simply doing her job of protecting public safety.

45. Haney (2018:4)

4. IN SEARCH OF RESPECTABILITY

1. See also Black and Keyes (2021:ch. 8)

2. Black and Keyes (2021); Sered and Norton Hawk (2014)

3. Soss et al. (2011)

4. Western (2006:22). Although the collective fate of subsequent birth cohorts has been negatively impacted by mass incarceration, my focus here is on the men who experienced the initial wave of the prison boom. While mass incarceration continues to shape the collective fate of marginalized men of color, the experiences of subsequent birth cohorts have been shaped by significant reductions in violent crime and a growing reform movement to scale back the war on drugs (Sharkey 2018).

5. Miller (2021:8)

6. Maruna (2001:7–8)

7. Jones (2018:5); Flores (2013)

8. The title of this chapter is a play on *In Search of Respect*, Philippe Bourgois's (1995) classic ethnography of crack entrepreneurs in Spanish Harlem.

9. Edin, Nelson, and Paranal (2004); Sampson and Laub (1993)

10. In her ethnographic study of formerly incarcerated young men in Philadelphia, Fader (2013:ch. 6) similarly finds that romantic relationships and fatherhood were not enough to keep the young men in her study from engaging in the underground economy.

11. Halushka (2020)

12. Halushka (2020)

13. Chris was one of only a few men who had sole custody of his children. His experience navigating the family court was also atypical when compared to the rest of the sample. However, his experience provides a window into how men's interpretation of the runaround shifts as they grow older and embrace identities as fathers.

14. It's not clear why ACS released Chris's kids to his mom and not to him. My assumption is that Chris's mom had been the kids' caregiver in the past, but I couldn't verify this.

15. Scattersite housing programs refer to "apartments scattered throughout the city in different buildings owned by private landlords. Non-profit providers hold contracts with government agencies to secure safe affordable units for tenants to move into and to also provide the social services support needed by tenants" (NYC Human Resources Administration n.d.:para. 9).

16. Sered and Norton-Hawk (2014)

17. See Flores (2013); Sered and Norton-Hawk (2014); Black and Keyes (2021)

18. Oscar's case was atypical in a number of ways. He reported an exceptional level of participation in prison-based rehabilitation programs. Although other men discussed participating in various programs, Oscar was an outlier in terms of the quantity and quality of his participation. He was also the only man I interviewed who took on an active leadership role in these kinds of programs. Because of his extraordinary level of participation, he earned parole as soon as he was eligible, which is unusual for someone convicted of felony murder. Oscar also had an exceptional level of family support. Where other men's relationships with family members deteriorated during incarceration, Oscar's relationship with his daughter and extended family remained strong throughout his two-decade sentence. Despite being an atypical case, Oscar's experience is still instructive for understanding how prison-based rehabilitation programs shape men's experiences of the runaround on the outside.

19. Maruna (2001)

20. Sered and Norton-Hawk (2014)

21. Sered and Norton-Hawk (2014:116)

22. Haney (2010); McKim (2017); Whetstone and Gowan (2017); Kaye (2019)

23. Whetstone and Gowan, (2017:92). Of course, these therapeutic practices are heavily gendered. McKim (2017) and Haney (2010) both provide accounts of how "gender-responsive" addiction programs control and coerce women in distinct ways.

24. Halushka (2017)

25. Brown (1991); Soss et al. (2011)

26. Maruna (2001)

27. Halushka (2016:85)

28. Halushka (2016:86)

29. Patillo (2007)

30. Jones (2018:5)

31. Randles (2020a,2020b)

32. Dads Take Your Child to School (n.d.)

33. A variety of studies have debunked "the premises that mothers and fathers parent differently as a result of essential gender differences and that men are essential for child development due to their exclusive ability to model healthy masculine behavior. . . . Overall, evidence does not support the claim that fathers are essential because they make indispensable and uniquely male contributions to childrearing due to their masculinity" (Randles 2020a:98). Indeed, negative development outcomes correlated with the absence of fathers are often confounded by other variables, such as the effects of family disruption and complexity or "the reduction in

resources associated with family disconnection" (Randles 2020a:98). See Randles (2020a) for an overview of the literature on the "essential father discourse."

34. "Getting over" is a phrase commonly used by study participants to describe a situation when someone manipulates the system to their advantage.

35. Louis fails to point out that "Joe" is making payments on what is in effect a high-interest loan to the state. See Haney (2018) and Black and Keyes (2021).

5. BECOMING PROFESSIONALLY POOR

1. Halushka (2020)

2. Welsh and Rajah (2014); Gurusami (2017); Williams and Rumpf (2020)

3. Sweet (2019, 2021); Gurusami (2017); Miller and Stuart (2017)

4. Halushka (2020)

5. Stuart (2016); Lens and Cary (2009)

6. In his ethnography of policing in LA's Skid Row neighborhood, Stuart (2016) shows how neighborhood residents learn to "see like a cop" in order to avoid police harassment. Residents turn the gaze of the police inward onto themselves, learning to avoid certain social relationships, daily routines, and bodily dispositions that might invite police contact. They also turn this gaze outward to police the behaviors of other neighborhood residents.

7. I borrow this insight from Menjivar and Lakhani (2016), who find that immigrants "change their lives not out of fear of deportation per se (arguably the ultimate form of exclusion) but in hopes of inclusion, of being considered as deserving of membership and accepted as legitimate members of society. The moment of legalizing—particularly if a positive outcome is anticipated—represents a validation of the ways these immigrants stake membership claims through their personal and social lives that distances them from negative anti-immigrant stereotypes" (1823).

8. K2 is a popular brand of synthetic marijuana or "spice." Spice refers to dried plant materials sprayed with synthetic cannabinoids that mimic the effects of THC. Spice is cheap and widely available in tobacco shops and bodegas across the city. It is popular among residents of residential treatment programs because it does not show up on drug tests.

9. Justin was younger than most of the other study participants by about a decade. Unlike other study participants, he had transitioned away from crime at a relatively early age, and his incarceration history was not as extensive as those of older study participants. However, Justin's views on the child support system were typical of the men I interviewed.

10. Sweet (2019, 2021); Welsh and Rajah (2014); Gurusami (2017); Williams and Rumpf (2020)

11. Sweet (2021:4)

12. Sweet (2019:417)

13. Although domestic violence and reentry represent distinct policy domains, the concept of "institutional legibility" describes a generalizable social process that

applies across multiple fields. Both women seeking domestic violence services and formerly incarcerated men must engage in bureaucratic labor to earn recognition as worthy citizens deserving of social services.

14. Pager (2007)

15. Scott (1998); Sweet (2019); Gurusami (2017)

16. Haney's (2022) ethnography of child support courts shows that judges actually give little regard to formal paperwork.

17. Bourdieu (1986)

18. Maruna (2001:158)

19. NYS Department of Corrections and Community Supervision (n.d.)

20. Legal Action Center (2019)

21. Legal Action Center (2019)

22. Legal Action Center (2019)

23. Legal Action Center (2019)

24. Legal Action Center (2016); NYS Department of Corrections and Community Supervision (n.d.)

25. Legal Action Center (2019:19–20)

26. Halushka (2020)

27. Halushka (2020)

28. Wyse (2013)

29. Gonzalez Van Cleve (2016)

30. Hughes (2018)

31. Soss et al. (2011); Sered and Norton-Hawk (2014)

32. This is in stark contrast to how the state intervenes in the lives of criminalized women. "Gender-responsive" rehabilitation for women prioritizes therapeutic interventions designed to "cure" women of their addictions to not only drugs and alcohol, but also abusive relationships, "unhealthy" desires, and dependence on welfare. These interventions sometimes include education and job training, but they primarily focus on cultivating "internal self-awareness and discovery," pushing women to confront "their personal experiences of pain and trauma" in order to find psychological healing and cultivate female "empowerment" (Haney 2010:129). By contrast, the state's governance of criminalized men tends to focus on cultivating their capacity to fulfill economic roles and responsibilities. While men also experience therapeutic interventions, such as anger management, substance abuse treatment, and responsible fatherhood classes, employment remains the centerpiece of rehabilitation for men. See Wyse (2013), Sered and Norton-Hawk (2014), Sweet (2019, 2021), and McKim (2017).

33. Piehowski and Phelps (2022:5); see also Gowan and Whetstone (2012); Miller (2014)

34. Wyse (2013:239–45)

35. Haney (2022:12)

36. Halushka (2016)

37. Russell-Brown (1998)

38. Sweet (2021:16); see also E. Goffman (1959)

39. Garland (1990:173), cited in Stuart (2016:16)

40. Menjívar and Lakhani (2016:1826).

41. Gibson-Light (2020)

42. Menjívar and Lakhani (2016:1826)

43. Gurusami (2017); Miller (2021); Miller and Stuart (2017)

44. Comfort et al. (2015)

45. Miller (2014:319)

46. Haney (2022)

47. Black and Keyes (2021)

6. BACKSLIDING

1. Definitions of "recidivism" vary. In some studies, recidivism is defined by rearrests. Other studies have more narrow definitions of recidivism that focus on convictions for new crimes that result in reincarceration. Whatever the definition, our policymakers gauge successful reentry based on the degree to which returning citizens continue to have contact with criminal legal authorities. When recidivism rates go down, it is an indication that returning citizens have desisted from crime and are no longer public safety risks.

2. Miller (2021)

3. Comfort et al. (2015)

4. Alper, Durose, and Markman (2018). However, not all arrests result in convictions and returns to prison. In a previous analysis, Durose, Cooper, and Snyder (2014) found that within three years, 50 percent of people released from prison in 2005 were returned to prison for new convictions or technical parole violations (versus 68 percent who were rearrested). By year five, 55 percent were returned to prison on new charges or violations (versus 77 percent who were rearrested).

5. Western (2018); Harding et al. (2019)

6. Miller (2021)

7. In addition to these eighteen men, four men I interviewed were rearrested on drug-related charges but were not sent back to prison. Of the four, one man had been released four years prior to our interview but had relapsed on heroin and was sentenced to a residential treatment facility as an intermediate sanction for a parole violation. The other three had been released from prison at least six years prior to our interview. However, they had recently been rearrested on drug-related charges and were sentenced to alternative-to-incarceration programs rather than prison.

8. Travis was the only man in the sample who was the primary caregiver for a disabled child. While many of Travis's struggles related to the difficulties of caring for his disabled son, his experience of persistent material hardships and recurrent episodes of the runaround was typical of other men in the sample.

9. Travis has two sons from previous relationships; one is 12 and the other is 18. They were born during the height of Travis's addiction, and he is estranged from both of them. He hopes to reunite all of his sons one day.

10. These numbers are based on Eric's accounts during class presentations and our informal discussions. I was able to partially corroborate these accounts by comparing them to a formal interview Eric gave for a policy report about the burdens of legal financial obligations. Since Eric's real name and picture appear in the report, I cannot provide a formal citation to the report without compromising Eric's confidentiality.

11. Eric's fear was not unfounded. He was once denied a job because he had an open charge on his record that he didn't know about. Eric had disclosed all of his convictions to a potential employer but didn't know about the open charge, which was out of state and several years old. When the employer conducted a background check, the open charge appeared on his record. Eric was accused of lying and was denied the job.

12. At the time, the median monthly rent in New York City was $1200 (Prisoner Reentry Institute 2013).

13. See also Harding et al. (2019); Western (2018); Black (2010)

14. Alper, Durose, and Markman (2018)

15. Comfort et al. (2015)

16. Chen and Meyer (2020)

CONCLUSION: CITIZENSHIP AND SOCIAL JUSTICE IN THE AGE OF MASS PRISONER REENTRY

1. Glenn (2002:52)

2. Glenn (2002:53)

3. S. Sered (2020)

4. S. Sered (2020:2; emphasis mine)

5. S. Sered (2020:6)

6. S. Sered (2020:6)

7. Hughes (2018); Headworth (2021)

8. See also Haney (2010); McKim (2017); Whetstone and Gowan (2017); S. Sered and Norton-Hawk (2014); Martin (2021)

9. Miller and Stuart (2017:533)

10. Foucault (1977); Garland (1990, 1997, 2001); Stuart (2016)

11. Brayne (2014)

12. Ezzell (2012)

13. Sweet (2019, 2021); see also Miller and Stuart (2017)

14. Gurusami (2017)

15. Miller and Stuart (2017:533); Gurusami (2017)

16. Miller and Stuart (2017:542)

17. Comfort et al. (2015)

18. DeParle (2021:para. 10)

19. Code for America (n.d.); DeParle (2021)

20. DeParle (2021)

21. DeParle (2021)

22. Miller and Stuart (2017)

23. Simes and Tichenor (2022)

24. Simes and Tichenor (2022:295)

25. Simes and Tichenor (2022:295)

26. M. Bell (2021:41)

27. M. Bell (2021:41)

28. Lara-Millán (2021, 2022)

29. Lara-Millán (2021, 2022)

30. Chen and Meyer (2020)

31. See also Harding et al. (2019); Western (2018); Black (2010)

32. Chen and Meyer (2020)

33. M. Bell (2021:40–41)

34. Chen and Meyer (2020:37)

35. Chen and Meyer (2020:38)

36. National Academies of Sciences, Engineering, and Medicine (2022)

37. Chen and Meyer (2020:38)

38. National Academies of Sciences, Engineering, and Medicine (2022:153)

39. The majority of inmates are held in state facilities (1.29 million), and the majority of those inmates are incarcerated for violent crimes (713,000) (Sawyer and Wagner 2020). See also Forman (2017); Pfaff (2017); Gottschalk (2015)

40. Forman (2017:228)

41. See also Western (2018, Ch. 5)

42. Western (2018)

43. Western (2018:180)

44. Western (2018:182)

45. Sharkey (2020:para. 11); See also D. Sered (2017)

46. D. Sered (2017)

47. Forman (2017)

48. Western (2018:182)

49. Western (2018:181)

50. Western (2018:182)

51. Sharkey (2018)

52. Sharkey (2020, 2018)

53. Executive Session on Community Corrections (2017:3); Scott-Hayward (2011)

54. Executive Session on Community Corrections (2017:3)

55. Executive Session on Community Corrections (2017:4)

56. Executive Session on Community Corrections (2017:4)

57. Harding et al. (2019)

58. Harding et al. (2019:230–31)

59. Herbert et al. (2015)

60. Harding et al. (2019:231)

61. Miller (2021)

62. Soss et al. (2011:307); Flores (2018)
63. Western (2018)
64. Harding et al. (2019:232)
65. Gumaer (2021); NYC Human Rights Commission (2015)
66. Doleac and Hansen (2020)
67. Schneider et al. (2022)
68. Berry, Nelson, and Nielsen (2017)
69. Prescott and Starr (2020)
70. Dimon (2021:para. 8)
71. Prescott and Starr (2020:2460)
72. Legal Action Center (n.d.); NYS Unified Court System (n.d.)
73. Legal Action Center (n.d.)
74. Harding et al. (2019:234); see also Lageson (2020)
75. Lageson (2020)
76. Bushway and Apel (2012)
77. Soss et al. (2011:303)
78. Western (2006)
79. Glasmeier (2020)
80. Bonnet (2019)
81. Bonnet (2019:1)
82. NYC Housing Plan (n.d.)
83. Cortes and Rogers (2010)
84. Mironova and Waters (2020)

REFERENCES

Alexander, Michelle. 2010. *The New Jim Crow: Mass Incarceration in the Age of Colorblindness*. New York: The New Press.

Allard, Scott W. 2008. "Rethinking the Safety Net: Gaps and Instability in Help for the Working Poor." *Focus* 26(1):27–32.

Alper, Mariel, Matthew R. Durose, and Joshua Markman. 2018. *2018 Update on Prisoner Recidivism: A 9-Year Follow-Up Period (2005–2014)*. Washington, DC: Bureau of Justice Statistics.

Anderson, Elijah. 1999. *The Code of the Street: Decency, Violence, and the Moral Life of the Inner City*. New York: W. W. Norton.

Auyero, Javier. 2011. "Patients of the State: An Ethnographic Account of Poor People's Waiting." *Latin American Research Review* 46:5–29.

Aviram, Hadar. 2015. *Cheap on Crime: Recession-Era Politics and the Transformation of American Punishment*. Oakland: University of California Press.

Bach, Trevor. 2020. "The 10 U.S. Cities with the Largest Income Inequality Gaps." *U.S. News and World Report*, September 21. https://www.usnews.com/news /cities/articles/2020-09-21/us-cities-with-the-biggest-income-inequality-gaps.

Barker, Kim. 2015. "A Choice for Recovering Addicts: Relapse or Homelessness." *New York Times*, May 30. https://www.nytimes.com/2015/05/31/nyregion/three-quarter -housing-a-choice-for-recovering-addicts-or-homelessness.html?referringSource= articleShare.

Barker, Kim. 2017. "Bills Passed to Help Tenants of New York 'Three-Quarter Homes.'" *New York Times*, February 1. https://www.nytimes.com/2017/02/01 /nyregion/bills-tenants-protection-three-quarter-homes-new-york.html?referring Source=articleShare.

Bell, Marina. 2021. "Abolition: A New Paradigm for Reform." *Law & Social Inquiry* 46(1):32–68.

Bell, Monica C. 2017. "Police Reform and the Dismantling of Legal Estrangement." *Yale Law Journal* 126(7):2054–2150.

Berrey, Ellen, Robert L. Nelson, and Laura Beth Nielsen. 2017. *Rights on Trial: How Workplace Discrimination Law Perpetuates Inequality*. Chicago: University of Chicago Press.

Black, Timothy. 2010. *When the Heart Turns Rock Solid: The Lives of Three Puerto Rican Brothers On and Off the Streets*. New York: Vintage.

Black, Timothy, and Sky Keyes. 2021. *It's a Setup: Fathering from the Social and Economic Margins*. New York: Oxford University Press.

Bonnet, François. 2019. *The Upper Limit: How Low-Wage Work Defines Punishment and Welfare*. Oakland: University of California Press.

Bourdieu, Pierre. 1986. "The Forms of Capital." Pp. 241–58 in *Handbook of Theory and Research for the Sociology of Education*, edited by J. Richardson. New York: Greenwood.

Bourgois, Philip. 1995. *In Search of Respect: Selling Crack in El Barrio*. New York: Cambridge University Press.

Brayne, Sarah. 2014. "Surveillance and System Avoidance: Criminal Justice Contact and Institutional Attachment." *American Sociological Review* 79(3):367–91.

Brown, J. David. 1991. "The Professional Ex-: An Alternative for Exiting a Deviant Career. *Sociological Quarterly* 32(2):219–30.

Bushway, Shawn D., and Robert Apel. 2012. "A Signaling Perspective on Employment-Based Reentry Programming." *Criminology and Public Policy* 11(1):21–50.

Cadigan, Michele, and Gabriela Kirk. 2020. "On Thin Ice: Bureaucratic Processes of Monetary Sanctions and Job Insecurity." *RSF Journal of the Social Sciences* 6(1):113–31.

Calavita, Kitty, and Valerie Jenness. 2014. *Appealing to Justice: Prisoner Grievances, Rights, and Carceral Logic*. Oakland: University of California Press.

Carson, E. Ann. 2018. *Prisoners in 2016*. Washington, DC: Bureau of Justice Statistics. https://www.bjs.gov/content/pub/pdf/p16.pdf.

Chen, Elsa Y., and Sophie E. Meyer. 2020. "Beyond Recidivism: Toward Accurate, Meaningful, and Comprehensive Data Collection on the Progress of Individuals Reentering Society." Pp. 13–28 in *Beyond Recidivism: New Approaches to Research on Prisoner Reentry and Reintegration*, edited by A. Leverentz, E. Y. Chen, and J. Christian. New York: NYU Press.

Clair, Matthew. 2020. *Privilege and Punishment: How Race and Class Matter in Criminal Court*. Princeton, NJ: Princeton University Press.

Clear, Todd R. 2007. *Imprisoning Communities: How Mass Incarceration Makes Disadvantaged Neighborhoods Worse*. New York: Oxford University Press.

Cobbina, Jennifer E. 2019. *Hands Up, Don't Shoot: Why the Protests in Ferguson and Baltimore Matter, and How They Changed America*. New York: NYU Press.

Code for America. n.d. "Improving Access to Food Assistance and How Benefits Are Delivered." San Francisco: Code for America. Accessed January 13, 2022. https://www.codeforamerica.org/programs/social-safety-net/food-benefits/.

Comfort, Megan. 2007. "Punishment Beyond the Legal Offender." *Annual Review of Law and Social Science* 3:271–96.

Comfort, Megan. 2008. *Doing Time Together: Love and Family in the Shadow of the Prison.* Chicago: University of Chicago Press.

Comfort, Megan, Adrea M. Lopez, Christina Powers, Alex H. Kral, and Jennifer Lorvick. 2015. "How Institutions Deprive: Ethnography, Social Work, and Interventionist Ethics among the Hypermarginalized." *RSF Journal of the Social Sciences* 1(1):100–119.

Cortes, Katherine, and Shawn Rogers. 2010. *Reentry Housing Options: The Policymakers' Guide.* New York: Council of State Governments Justice Center. https://csgjusticecenter.org/wp-content/uploads/2020/02/Reentry_Housing_Options-1.pdf.

Dads Take Your Child to School Day. n.d. "About Us." Accessed January 13, 2022. https://dadstakeyourchildtoschoolday.com/about-us.

De Giorgi, Alessandro. 2017. "Back to Nothing: Prisoner Reentry and Neoliberal Neglect." *Social Justice* 44(1):83–120.

DeMichele, Matthew. 2014. "Studying the Community Corrections Field: Applying Neo-Institutional Theories to a Hidden Element of Mass Social Control." *Theoretical Criminology* 18(4):546–64.

DeParle, Jason. 2021. "How Tech Is Helping Poor People Get Government Aid." *New York Times*, December 8, 2021. https://www.nytimes.com/2021/12/08/us/politics/safety-net-apps-tech.html.

Desmond, Matthew. 2014. "Relational Ethnography." *Theory and Society* 43:547–79.

Desmond, Matthew. 2015. "Severe Deprivation in America: An Introduction." *RSF Journal of the Social Sciences* 1(1):1–11.

Desmond, Matthew. 2016. *Evicted: Poverty and Profit in the American City.* New York: Crown.

Dimon, Jamie. 2021. "If You Paid Your Debt to Society, You Should Be Able to Work." *New York Times*, August 4, 2021. https://www.nytimes.com/2021/08/04/opinion/clean-slate-incarceration-work.html.

Doleac, Jennifer, and Benjamin Hansen. 2020. "The Unintended Consequences of 'Ban the Box': Statistical Discrimination and Employment Outcomes When Criminal Histories Are Hidden." *Journal of Labor Economics* 38(2):321–74.

Durose, Matthew, Alexia D. Cooper, and Howard N. Snyder. 2014. *Recidivism of Prisoners Released in 30 States in 2005: Patterns from 2005 to 2010.* Washington DC: Bureau of Justice Statistics.

Edin, Kathryn, Timothy J. Nelson, and Rechelle Paranal. 2004. "Fatherhood and Incarceration as Potential Turning Points in the Criminal Careers of Unskilled Men." Pp. 46–75 in *Imprisoning America: The Social Effects of Mass Incarceration*, edited by M. Patillo, D. Weiman, and B. Western. New York: Russell Sage Foundation.

Eife, Erin, and Gabriela Kirk. 2020. "'And You Will Wait . . .'": Carceral Transportation in Electronic Monitoring as Part of the Punishment Process." *Punishment and Society.* 23(1):69–87.

Emerson, Robert M., Rachel I. Fretz, and Linda L. Shaw. 2011. *Writing Ethnographic Field Notes.* 2nd ed. Chicago: University of Chicago Press.

Emirbayer, Mustafa. 1997. "Manifesto for a Relational Sociology." *American Journal of Sociology*. 103(2):281–317.

Executive Session on Community Corrections. 2017. *Toward an Approach to Community Corrections for the 21st Century: Consensus Document of the Executive Session on Community Corrections*. Cambridge, MA: Program in Criminal Justice Policy and Management, Harvard Kennedy School.

Ezzell, Matthew B. 2012. "'I'm in Control': Compensatory Manhood in a Therapeutic Community." *Gender and Society* 26(2):190–215.

Fader, Jamie J. 2013. *Falling Back: Incarceration and Transitions to Adulthood among Urban Youth*. New Brunswick, NJ: Rutgers University Press.

Fairbanks, Robert. 2009. *How It Works: Recovering Citizens in Post-Welfare Philadelphia*. Chicago: University of Chicago Press.

Feeley, Malcolm, and Jonathan Simon. 1992. "The New Penology: Notes on the Emerging Strategy of Corrections and Its Implications." *Criminology* 30(4): 449–74.

Feeley, Malcolm M. 1979. *The Process Is the Punishment: Handling Cases in a Lower Criminal Court*. New York: Russell Sage Foundation.

Flores, Edward Orozco. 2013. *God's Gang: Barrio Ministry, Masculinity, and Gang Recovery*. New York: NYU Press.

Flores, Edward Orozco. 2018. *"Jesus Saved an Ex-Con": Political Activism and Redemption after Incarceration*. New York: NYU Press.

Forman, James, Jr. 2017. *Locking Up Our Own: Crime and Punishment in Black America*. New York: Farrar, Straus, and Giroux.

Foucault, Michel. 1977. *Discipline and Punish: The Birth of the Prison*. New York: Vintage.

Garland, David. 1990. *Punishment and Modern Society*. Chicago: University of Chicago Press.

Garland, David. 1997. "'Governmentality' and the Problem of Crime: Foucault, Criminology, Sociology. *Theoretical Criminology* 1(2):173–214.

Garland, David. 2001. *The Culture of Control: Crime and Social Order in Contemporary Society*. Chicago: University of Chicago Press.

Geller, Amanda, Irwin Garfinkel, and Bruce Western. 2011. "Paternal Incarceration and Support for Children in Fragile Families." *Demography* 48:25–47.

Gibson-Light, Michael. 2020. "Sandpiles of Dignity: Labor Status and Boundary-Making in the Contemporary American Prison." *RSF Journal of the Social Sciences* 6(1):198–216.

Glasmeier, Amy K. 2020. *Living Wage Calculator*. Massachusetts Institute of Technology. https://livingwage.mit.edu/metros/35620.

Glenn, Evelyn Nakano. 2002. *Unequal Freedom: How Race and Gender Shaped American Citizenship and Labor*. Cambridge, MA: Harvard University Press.

Goddard, Tim. 2012. "Post-Welfarist Risk Managers? Risk, Crime Prevention, and the Responsibilization of Community-Based Organizations." *Theoretical Criminology* 16(3):347–63.

Goffman, Alice. 2014. *On the Run: Fugitive Life in an American City*. Chicago: University of Chicago Press.

Goffman, Erving. 1959. *The Presentation of Self in Everyday Life*. New York: Anchor.

Goffman, Erving. 1961. *Asylums: Essays on the Social Situation of Mental Patients and Other Inmates*. New York: Anchor.

Gonzalez Van Cleve, Nicole. 2016. *Crook County: Racism and Injustice in America's Largest Criminal Court*. Stanford, CA: Stanford University Press.

Gottschalk, M. 2015. *Caught: The Prison State and the Lockdown of American Politics*. Princeton, NJ: Princeton University Press.

Gowan, Teresa, and Sarah Whetstone. 2012. "Making the Criminal Addict: Subjectivity and Social Control in a Strong-Arm Rehab." *Punishment and Society* 14(1):69–93.*

Gumaer, Timothy A. 2021. *NYC Imposes New Limits on Use of Criminal History in Hiring and Employment*. New York: Fox Rothschild, LLP. https://www.fox rothschild.com/publications/nyc-imposes-new-limits-on-use-of-criminal-history -in-hiring-and-employment.

Gurusami, Susila. 2017. "Working for Redemption: Formerly Incarcerated Black Women and Punishment in the Labor Market." *Gender and Society* 31(4):433–56.

Gustafson, Kaaryn. 2009. "The Criminalization of Poverty." *Journal of Criminal Law and Criminology* 99:643–716.

Halushka, John. 2016. "Work Wisdom: Teaching Former Prisoners How to Negotiate Workplace Interactions and Perform a Rehabilitated Self." *Ethnography* 17(1):72–91.

Halushka, John. 2017. "Managing Rehabilitation: Negotiating Performance Accountability at the Frontlines of Reentry Service Provision." *Punishment and Society* 19(4):482–502.

Halushka, John. 2020. "The Runaround: Punishment, Welfare, and Poverty Governance After Prison." *Social Problems* 67(2):233–50.

Hamlin, Madeleine, and Gretchen Purser. 2021. "'A Program, Not the Projects': Reentry in the Post-Public Housing Era." *Journal of Contemporary Ethnography* 50(6):806–34.

Haney, Lynne. 2010. *Offending Women: Power, Punishment, and the Regulation of Desire*. Berkeley: University of California Press.

Haney, Lynne. 2018 "Incarcerated Fatherhood: The Entanglements of Child Support Debt and Mass Incarceration." *American Journal of Sociology* 124:1–48.

Haney, Lynne. 2022. *Prisons of Debt: The Afterlives of Incarcerated Fathers*. Oakland: University of California Press.

Hannah-Moffat, Kelly. 2005. "Criminogenic Needs and the Transformative Risk Subject: Hybridizations of Risk/Need in Penality." *Punishment and Society* 7(1):29–51.

Harding, David J., Jeffery D. Morenoff, and Jessica J. B. Wyse. 2019. *On the Outside: Prisoner Reentry and Reintegration*. Chicago: University of Chicago Press.

Hays, Sharon. 2003. *Flat Broke with Children: Women in the Age of Welfare Reform*. New York: Oxford University Press.

Headworth, Spencer. 2019. "Getting to Know You: Welfare Fraud Investigation and the Appropriation of Social Ties." *American Sociological Review* 84:171–96.

Headworth, Spencer. 2021. *Policing Welfare: Punitive Adversarialism in Public Assistance*. Chicago: University of Chicago Press.

Herbert, Clair W., Jeffery D. Morenoff, and David J. Harding. 2015. "Homelessness and Housing Insecurity among Former Prisoners." *RSF Journal of the Social Sciences* 1(2):44–79.

Herd, Pamela, and Donald P. Moynihan. 2018. *Administrative Burden: Policymaking by Other Means*. New York: Russell Sage Foundation.

Hopper, Kim, John Jost, Terri Hay, Susan Welber, and Gary Haugland. 1997. "Homelessness, Severe Mental Illness, and the Institutional Circuit." *Psychiatric Services* 48:659–65.

Hughes, Cayce C. 2018. "From the Long Arm of the State to Eyes on the Street: How Poor African American Mothers Navigate Surveillance in the Social Safety Net." *Journal of Contemporary Ethnography* 48(3):339–76.

Jerolmack, Colin, and Shamus Khan. 2014. "Talk Is Cheap: Ethnography and the Attitudinal Fallacy." *Sociological Methods and Research* 43:178–209.

Jones, Nikki. 2018. *The Chosen Ones: Black Men and the Politics of Redemption*. Oakland: University of California Press.

Kasdan, Alexa, and Sondra Youdelman. 2008. *Missing the Mark: An Examination of NYC's Back to Work Program and Its Effectiveness in Meeting Employment Goals for Welfare Recipients*. New York: Community Voices Heard. http://www.cvhaction.org/sites/default/files/Missing%20the%20Mark%20-%20Executive%20Summary.pdf.

Kaye, Kerwin. 2019. *Enforcing Freedom: Drug Courts, Therapeutic Communities, and the Intimacies of the State*. New York: Columbia University Press.

Kohler-Hausmann, Issa. 2018. *Misdemeanorland: Criminal Courts and Social Control in an Age of Broken Windows Policing*. Princeton, NJ: Princeton University Press.

Lageson, Sarah Esther. 2020. *Digital Punishment: Privacy, Stigma, and the Harms of Data-Driven Criminal Justice*. New York: Oxford University Press.

Lara-Millán, Armando. 2021. *Redistributing the Poor: Jails, Hospitals, and the Crisis of Law and Fiscal Austerity*. New York: Oxford University Press.

Lara-Millán, Armando. 2022. "The Administrative Disappearing of State Crisis: The Resolution of Prison Realignment in Los Angeles County." *American Journal of Sociology* 127(5):1460–1506.

Lara-Millán, Armando, and Nicole Gonzalez Van Cleve. 2017. "Interorganizational Utility of Welfare Stigma in the Criminal Justice System." *Criminology* 55:59–84.

Legal Action Center. 2009. *After Prison: Roadblocks to Reentry—2009 Update*. New York: Legal Action Center. http://www.lac.org/roadblocks-to-reentry/index.php.

Legal Action Center. 2016. *How to Gather Evidence of Rehabilitation*. New York: Legal Action Center. https://www.lac.org/assets/files/How-to-Gather-Evidence-of-Rehabilitation.pdf.

Legal Action Center. 2019. *Lowering Criminal Record Barriers*. New York: Legal Action Center. https://www.lac.org/assets/files/Lowering_Criminal_Record_Barriers.pdf.

Legal Action Center. n.d. "FAQs: Criminal Legal." New York: Legal Action Center. Accessed January 13, 2022. https://www.lac.org/faqs.

Legal Services for Prisoners with Children. 2012. *Child Custody and Visiting Rights Manual for Incarcerated Parents.* San Francisco: Legal Services for Prisoners with Children. https://www.courts.ca.gov/documents/BTB_23_4K_3.pdf.

Lens, Vicki, and Colleen Cary. 2009. "Negotiating the Discourse of Race within the United States Welfare System." *Ethnic and Racial Studies* 33(6):1032–48.

Lerman, Amy E., and Vesla M. Weaver. 2014. *Arresting Citizenship: The Democratic Consequences of American Crime Control.* Chicago: University of Chicago Press.

Lubet, Steven. 2017. *Interrogating Ethnography: Why Evidence Matters.* New York: Oxford University Press.

Lucken, Karol. 1997. "Privatizing Discretion: 'Rehabilitating' Treatment in Community Corrections." *Crime and Delinquency* 43(3):243–59.

Lynch, Mona. 2000. "Rehabilitation as Rhetoric: The Ideal of Reformation in Contemporary Parole Discourse and Practices." *Punishment and Society* 2(1):40–65.

Manza, Jeff, and Christopher Uggen. 2006. *Locked Out: Felon Disenfranchisement and American Democracy.* New York: Oxford University Press.

Martin, Laim. 2013. "Reentry within the Carceral: Foucault, Race, and Prisoner Reentry." *Critical Criminology* 21:493–508.

Martin, Laim. 2021. *Halfway House: Prisoner Reentry and the Shadow of Carceral Care.* New York: NYU Press.

Maruna, Shadd. 2001. *Making Good: How Ex-convicts Reform and Rebuild Their Lives.* Washington DC: American Psychological Association.

Marwell, Nicole P. 2004. "Privatizing the Welfare State: Nonprofit Community-Based Organizations as Political Actors." *American Sociological Review* 69(2): 265–91.

Mauer, Marc, and Meda Chesney-Lind, eds. 2002. *Invisible Punishment: The Collateral Consequences of Mass Imprisonment.* New York: The New Press.

McKay, Tasseli, Megan Comfort, Christine Lindquist, and Anupa Bir. 2019. *Holding On: Family and Fatherhood during Incarceration and Reentry.* Oakland: University of California Press.

McKernan, Patricia. 2017. "Homelessness and Prisoner Reentry: Examining Barriers to Housing Stability and Evidence Based Strategies that Promote Improved Outcomes." *Journal of Community Corrections* 27(1):7–14.

McKim, Allison. 2017. *Addicted to Rehab: Race, Gender, and Drugs in the Era of Mass Incarceration.* New Brunswick, NJ: Rutgers University Press.

Menjivar, Cecilia, and Sarah M. Lakhani. 2016. "Transformative Effects of Immigration Law: Immigrants' Personal and Social Metamorphoses through Regularization." *American Journal of Sociology* 121(6):1818–55.

Middlemass, Keesha. 2017. *Convicted and Condemned: The Politics and Policies of Prisoner Reentry.* New York: NYU Press.

Miller, Reuben Jonathan. 2014. "Devolving the Carceral State: Race, Prisoner Reentry, and the Micro-politics of Urban Poverty Management." *Punishment and Society* 16(3):305–35.

Miller, Reuben Jonathan. 2021. *Halfway Home: Race, Punishment, and the Afterlife of Mass Incarceration*. New York: Little, Brown.

Miller, Reuben Jonathan, and Forrest Stuart. 2017. "Carceral Citizenship: Race, Rights, and Responsibility in the Age of Mass Supervision." *Theoretical Criminology* 21(4):532–48.

Mironova, Oksana, and Thomas J. Waters 2020. "Social Housing in the U.S." New York: Community Service Society. https://www.cssny.org/news/entry/social-housing-in-the-us.

National Academies of Sciences, Engineering, and Medicine. 2022. *The Limits of Recidivism: Measuring Success after Prison*. Washington, DC: The National Academies Press.

New York Public Welfare Association (NYPWA). 2009. *Grappling with Safety Net Assistance for Single Adults*. Albany: New York Public Welfare Association.

Norton-Hawk, Maureen, and Susan Starr Sered. 2014. *Can't Catch a Break: Gender, Jail, Drugs, and the Limits of Personal Responsibility*. Oakland: University of California Press.

NYC Department of Homeless Services. 2021. "Single Adults: The Shelter System." New York: NYC Department of Homeless Services. https://www1.nyc.gov/site/dhs/shelter/singleadults/single-adults-shelter.page.

NYC Housing Plan. n.d. "Problem: Our Current Affordable Housing Crisis." New York: NYC Housing Plan. Accessed January 13, 2022. https://www1.nyc.gov/site/housing/problem/problem.page.

NYC Human Resources Administration. n.d. "Supportive Housing." New York: NYC Human Resources Administration. Accessed January 13, 2022. https://www1.nyc.gov/site/hra/help/supportive-housing.page.

NYC Human Rights Commission. 2015. "Fair Chance Act." New York: NYC Human Rights Commission. Accessed January 13, 2022. https://www1.nyc.gov/site/cchr/law/fair-chance-law.page.

NYS Department of Corrections and Community Supervision. n.d. "Certificates of Relief/Good Conduct & Restoration of Rights." Albany: NYS Department of Corrections and Community Supervision. Accessed January 13, 2022. https://doccs.ny.gov/certificate-relief-good-conduct-restoration-rights.

NYS Department of Corrections and Community Supervision. 2020. *Special Conditions—Parolee Driving Privileges*. Albany: NYS Department of Corrections and Community Supervision. https://doccs.ny.gov/system/files/documents/2020/11/9102.pdf.

NYS Office of the Governor. 2012. "Governor Cuomo Announces 'Work for Success' Employment Initiative for Formerly Incarcerated. Albany: NYS Office of the Governor. https://www.governor.ny.gov/news/governor-cuomo-announces-work-success-employment-initiative-formerly-incarcerated.

NYS Unified Court System. n.d. "Cannabis (Marihuana) and Expungement under New York State Law." Albany: NYS Unified Court System. Accessed January 13, 2022. https://nycourts.gov/courthelp/Criminal/marihuanaExpunge.shtml.

Pager, Devah. 2007. *Marked: Race, Crime, and Finding Work in an Era of Mass Incarceration*. Chicago: University of Chicago Press.

Paik, Leslie. 2021. *Trapped in a Maze: How Social Control Institutions Drive Family Poverty and Inequality*. Oakland: University of California Press.

Patillo, Mary. 2007. *Black on the Block: The Politics of Race and Class in the City*. Chicago: University of Chicago Press.

Petersilia, Joan. 2003. *When Prisoners Come Home: Parole and Prisoner Reentry*. New York: Oxford University Press.

Pfaff, John. 2017. *Locked In: The True Causes of Mass Incarceration and How to Achieve Real Reform*. New York: Basic Books.

Phelps, Michelle S., and Ebony L. Ruhland. 2021. "Governing Marginality: Coercion and Care in Probation." *Social Problems* 69(3):799–816.

Piehowski, Victoria, and Michelle S. Phelps. 2022. "Strong-Arm Sobriety: Addressing Precarity through Probation." *Law and Social Inquiry*, first published on September 5, 2022 as https://doi.org/10.1017/lsi.2022.49.

Polkey, Chesterfield. 2019. "Most States Have Ended SNAP Ban for Convicted Drug Felons." Washington, DC: National Conference of State Legislatures. https://www.ncsl.org/blog/2019/07/30/most-states-have-ended-snap-ban-for-convicted-drug-felons.aspx.

Prescott, J. J., and Sonja B. Starr. 2020. "Expungement of Criminal Convictions: An Empirical Study." *Harvard Law Review* 133(8):2460–2555.

Prisoner Reentry Institute. 2013. *Three-Quarter Houses: The View from the Inside*. New York: John Jay College of Criminal Justice. http://johnjayresearch.org/pri/files/2013/10/PRI-TQH-Report.pdf.

Randles, Jennifer. 2020a. "Role Modeling Responsibility: The Essential Father Discourse in Responsible Fatherhood Programming and Policy." *Social Problems* 67(1):96–112.

Randles, Jennifer. 2020b. *Essential Dads: The Inequalities and Politics of Fathering*. Oakland: University of California Press.

Rios, Victor. 2011. *Punished: Policing the Lives of Black and Latino Boys*. New York: NYU Press.

Russell-Brown, Katheryn K. 1998. *The Color of Crime: Racial Hoaxes, White Fear, Black Protectionism, Police Harassment, and Other Macroaggressions*. New York: NYU Press.

Sampson, Robert J., and Dawn Jeglum Bartusch. 1998. "Legal Cynicism and (Subcultural?) Tolerance of Deviance: The Neighborhood Context of Racial Differences." *Law and Society Review* 32(4):777–804.

Sampson, Robert J., and John H. Laub. 1993. *Crime in the Making: Pathways and Turning Points through Life*. Cambridge, MA: Harvard University Press.

Sawyer, Wendy, and Peter Wagner. 2020. "Mass Incarceration: The Whole Pie 2020." Northampton, MA: Prison Policy Institute. https://www.prisonpolicy.org/reports/pie2020.html?c=pie&gclid=CjoKCQiAuP-OBhDqARIsAD4XHpcFc_rbkuztX5XJCopNXolqru2sr_fx37OLG3DjxHOwuOk-3nz9IdkaApuFEALw_wcB.

Schneider, Lesley E., Mike Vuolo, Sarah E. Lageson, and Christopher Uggen. 2022. "Before and after Ban the Box: Who Complies with Anti-Discrimination Law?" *Law and Social Inquiry* 47(3):749–82.

Schott, Liz. 2020. "State General Assistance Programs Very Limited in Half the States and Nonexistent in Others, Despite the Need." Washington, DC: Center on Budget and Policy Priorities. https://www.cbpp.org/research/family-income -support/state-general-assistance-programs-are-weakening-despite-increased.

Schrock, Douglas, and Michael Schwalbe. 2009. "Men, Masculinity, and Manhood Acts." *Annual Review of Sociology* 35:277–95.

Scott, James C. 1998. *Seeing Like a State: How Certain Schemes to Improve the Human Condition Have Failed.* New Haven, CT: Yale University Press.

Scott-Hayward, Christine S. 2011. "The Failure of Parole: Rethinking the Role of the State in Reentry." *New Mexico Law Review* 41(2):421–65.

Seeds, Christopher. 2017. "Bifurcation Nation: American Penal Policy in Late Mass Incarceration." *Punishment and Society* 19(5):590–610.

Seim, Josh. 2016. "Short-Timing: The Carceral Experience of Soon-to-Be-Released Prisoners." *Punishment & Society* 18:442–58.

Seim, Josh. 2020. *Bandage, Sort, and Hustle: Ambulance Crews on the Front Lines of Urban Suffering.* Oakland: University of California Press.

Seim, Josh, and David J. Harding. 2020. "Parolefare: Post-Prison Supervision and Low-Wage Work." *Russell Sage Foundation Journal of Social Science* 6(1):173–95.

Sered, Danielle. 2017. *Accounting for Violence: How to Increase Safety and Break Our Failed Reliance on Mass Incarceration.* New York: Vera Institute of Justice.

Sered, Susan Starr. 2020. "Diminished Citizenship in the Era of Mass Incarceration." *Punishment and Society* 23(2):218–40.

Sered, Susan Starr, and Maureen Norton-Hawk. 2014. *Can't Catch a Break: Gender, Jail, Drugs, and the Limits of Personal Responsibility.* Oakland: University of California Press.

Sered, Susan Starr, and Maureen Norton-Hawk. 2019. "Women on the Institutional Circuit: A 9-Year Qualitative Study." *Journal of Correctional Health Care* 25(1):25–36.

Shannon, Sarah K., Christopher Uggen, Jason Schnittker, Melissa Thompson, Sara Wakefield, and Michael Massoglia. 2017. "The Growth, Scope, and Spatial Distribution of People with Felony Records in the United States, 1948–2010." *Demography* 54(1):795–1818.

Sharkey, Patrick. 2018. *Uneasy Peace: The Great Crime Decline, the Renewal of City Life, and the Next War on Violence.* New York: W. W. Norton.

Sharkey, Patrick. 2020. "Why Do We Need the Police?" *Washington Post*, June 12, 2020. https://www.washingtonpost.com/outlook/2020/06/12/defund-police -violent-crime/?arc404=true.

Simes, Jessica T., and Erin Tichenor. 2022. "'We're Here to Help': Criminal Justice Collaboration among Social Service Providers across the Urban-Rural Continuum." *Social Service Review* 96(2):268–307.

Simon. Jonathan. 1993. *Poor Discipline: Parole and the Social Control of the Underclass, 1890–1990*. Chicago: University of Chicago Press.

Small, Mario. 2009. "How Many Cases Do I Need? On the Science and Logic of Case Selection in Field Research." *Ethnography* 10(1):5–38.

Smith, Steven Rathgeb, and Michael Lipsky. 1994. *Nonprofits for Hire: The Welfare State in the Age of Contracting*. Cambridge, MA: Harvard University Press.

Smoyer, Amy B., Danya E. Keene, Maribel Oyola, and Ashley C. Hampton. 2021. "Ping-Pong Housing: Women's Post-Incarceration Trajectories." *Affilia* 36(3):336–56.

Soss Joe, Richard C. Fording, and Sanford F. Schram. 2011. *Disciplining the Poor: Neoliberal Paternalism and the Persistent Power of Race*. Chicago: University of Chicago Press.

Stevenson, Bryan. 2014. *Just Mercy: A Story of Justice and Redemption*. New York: Spiegel & Grau.

Stewart, Nikita. 2019. "Shuffled among Homeless Shelters, and Not Told Why." *New York Times*, June 13, 2019. https://www.nytimes.com/2019/06/13/nyregion/nyc-homeless-shelters-transfers.html.

Stuart, Forrest. 2016. *Down, Out, and Under Arrest: Policing and Everyday Life in Skid Row*. Chicago: University of Chicago Press.

Sweet, Paige L. 2019. "The Paradox of Legibility: Domestic Violence and Institutional Survivorhood." *Social Problems* 66(3):411–27.

Sweet, Paige L. 2021. *The Politics of Surviving: How Women Navigate Domestic Violence and Its Aftermath*. Oakland: University of California Press.

Testa, Alexander, and Dylan B. Jackson. 2019. "Food Insecurity among Formerly Incarcerated Adults." *Criminal Justice and Behavior* 46(10):1493–1511.

Travis, Jeremy. 2005. *But They All Come Back: Facing the Challenges of Prisoner Reentry*. Washington, DC: The Urban Institute Press.

Turetsky, Viki. 2007. *Staying in Jobs and Out of the Underground: Child Support Policies that Encourage Legitimate Work*. Washington, DC: Center for Law and Social Policy. http://www.clasp.org/admin/site/publications/files/0349.pdf.

Tyler, Tom R. 2006. *Why People Obey the Law*. Princeton, NJ: Princeton University Press.

Uggen, Christopher. 2000. "Work as a Turning Point in the Life Course of Criminals: A Duration Model of Age, Employment, and Recidivism." *American Sociological Review* 65(4):529–46.

Urban Institute. 2020. "Measuring Inclusion in America's Cities." Washington, DC: Urban Institute. https://apps.urban.org/features/inclusion/?topic=map.

US Census Bureau. 2018. "Census Bureau Reveals Fastest-Growing Large Cities." Washington, DC: U.S. Census Bureau. https://www.census.gov/newsroom/press-releases/2018/estimates-cities.html#table3.

Visher, Chrity A., and Jeremy Travis. 2003. "Transitioning from Prison to Community: Understanding Individual Pathways." *Annual Review of Sociology* 29:89–113.

Wacquant, Loïc. 2009. *Punishing the Poor: The Neoliberal Government of Social Insecurity*. Durham, NC: Duke University Press.

Wacquant, Loïc. 2010. "Prisoner Reentry as Myth and Ceremony." *Dialectic Anthropology* 34:605–20.

Wang, Emily A., Gefei A. Zhu, Linda Evans, Amy Carroll-Scott, Rani Desai, and Lynn E. Fielinn. 2013. "A Pilot Study Examining Food Insecurity and HIV Risk Behaviors among Individuals Recently Released from Prison." *AIDS Education and Prevention* 25(2):112–23.

Welsh, M., and Rajah, V. 2014. "Rendering Invisible Punishments Visible: Using Institutional Ethnography in Feminist Criminology." *Feminist Criminology* 9(4): 323–43.

Werth, Robert. 2011. "'I Do What I'm Told, Sort Of': Reformed Subjects, Unruly Citizens, and Parole. *Theoretical Criminology* 16(3):329–46.

Werth, Robert. 2013. "The Construction and Stewardship of Responsible Yet Precarious Subjects: Punitive Ideology, Rehabilitation, and 'Tough Love' among Parole Personnel." *Punishment and Society* 15(3):219–46.

Western, Bruce. 2006. *Punishment and Inequality in America*. New York: Russell Sage Foundation.

Western, Bruce. 2018. *Homeward: Life in the Year After Prison*. New York: Russell Sage Foundation.

Western, Bruce, Anthony A. Braga, Jaclyn Davis, and Catherine Sirois. 2015. "Stress and Hardship after Prison. *American Journal of Sociology* 120(5):1512–47.

Whetstone, Sarah, and Teresa Gowan. 2017. "Carceral Rehab as Fuzzy Penality: Hybrid Technologies of Control in the New Temperance Crusade." *Social Justice* 44(2–3):83–112.

Williams, Quintin, and Cesraea Rumpf. 2020. "What's after Good? The Burdens of Post-Incarceration Life." *Journal of Qualitative Criminal Justice and Criminology* 8:285–312.

Wiseman, Jacqueline P. 1979. *Stations of the Lost: The Treatment of Skid Row Alcoholics*. Chicago: University of Chicago Press.

Wyse, Jessica B. 2013. "Rehabilitating Criminal Selves: Gendered Strategies in Community Corrections." *Gender and Society* 27(2):231–55.

INDEX

Men with first names only are formerly incarcerated people. *fig.* indicates tables.

child custody, 43, 109–10, 156, 204n1011
child support: overview, 8, 65; arrears,
65–66, 71, 106, 123, 131–32; being mindful in court, 142–43; and deserving
poor, 131–33; and driver's licenses, 66,
71, 73, 107; and employment, 143–44;
and engaged fathers, 66–67; and evasive
treatment, 64–66, 71–73, 202n2; and
incarceration, 66; and interviewees,
4fig.; and judges, 142–43, 150; as money
to state, 73, 122; and recidivism, 72;
rectifying, 107; and Responsible Fatherhood programs, 43; sanctions for, 11;
and wages garnished, 123
Chris, 107–11, 204n1011
circulation, 29, 30–32, 42, 45, 54, 71–72, 156
citizenship, 10, 11–12, 174–78, 196n5,
197n34
civil rights, 175, 177
class, 203n38
clerical errors, 52, 62–64, 112
Code for America, 179
cognitive capacity, 75–76, 84
collective action, 126
community-based providers overview:
criminalizing poverty, 40; funds for, 35,
39, 43, 46–47; history of, 34–35; and
HRA, 41; numbers of programs, 35; as
prominent in reentry, 33–34; as rehabilitation, 35, 36; support for, 189; and
unemployment, 37–38
compensatory manhood acts, 78, 80–85,
202n20
compliance costs, 55, 59, 61–62, 70
compliance tests, 140–42
conflicting obligations, 55–58
confrontations, 78, 80–85
criminalized poverty, 40
criminal legal system, 5, 9–10, 13, 196n9,
203n43
criminal record stigma: overview, 7; and
certificates, 139; and housing, 166; and
institutionally legible, 135–36; vs. internal barriers, 120; and limiting access to
records, 38; and performances, 147–48;
protecting people from, 189–91; as
punishment, 153
culture of poverty, 120–24

Cuomo, Andrew, 37
curfews, 56, 67–69, 95
Curtis, 44, 49, 55–56, 104

Darius, 60
deadbeat dads, 131–32
Deanna (Second Chances worker), 85–86
debt, 8, 164, 177
decisions from gatekeepers, 13–14, 135
dehumanization, 85–86, 87–88, 90–91, 94
Department of Social Services (DSS), 65,
66, 122, 202n2
deprivation, severe, 75–77, 155–59, 202n11
deserving immigrants, 206n7
deserving poor, 116, 130–34, 149
Desmond, Matthew, 202n11
diminished citizenship, 174–78
discipline, 149–51
discrimination, 189–90. See also criminal
record stigma
disempowerment, 53, 54, 73
Dismantling Mass Incarceration event,
18–19
disrespect, 14, 74, 84
distrust, 72–73, 85–86, 92–93, 96–97,
111–12, 126, 151
documents. See paperwork
domestic care work, 11
Donnell, 81
drugs: economics and independence, 72, 73,
77, 100, 101, 103; and federal assistance,
40; K2, 131, 206n8; and parole conditions, 44; and public housing, 125; war
on drugs, 184; weed and addiction
treatment, 37. See also substance abuse
treatment
Duane, 141
Dwight, 44, 46–47, 68–69, 112–13, 133–34

Eddie, 62, 160
Eduardo, 90, 98–99, 133–34
education, 125, 138
Emirbayer, Mustafa, 197–98n45
employment: barriers to, 119–20, 160–61;
vs. community program obligations,
59–60, 69–70; and criminal record
stigma, 190–91; as difficult to find, 76;
and job interviews, 146–48, 160; as

Medicaid, 1, 28, 46, 48, 152
Menjivar, Cecilia, 206n7
men of color, 5, 7, 9–10. *See also* African
    Americans
MetroCards, 42, 59, 81–85
Meyer, Sophie, 182
Michael, 112
Miguel, 89–90
Miller, Reuben Jonathan, 10, 102, 150, 177
minimum wage, 192–93
mobile apps, 179
Moynihan, Donald P., 12, 74

neighborhoods, 165–67
neoliberalism, 35
neoliberal paternalism, 10–11
neoliberal penality, 9–10
nervous breakdowns, 96
New York City overview, 17, 192, 193,
    198n56
noncompliance. *See* failure to comply;
    sanctions for noncompliance
Norton-Hawk, Maureen, 31

obligations, conflicting, 55–58
Office of Child Support Enforcement, 42,
    65–66, 123
"one stop" service model, 179–80
Orlando, 133
Oscar, 113–17, 137, 141–42, 205n18

paperwork, 28, 53, 129, 135–39, 150, 191. *See
    also* bureaucratic labor
parents. *See* fathers
parents in prison, 8
Parents in Transition Program, 16–17
parole: and ankle bracelets, 95; and class,
    203n38; and community-based pro-
    viders, 36–37; curfews, 95; and drugs,
    44; and employment, 200n41; fees for
    meetings, 115; fulfilling obligations of,
    33; and housing, 44; as institutional
    circuit, 2; intolerance of, 79; as law
    enforcement, 34; promoting success,
    187–88; and recidivism, 92, 93, 95,
    140–41; as social work, 34; waiting at
    offices, 89, 108, 141–42; and "work first"
    approach, 38

parole officers (PO): and community-
    based providers, 38–39; as helpful, 106;
    and informal mechanisms of social
    control, 34, 141–42; jobs of, 126, 143;
    obligations to, 55, 58, 60, 108; power of,
    86, 92, 95–97, 140–41, 204n44; pro-
    tecting jobs, 92, 96; and recidivism,
    140–41; resource referrals, 34–35; and
    risk management, 200n36; surveilling
    housing facilities, 50; and
    unemployment/employment, 38–39
paternalism, 10–11, 50
Paul, 135–36
performing rehabilitation, 129, 140–43, 146
personal liberties, 175
Personal Responsibility and Work Opportu-
    nity Reconciliation Act (PRWORA), 40
Peter, 37, 140–41, 152–53, 162
plea bargains, 196n9
police, 34, 165, 180, 206n5
positivity, 101, 112
post-traumatic stress disorder (PTSD), 165
poverty: criminalized, 40; culture of,
    120–24; deserving poor, 116, 130–34,
    149; as disease, 152; as emasculating,
    77–78; and hunger, 7; and neighbor-
    hoods, 76; and neoliberal paternalism,
    10–11; and neoliberal penalty, 9; poverty
    line, 7; reentry as, 7, 155; and success,
    150, 153–54, 156–57, 163–64, 171–72. *See
    also* severe deprivation
poverty governance, 8–9, 10–11, 30–32
power, 54, 77, 88, 90–91. *See also* parole
    officers: power of
prison. *See* incarceration
prison-based rehabilitation programs,
    113–15
privacy, 86
privatization, 35
procedural hassles, 88
procedural injustice, 87–97
procedural justice, 87, 202–3n29
procedural punishment, 12, 13, 14, 87
professionally poor: overview, 2, 6, 128–29;
    bureaucracy and legibility, 129–35; and
    discipline, 149–51; discipline and the
    runaround, 149–51; getting on paper,
    135–39; performing rehabilitation,

Schram, Sanford, 10

Second Chances: benefits of, 188–89; and culturally competent staff, 41, 118–19, 198n60; Halushka fieldwork overview, 18–22; and HRA, 42; as important support, 162; MetroCards, 59, 81–85; "one stop" service model, 179–80; pace at, 167; Parents in Transition Program, 16–17; and parole officers, 38–39; politics of, 125–26; Responsible Fatherhood program, 42–43, 122–24; and self-help, 101; and Single Stop technology, 179; staff struggles, 162–67. *See also* Workforce Development Workshop

security, 89

segregated neighborhoods, 76

Seim, Josh, 200n41

Selena (Second Chances worker), 38–39, 57

self-doubt, 119

self-help, 101, 114, 116, 119–20

Sered, Susan Starr, 31, 174

severe deprivation, 75–77, 155–59, 202n11

Sharkey, Patrick, 186

Shaun, 125

Simon, Jonathan, 34

Single Stop, 178–79

smart-on-crime movement, 35–36, 37–38, 188

social adversity mitigation, 185

social control: circularity of, 32; fees for supervision, 10, 44, 115; of gatekeepers (overview), 86–87; as gendered regime, 9–10; and idealized masculine citizens, 11–12; through institutional displacement, 31; institutions network list, 31; surveillance, 10, 34, 180; in transitional housing, 49–50. *See also* failure to comply; sanctions for noncompliance

social housing, 193–94

social justice model of reentry: carceral state shrinkage, 183–88; investing in public infrastructure, 188–94; redefining success, 181–83; reducing the runaround, 178–81

social rights, 174–75, 177

social welfare policy, 9

social workers, 64

sociology, 197–98n45

Soss, Joe, 10

speech patterns, 142, 143

sponsors, 118–19

Stanley, 124–25

Stephan, 92, 203n38

stereotypes, 14, 90–91, 98, 130, 134, 142, 145–46, 206n7

"stop and frisk," 126

street-level bureaucrats, 130, 140

structural issues, 125–26

Stuart, Forrest, 10, 177, 206n5

subject effects: aggravation over waiting, 90–91; controlling emotions, 140–42; dehumanization, 85–86, 87–88, 90–91, 94; of incarceration, 94; parole as numbers game, 92; and PO's power, 95–97; and severe deprivation, 75–77; as subjective, 74–75; verbal aggression and confrontations, 78, 80–85

substance abuse treatment: overview, 118–20, 175; as bureaucratic barrier, 60; as exploitative, 48, 61; and housing access, 45–46; as low-cost housing, 2, 130; as mandated, 55; and Medicaid, 28; and parole, 36–37, 44; as punishment, 200n36; as redundant, 60; and relapse, 48; as time consuming, 55; and time management, 1–2; and weed smokers, 37

substantive citizenship, 174

success: and earning inclusion, 149–50; and marginalization, 153–54; metrics of, 172; and poverty, 150, 153–54, 156–57, 163–64, 171–72; and quality of life, 182–83; redefining, 181–83

Supplemental Nutrition Assistance Program (SNAP), 40, 42, 46–47, 59, 82. *See also* food stamps

surveillance, 10, 34, 180

survivors, 134, 185

Sweet, Paige, 129, 134, 148

Sylvia (OCSE staff), 142

symbolic debt, 177

system abuse, 133–34

technology, 34, 178–79, 191

therapeutic interventions and gender, 207n32

thick public safety, 185–86

Founded in 1893,
UNIVERSITY OF CALIFORNIA PRESS
publishes bold, progressive books and journals
on topics in the arts, humanities, social sciences,
and natural sciences—with a focus on social
justice issues—that inspire thought and action
among readers worldwide.

The UC PRESS FOUNDATION
raises funds to uphold the press's vital role
as an independent, nonprofit publisher, and
receives philanthropic support from a wide
range of individuals and institutions—and from
committed readers like you. To learn more, visit
ucpress.edu/supportus.